Press Box Red

Press Box Red

The Story of
Lester Rodney, the
Communist Who
Helped Break the
Color Line in
American Sports

Irwin Silber

FOREWORD BY JULES TYGIEL

Temple University Press Philadelphia

Temple University Press, Philadelphia 19122
Copyright © 2003 by Irwin Silber
All rights reserved
Published 2003
Printed in the United States of America

∞ The paper used in this publication meets the requirements of the
American National Standard for Information Sciences—Permanence of
Paper for Printed Library Materials, ANSI Z39.48-1984

Library of Congress Cataloging-in-Publication Data

Silber, Irwin, 1925–
    Press box red : the story of Lester Rodney, the communist who helped break the
    color line in American sports / Irwin Silber ; foreword by Jules Tygiel.
        p.   cm.
    Includes bibliography and index.
    ISBN 1-56639-973-4 (cloth : alk. paper) — ISBN 1-56639-974-2 (pbk : alk. paper)
        1. Rodney, Lester, 1911– . 2. Sportswriters—United States—Biography.
    3. Communists—United States—Biography. 4. Baseball—United States—History.
    5. Discrimination in sports—United States—History. 6. Daily worker (New York, N.Y.).
    I. Rodney, Lester, 1911– . II. Title.

    GV742.42.R63S55 2003
    070.4′49796′092—dc21
    [B]
                                                                    2003040182

Contents

Foreword

SOMETHING WONDERFUL HAPPENED in the world of sports in 1997. Amid the hoopla and commercial sensationalism that characterized much of the fiftieth anniversary celebration of Jackie Robinson's historic debut with the Brooklyn Dodgers, Lester Rodney was rediscovered. To his neighbors in the Rossmoor retirement community in Walnut Creek, California, Rodney was known as a warm, friendly, former journalist who loved watching sports and playing tennis and who submitted occasional articles and opinion pieces to the *Rossmoor News*. Few knew that he had once been a well-known, indeed notorious, New York sportswriter or suspected the place that he held in baseball history. But as the Robinson commemorations approached, a national spotlight began to shine on Rodney. He appeared as a featured speaker and participant at the milestone Jackie Robinson conference held at Long Island University and again at a symposium sponsored by the Society for American Baseball Research at San Francisco State University. The *New York Times* praised his coverage of the Robinson story as among the most accurate of the era. Rodney even appeared on CNN's *Early Prime* and several times on ESPN.

In part, Rodney's moment of celebrity was due to his longevity. Having survived into his eighties, he had outlived most of the other sportswriters who had covered the integration beat. But, more significantly, the Ross-moor residents learned, Rodney had not simply been a commentator on the most significant sports story of the century but a catalyst. In the 1930s, when most sportswriters had remained silent about what Rodney had called "The Crime of the Big Leagues," he had launched a campaign that exposed the injustice and hypocrisy of baseball's color line to millions of Americans. Even more remarkable, they learned that Rodney had performed this service as the sports editor of the *New York Daily Worker,* the organ of the American Communist Party. Lester Rodney, a seemingly mild-mannered reporter, had been a "Red"—a Communist who had inhabited the New York press boxes and covered sports with a thoroughly professional and singular perspective—and in doing so had helped to transform not just baseball and American athletics but the broader society as well.

Perhaps no story from the world of sports is more familiar than the Jackie Robinson saga. The tale, as usually told, justifiably credits Brooklyn Dodgers president Branch Rickey with the courage and inspiration to buck the baseball establishment and end the major leagues' long-standing ban on African American players. In 1945, Rickey tabbed Jackie Robinson, a former four-sport collegiate athletic standout at UCLA, to spearhead the integration of baseball. Over the next two seasons, first in the minor leagues at Montreal and in 1947 with the Brooklyn Dodgers, Robinson crafted one of the most enduring legends in American history, triumphing in his performance on the field and opening the gates for a flood of African American athletes not just in baseball but across the sports spectrum. The Rickey-Robinson alliance established an important precursor for the national Civil Rights movement of the 1950s and 1960s.

In most retellings of this saga, however, an important element is omitted; for the sustained campaign to integrate baseball did not begin with Branch Rickey in 1945 but nine years earlier in 1936, in the mind of Lester Rodney, a twenty-five-year-old journalist who had unexpectedly found himself the sports editor of the Communist *Daily Worker* newspaper. That Rodney, an inexperienced writer and non–Party member, raised in a Republican household, would become the paper's sports editor is surprising;

that the *Daily Worker* would even have a sports section is astonishing. These developments stemmed from a critical shift in Communist Party strategy in the midst of the Great Depression. In July 1935, the Communist Third International meeting in Moscow had urged party members world-wide to create a "popular front" with other forces on the political left in their respective countries. In the United States this meant recasting communism, in the words of party leader Earl Browder, as "Twentieth-Century Americanism." The *Daily Worker* itself had to be reconceived from an organ that primarily addressed the party faithful to one that appealed to a broader mass of Americans who would be sympathetic to issues of radical social change. What better way to court a working-class readership than to highlight coverage of baseball and other sports that workers enjoyed?

Many of the ideologues who ran the paper, however, had little understanding or knowledge of American sports. Their earliest once-a-week efforts proved heavy-handed and propaganda-laden. Reading these dispatches prompted Rodney, a freelance (read unemployed) writer, to send a letter suggesting a different approach. Rodney had grown up in Brooklyn, an avid athlete and fan. In high school he had run track (well enough to be offered a scholarship to Syracuse University) and played on the basketball team. He had also played semi-professional baseball. And like most Brooklyn boys, he was an avid sports fan with a fervid devotion to the Dodgers, devouring daily sports pages and soaking up insights and information. Rodney believed that a sports page, even one in a Communist newspaper, must not only critique the flaws of capitalist athletics but also convey the love of the games that drew fans to them. To Rodney, sport was not an "opiate for the masses" but an important component of people's lives and culture. His enthusiasm convinced the editors of the *Daily Worker* to entrust him with responsibility for a new daily sports section.

The *Daily Worker* sports page, however, would be different from those of the more mainstream dailies. Although Rodney attended and covered sporting events assiduously and wrote lively accounts of the games, he emphasized not so much their results but the social issues that surrounded them. And Rodney immediately recognized that one issue above all others could simultaneously attract readers, advance the interests of social justice, and serve the needs of the Communist Party—the unconscionable exclusion of African American athletes from the ranks of organized baseball.

Although few people today would dispute the obvious inequity of baseball's color line, the ban was not a major topic of discussion in the mid-1930s. White sportswriters might occasionally comment on the matter; the black weekly press would more regularly rail against it. But most people accepted segregation as the natural order of things. Rodney saw this sociological vacuum as a remarkable opportunity. From the beginning of his tenure as sports editor in August 1936, the integration of baseball became the signature issue of the *Daily Worker* sports page. Like the Communist campaign to free the Scottsboro Boys, nine young African Americans sentenced to death in Alabama on trumped-up rape charges, baseball integration offered the Party a rallying cry that enabled it both to advance the cause of social justice and to attract positive attention to itself. On these issues, ignored by most others, the Communists unquestionably held the moral high ground. Rodney can honestly state in retrospect, "I was in it because I wanted the damn ban to end, to bring elementary democracy to the game I loved, and to see the banned players get their chance to show they belonged." At the same time, the Communist Party gained a platform from which to attract members and enhance its visibility in what they hoped would be the fertile recruiting grounds of African American communities.

The campaign begun by Rodney, and inherited by writers like Bill Mardo and Nat Low when Rodney marched off to fight in the Pacific in World War II, consisted of equal parts confrontation and education. *Daily Worker* correspondents forced baseball officials such as Commissioner Kennesaw Mountain Landis, National League president Ford Frick, and numerous owners to deny—despite all evidence to the contrary—the existence of a color line. They asked players and managers for their opinions and trumpeted their positive responses in blaring headlines. Of added significance, the *Daily Worker,* alone among the non–African American press, publicized the exploits of players in the Negro Leagues, the existence of which was often just a rumor to most whites. Rodney's accounts and an-

nouncements of Negro League games and his focus on the injustice of excluding such players as Satchel Paige and Josh Gibson shone a needed
light on black baseball. The *Worker* also spearheaded a drive to amass petitions, eventually signed by more than 1 million people, protesting blacks'
exclusion from the game.

Why has this facet of the integration of baseball, so painstakingly
described in *Press Box Red,* generally been ignored in the standard re-
creations of the Robinson story, particularly in its earliest versions? Dodgers president Branch Rickey, not only the architect of baseball integration
but, along with Robinson himself, the primary creator of the legend that
surrounds these events, vehemently rejected any suggestions that political
agitation had influenced him. In 1945, Rickey, a staunch anti-Communist
and skilled self-promoter, authorized sportswriter Arthur Mann, a close
friend, to write the first official version of the Robinson signing for publication. In the draft manuscript, Mann expressed his eyewitness perception
that on arriving in Brooklyn in 1942, "Rickey was besieged by telephone
calls, telegrams and letters of petition on behalf of black ballplayers," and
that "this staggering pile of missives were so inspired to convince him that
he and the Dodgers had been selected as a kind of guinea pig." Rickey, in a
strongly written marginal comment, adamantly instructed Mann to remove
this assertion. Robinson, who increasingly allied himself with anti-Communist forces (and who was not part of the New York scene in the years before his signing), also never credited Rodney or the Communists. Since
the Robinson story played itself out against the backdrop of the post–
World War II Red Scare and repression of the Communist Party, suppress-
ing the Party's role in the integration campaign proved relatively easy, and
even desirable, for those who portrayed this story as a harbinger of future
racial progress.

Others, however, readily recognized the significance of the almost
decade-long agitation. Larry MacPhail, an owner of the New York Yankees, repeatedly blamed "certain groups in this country including political
and social-minded drumbeaters," who "single out baseball for attack because it offers a good publicity medium," for forcing the major leagues to
confront what he dismissively called "the Race Question." Dan Dodson, a

sociologist who worked with Rickey on planning baseball's great experiment, admitted that political pressure groups "contributed to the initiation of the venture and the venture was far less difficult" due to this reality.

Some have questioned how influential the *Daily Worker,* with its limited circulation, could have been. But the impact of the *Worker* extended far beyond its immediate readership. Based in New York City at a time when interest in communism was at its peak, the newspaper had wide visibility. In addition, other elements of the Party apparatus picked up on Rodney's campaign, publicly picketing ballparks, collecting signatures on petitions, and spreading the issue through the trade union movement, where Communist organizers had considerable influence. Rodney also worked in concert with sportswriters from the black weeklies, who increasingly in the late 1930s and 1940s stepped up their agitation. Rodney and Wendell Smith of the *Pittsburgh Courier* and other black reporters exchanged information and reprinted each other's scoops, giving them wider exposure and providing Smith with an outlet in the all-important New York market. In addition, mainstream newspapers sometimes publicized Rodney's stories —most memorably in 1942, when the *New York Daily News* divulged his interview with Leo Durocher, revealing the Dodgers manager's acceptance of black players.

Rodney's greatest contributions stemmed from the integration campaign, but his singular role as a Communist sportswriter (Rodney did quickly become a Party member) extended beyond this single issue. The very notion of a Communist covering sports conjures up images of a furtive figure, skulking around the field and press box, spouting propaganda at unsuspecting athletes and spectators. Rodney, however, defied this stereotype. He was a regular working journalist, a full-fledged and accepted member of the Baseball and Basketball Writers' Associations. Everyone knew that he worked for the *Daily Worker* (although some athletes did not realize that this was a Communist journal). Rodney won acceptance and respect from players and fellow sportswriters for his broad knowledge of sports and his reportorial skills and honesty. His modesty, good nature, and humor made him a welcome figure at ballparks and arenas.

Baseball dominated sports coverage in the *Daily Worker,* as it did in most newspapers of the era. But Rodney reported on other sports as well. He wrote on boxing, tracing the careers of fighters such as Henry Armstrong and Joe Louis. At Louis's training camp before the boxer's famed rematch with German Max Schmeling, he arranged a meeting between Louis and African American novelist Richard Wright. Wright's view of the historic fight and its impact on black America appeared in the *Daily Worker* and is excerpted in these pages. At the fight itself, Rodney sat in the press section at ringside as Louis demolished both Schmeling and Hitler's myth of Aryan supremacy. He returned from the army in time to witness Robinson's 1947 debut with the Dodgers and to cover the fabled Boys of Summer in their heyday. In the early 1950s, Rodney emerged as one of the most astute commentators on college basketball's point-shaving scandals, focusing his ire not so much on the players as on the athletic system that had manipulated and victimized them.

The recollections that comprise this volume, lovingly assembled and edited by fellow former Communist Irwin Silber, capture the essence of Lester Rodney as sportswriter and humanitarian. Even in his nineties, Rodney remains an astute observer, his sharp social conscience tempered by his gentle, self-deprecating manner. Like most good sportswriters, Rodney is at heart a great storyteller. Witness his accounts of the Brooklyn Dodgers cutting down a runner at home plate or Joe DiMaggio facing Satchel Paige in a 1949 showdown. But Rodney always adds an analytical dimension that enriches our understanding of the moment. His insights into the famed athletes that he observed and often befriended—DiMaggio, Paige, Robinson, Roy Campanella, Joe Louis, Henry Armstrong and Nat Holman (Original Celtics basketball star and famed coach of CCNY's "Cinderella" team), among others—offer fresh perspectives on their careers.

Nor is Rodney blind or sparing toward his own early faith in Communism as a panacea for the ills of the world. He disparages many Party members, not excluding himself, as "rigid simpletons" and "victims of do-it-yourself brainwashing" for their naïveté, obtuseness, and unwillingness to confront the realities of the Soviet Union. Following Nikita Khrushchev's 1956 report revealing beyond any possible doubt the evils of Stalinism, Rodney and other *Daily Worker* employees sided with reformers who sought to wrest control of the Party from traditional hardliners. When the old guard prevailed and shut down the *Worker,* Rodney resigned his membership.

Rodney's remarkable life illustrates the impulses that drew men and women of intelligence and conscience into the Communist Party during the maelstrom of the Great Depression, their rejection of the racism so prevalent in that era, and their commitment to social justice. The sins of the American Communists were deep and numerous; but their virtues and contributions were also manifold. Lester Rodney embodies the best of this heritage. Today, more than sixty-five years after he launched the campaign that helped end Jim Crow in baseball, he maintains his values and his resolution. Rodney's memoirs remind us that the never-ending battle for a more just society can be effectively waged from even the most unexpected vantage points.

Jules Tygiel

Acknowledgments

THIS IS A BOOK that Lester Rodney should have written. But at the age of eighty-seven—which is when I started badgering him to write his story—Lester was full of reasons not to: He was too old. Who would want to read it? And even if there were readers, who would want to publish it?

I was convinced, however, that there was a great story in Lester's twenty-two years as the editor of the *Daily Worker*'s sports section and as the paper's foremost—for the most part, only—sportswriter. So I offered to "write" it on the condition that he would cooperate in a series of taped interviews and by going through his files to lend me his letters, columns, and articles, as well as whatever articles he could find that were written about him. In the end, much of *Press Box Red* is in Lester's own voice, taken from the transcripts of more than thirty hours of recorded interviews.

My agent, Sam Stoloff, with the Frances Goldin Agency, is both an avid baseball fan and an inveterate political activist. Sam immediately grasped the book's unique character and did yeoman work in suggesting changes to both the prospectus and the manuscript and in finding a publisher. Within weeks the publisher I wanted most—Temple University

Press, sparked by its enthusiastic senior acquisitions editor, Micah Kleit—expressed serious interest. We were on our way.

The photos and graphics—with one or two exceptions—are from the pages of the *Daily Worker,* graciously provided to us by Tim Wheeler. Tim is the current editor of the *People's Weekly World* in New York, which maintained the *Daily Worker*'s files.

Both the Tamamint Library at New York University and the library at the University of California in Berkeley were extremely helpful in facilitating my research into the files of the *Daily Worker*. My son, Joshua Silber, did yeoman's work nailing down sources for quotations.

An earlier oral history of Lester Rodney by Paul Buhle and Michael Fermanowski, *Baseball and Social Conscience*, written under the auspices of the oral history program at the University of California in Los Angeles, was a valuable source for additional information. Lester was also the subject of two M.A. theses during the 1990s: Kelly Elaine Rusinack of Clemson University wrote "Baseball on the Radical Agenda: The Daily and Sunday Worker on the Desegregation of Major League Baseball, 1933 to 1947," and Martha Shoemaker of the University of Nevada–Las Vegas wrote "Propaganda or Persuasion: The Communist Party and Its Campaign to Integrate Baseball." Both were generous in offering me excerpts from their research.

Bill Mardo, a sportswriter for the *Daily Worker* from 1942 to 1951, provided significant insights about the paper's coverage, the campaign to break the color line in baseball, and Lester's role in these and other events.

I especially want to thank Jules Tygiel, author of *Baseball's Great Experiment: Jackie Robinson and His Legacy,* for his indispensable support and constructive suggestions.

Press Box Red

OUTLAWED BY BASEBALL!

The Crime of the Big Leagues!

●

The newspapers have carefully hushed it up!

One of the most sordid stories in American sports!

Though they win laurels for America in the Olympics—though they have proven themselves outstanding baseball stars—Negroes have been placed beyond the pale of the American and National Leagues.

Read the truth about this carefully laid conspiracy!

Beginning next Sunday the SUNDAY WORKER will rip the veil from the "Crime of the Big Leagues"—mentioning names, giving facts, sparing none of the most sacred figures in baseball officialdom.

STARTING IN THE AUGUST 16th ISSUE OF THE

SUNDAY WORKER

Chapter 1

The *Daily Worker* Starts a Sports Section

H OW DID THE *DAILY WORKER,* a small, radical newspaper published by the much-maligned U.S. Communist Party, come to play a major role in ending the color ban in baseball?

This unlikely story begins in 1936, when the Greenwich Village campus of New York University (NYU)—like most other colleges and universities in New York at the time—was awash in radical newspapers and left-wing pamphlets. Despite three years of Franklin Roosevelt's New Deal, the Great Depression remained a somber reality for the country at large, and there was no shortage of Communists, socialists, Trotskyists, anarchists, and sundry radicals to hawk newspapers and hand out leaflets explaining what they believed were the causes of America's economic woes and offering revolutionary solutions.

One evening in the early winter of 1936, an energetic member of the Young Communist League (YCL) managed to shove a copy of the *Daily Worker* into the hands of Lester Rodney, a twenty-four-year-old NYU night school student from Brooklyn who had never paid attention to a Communist newspaper before. Glancing through the paper with a curiosity enhanced by the charged campus political atmosphere, Rodney discovered that the *Daily Worker* had a once-a-week sports section—but one like no other he had ever seen. Little did he know that in less than a year he would be the paper's sports editor, let alone that he would hold that position for more than two decades and, in the process, play a seminal role in changing the face of American professional sports forever.

Although prior to 1936 the *Daily Worker* carried only the occasional sports piece, the Communist Party itself paid considerable attention to the subject. Until the early 1930s, the Party's membership was made up largely of European immigrants who had brought with them a tradition of workers' sports associations, organized principally by socialist and Communist parties. In some Central European countries, membership in such organizations numbered in the hundreds of thousands. The main sports these immigrants enjoyed playing and watching were soccer, volleyball, gymnastics, and track and field.

In 1927, acknowledging their own members' interest in sport and trying to reach out to others of similar national background, the U.S. Communist Party helped establish the Labor Sports Union (LSU), whose purpose was "to encourage athletic activities by workers and win them away from the bosses who utilize the Amateur Athletic Union and similar bodies to spread anti-union activity" (Naison 1979, 49). While the *Daily Worker* occasionally reported on the LSU's activities—one can find there the announcement of an "Eastern District Wrestling Meet" and a "Workers' Table Tennis Meet," along with the standings of the Metropolitan Workers' Basketball League and the schedule of the Metropolitan Workers' Soccer League (February 3, 1933)—regular Communist coverage of sports was to be found only in the pages of the Young Communist League's monthly newspaper, the *Young Worker*.

But while the *Young Worker* was anxious to reach into the ranks of the vast majority of American workers whose interest in sports had more to do with baseball, boxing, basketball, and football, its view of sports was strictly traditional party-line. "It is the American workers who are mostly the victims of bourgeois sport, commercialism, professionalism, and corruption," the *Young Worker* proclaimed, "and [it is] among them that the work must be carried on." What the paper meant by the "work" was typified by an article on the 1928 World Series, whose theme was the following: "Through the means of this professional capitalist 'sport,' the capitalists were able to hoodwink the greater part of the American workers to eat, sleep and talk nothing . . . but baseball for a week. . . . Baseball is still a method used to distract workers from their miserable conditions." The paper's view of boxing was no different. Boxing champions and contenders were "Dope Peddlers" who were "tools of the bosses in doping the workers to forget the class struggle" (*Young Worker,* May 1930).

Writers for the *Daily Worker* were no less dogmatic. One summer day in 1933, staff writer Ben Field ventured out to report on a Dodgers–Giants game at Brooklyn's Ebbets Field. Noting the typically raucous comments of the fans as they responded to the ebb and flow of the game, Field wrote: "Are these 'bad elements?' Many are workers who have so identified themselves with their team that they cannot sleep or eat when the team loses. The leanness of American life under capitalism drives them to this fever." Nevertheless, Field did make a certain kind of history when he wrote: "You spot a few Negro fans. Negro workers make good athletes. But where are the Negroes on the field? The Big Leagues will not admit Negro players. There is something else to chalk up against capitalist-controlled sports." It was the first time that the *Daily Worker* highlighted the issue that, a few years later, would become one of the hallmarks of its sports section (*Daily Worker,* August 29, 1933).

Six months later, after a reader criticized the *Daily Worker* for "creating radical propaganda in a sports column," Simon Gerson, writing on behalf of the editors, responded:

> It is unquestionably true that American workers are greatly interested in professional sports, far too much, in fact, for their own class interest. Does this mean that the *Daily Worker*, a Communist newspaper . . . that must be the agitator and organizer of American workers and farmers should report professional sports in the same fashion as the capitalist press? That would mean . . . to accept the theory that sports are "neutral," "above classes," to accept the theory of the "democracy of the gymnasium." Do you honestly believe that you and I are "equals" of J.P. Morgan once we all put on gym shorts?

> I don't believe that Blondie Ryan [of the Giants], for example, is a conscious agent of the capitalist class seeking to dope the workers with his swell infielding. That would be the sheerest nonsense. But when a couple of dozen Blondie Ryans and Bill Terrys, with the aid of hundreds of sportswriters, rivet the attention of millions of workers upon themselves rather than upon unemployment, wage cuts and wars, then we can draw the conclusion that Ryan, et al, unconsciously serve the purposes of the ruling class. (*Daily Worker,* January 2, 1934)

But this classically doctrinaire view—not just about sports but about popular culture more generally—was about to change. On July 25, 1935, at the historic Seventh World Congress of the Communist Third International (Comintern) held in Moscow, the assembled seventy-six Communist Parties of the world adopted a major shift in political outlook. Spurred by the growth of fascism and the rise of Hitler in Germany, the Comintern dropped its previous focus on the promotion of world revolution in favor of building in every country a broad-based Popular Front against war and fascism. Unstated but implicit in this sea change was a tacit acknowledgment that the concept of a world socialist revolution led and orchestrated by the world's Communist Parties—the Comintern's principal founding goal—was not then a viable proposition. More explicit in the new approach was the view that Communist Parties should no longer divorce themselves from their respective national traditions and culture. For the U.S. Communist Party in particular, it meant a new and heightened emphasis on what was already a nominal goal—the Party's Americanization.

One of the first to realize the significance of this change in the Party's view of sports was the novelist and *Daily Worker* columnist Mike Gold. (Gold's novel, *Jews without Money,* had made him a celebrity not only in Party ranks but also in broader literary circles.) Barely a month after the Comintern Congress, Gold turned his fire on those *Daily Worker* readers who had registered opposition to the idea of instituting regular sports coverage in the paper.

> Many of them seemed to think that with the NRA breaking up [the National Recovery Act was one of the first measures taken by the

Roosevelt administration in 1933 to combat the depression] and with war and fascism on the horizon, it was a waste of time and valuable space to discuss baseball. Snobbism! In the circles in which these comrades move, they never meet anybody who is interested in baseball. It happens, however, that baseball is the American national game. I would say that nine out of every ten American workers follow it intensely, as well as other sports.

You can condemn them for it, if you are built that way, and you can call baseball a form of bourgeois opium for the masses. But that doesn't get around the fact that . . . the vast ocean of Americans of whom we are as yet a minority, adore baseball. What are we going to do, insist that they give up this taste? Are we going to maintain our isolation and make Americans stop their baseball before we will condescend to explain Communism to them? When you run the news of a strike alongside the news of a baseball game, you are making American workers feel at home. It gives them the feeling that Communism is nothing strange and foreign. . . . Let's loosen up. Let's begin to prove that one can be a human being as well as a Communist. (*Daily Worker,* August 31, 1935)

One spin-off of the turn to Popular Front politics was a decision to begin a weekend edition of the *Daily Worker* that would be aimed at reaching a broader audience than the daily paper did. The editors then solicited suggestions from readers on what they would like to see in the new edition. Reflecting the changing nature of American communism was an outpouring of ideas emphasizing the need for a popular writing style and a focus on such topics as movie and book reviews, cartoons, a woman's page, and human interest stories with a political slant. Particularly noteworthy was a pronounced sentiment in favor of a sports section.

The first issue of the new Sunday edition of the *Daily Worker* appeared January 12, 1936, and surely must have startled regular readers. Opening its new tabloid-size pages, they found cartoons, comic strips, catchy headlines, new bylines (along with some old ones), and features that undoubtedly caused many to look at the front page to make sure they were reading the *Daily Worker* and not the *Daily News.* In addition to three full pages of movie, theater, and music reviews, there were feature articles dealing with great moments in American history, a woman's page featuring household hints, recipes, articles on parenting, and short fiction with a working-class bent.

Most astonishing of all, perhaps, were the two full pages devoted to sports. Gone were the ponderous dismissals of professional sports as nothing but an ideological tool of the bosses and the patronizing comments about the fans who came out to the games. It was probably one of the first issues of this new weekend edition of the *Daily Worker* that Rodney found himself thumbing through on a January winter's night on the NYU campus.

Lester Rodney: By the time I got to NYU in the thirties, I still didn't know much about communism. I was working odd depression-type jobs by day and going to NYU at night. I wasn't looking for a degree or anything, just picking a few courses that interested me: journalism, sociology, political science. But you couldn't avoid the political discussions that went on everywhere. I used to argue with the Communists at first. I'd use the same arguments that people later used against me, like "You can't change human nature." Things like that.

I think the stock market crash of '29, which instantly wrecked my family's placid middle-class existence, began to make me a little more open to radical ideas, though the word *communist* was still completely off my radar screen. What you might call my political epiphany came one day when I was walking along Forty-second Street near Grand Central Station. There, just beneath the overpass, was a guy on a little platform making a speech. He was a Communist. But he wasn't at all like the popular image I had of Communists. He must have been in his early thirties, kind of tweedy, and he wasn't shouting. The way he talked was more like chatting with a circle of maybe thirty or forty people around him. He was saying something along the lines of "Don't you think it's ridiculous for a country as rich as ours to have so many people out of work? We Communists believe there are reasonable alternatives to the callous capitalism that benefits the few and keeps creating wars and economic crises. Do you know what socialism is, what it proposes?" That kind of talk.

When the speaker stepped down, I went over and asked him some question; I don't even remember what it was. I guess he saw me as a prime, young potential convert because he said, "Let's have some coffee and cake at the Automat and we can talk some more." We talked for a half hour. What impressed me especially was the patient way he answered all my questions about the Party, never pushing me or trying to sign me up.

I've thought of him often since then, but I never saw him again. Never even knew his name. What an asset he must have been to the Party. I suppose it doesn't follow psychological patterns to say that one person, or one incident, can give you a decisive push in a life-changing direction. But I think he did. Maybe it shows I was ready to be pushed.

Anyway, from then on I began seriously examining the political ideas I was encountering. Then I began reading more. That's when I read the *Daily Worker* for the first time. Some of the language was pretty heavy-handed, but I kind of liked what they were saying. I guess it stirred up some latent anti-capitalist feelings in me.

Rodney wasn't nearly as enthusiastic about the *Daily Worker*'s weekend sports section. When Rodney told the paper's news hawks on campus what he thought, they suggested he pass his opinions on to the editor.

LR: The writing at the time was kind of stilted, certainly as compared to the breezy style of the usual sports page.

Part of the problem was the limitations of writing about sports just once a week. They couldn't really cover events. And when they did feature pieces and analysis they sometimes slipped back into the denouncing-the-system mode. They seemed uneasy about sports, as though they'd be criticized by some Party higher-up if they really got into it.

There was a certain amount of that, but it's been exaggerated. There were sensible people there with mixed feelings about sports or who were secretly sports fans. Real sports fans. And sometimes you don't even know who they are. Like the Party leaders. For instance, William Z. Foster. Rigid sectarian. "Towards a Soviet America." And there's Earl Browder. "Communism Is Twentieth-Century Americanism." Who'd you think would be the sports fan? If I got in the elevator with Foster and he's going to the ninth floor [where the top leadership had their offices] and I was going to the eighth floor [where the *Daily Worker* was located], he'd immediately start chatting baseball with me. What'd you think of that catch last night? Do you think St. Louis is the best team you ever saw? That's William Z. Foster. Earl Browder, he'd stand there, tap his foot, lips pursed, unapproachable. He had no interest in sports. Never spoke to me. Isn't that funny?

And they also had some good writers. The best was Charlie Dexter, who was fifteen or twenty years older than me. He was the culture and feature editor then. The main thing, though, was he knew sports. His hand kept them in the real world. In fact, he wrote so many of the articles he had to use a couple of different names.

Still, the paper often gave the feeling of carping at the sports scene rather than showing a love and understanding for sports per se, which for me was not a contradiction with their general view of the world. You want a purer thing, a better thing that isn't tainted by money, but you still love dancing, let's say, for dancing's sake. You don't shy away from it as an opiate of the masses. So I wrote them a letter pointing out some ways they could improve their sports stuff.

But I made one mistake. I put my return address on the envelope. So a couple of days later a letter comes back from the editor, Clarence Hathaway, inviting me in. Hathaway was a hard-drinking guy from Minnesota. Broke a chair once over some socialist's head in Madison Square Garden. He wasn't the caricature Communist at all. So I go up to the *Daily Worker* building and Hathaway takes me right into his office. He was the first guy I spoke to.

Of course, I didn't say, "Here's an article the way I would write it." But I guess that was implicit in our conversation. What I said was something like, "I've begun to read your paper and I've become interested in what it has to say. But I cringe a little when I read the sports pages because I'm a sports fan." I made some specific suggestions, but the main thing I said was they needed a change in attitude. "You guys are focusing on the things that are wrong in sports," I told him. "And there's plenty that's wrong. But you wind up painting a picture of professional athletes being wage slaves with no joy, no élan—and that's just as wrong. Of course there's exploitation, but the professional athlete, the professional baseball player, still swells with joy when his team wins. They hug each other. That's not put on. That's not fake. That's beyond all the social analysis of the game. The idea of people coming together, blending their skills into a team, getting the best out of each other—and winning. That's a remarkable feeling. That's a wonderful human thing. And you must never forget that. The way I would write about sports if I were writing for the *Daily Worker*, that would never be absent. Along with social criticism. They're not contradictory."

I felt they needed to see the fun side of sports and the beauty, too. I mean, what's more beautiful and symmetrical than a 6–4–3 double play perfectly executed, where the shortstop fields a ground ball and flips it toward second base in one motion, the second baseman takes the throw in stride, pivots, avoids the oncoming base runner, and fires it to first in time. And they do it time and again. Beautiful to see. Anyway, after we talked for a while, Hathaway said, "Why don't you write some stuff for our weekly sports section?" And that's how I came to the *Daily Worker*. I might never have wound up there if I hadn't written that letter. Who the hell knows?

Once Rodney started writing for the *Daily Worker*'s once-a-week sports section, its tone began to change. His love for and knowledge of sports affected everyone on the staff, not only those who wrote sports. Readers loved it and wrote in to say so. It didn't take Hathaway long to realize he had a winner going for him, and he soon proposed making sports a daily feature. The editors were pretty much all for it, but some in the Party hierarchy were opposed, considering it a waste of precious space in a mostly eight-page daily paper.

The most outspoken opponent was Betty Gannett, one of the Communist Party's main ideologues, who never got used to the sports page. "This is ridiculous," Rodney remembers her saying. "It's kid stuff. Does it make sense for a hard-pressed, radical paper to give one-eighth of its space to games?"

Finally the editors decided to poll the readers on the issue. A year earlier, just taking such a poll would have been unthinkable. But by now, Party leaders had already begun to see the positive results of the Popular Front: a marked increase in young people coming into the Party; wider distribution of their press; a new respectability. Nevertheless, the outcome of the poll—6 to 1 in favor of a daily sports section—was an eye-opener. And so the die was cast. Nine months after its weekend edition started covering sports, the *Daily Worker* launched a daily sports section.

LR: Shortly after the poll, Hathaway called me into his office and told me they were going to start a daily sports section. By then that wasn't a big surprise. What was a surprise was when he asked me if I'd be interested in being the editor. By then I had emerged as the writing star of Sunday sports. But I wasn't a Party member. And it was just taken for granted that paid staff members would be Party members. So long as I was a volunteer, that was no problem. So it was very unusual to get a full-time writer/editor on staff who wasn't in the Party. Maybe because it was sports. I did get an informal ideological quiz. But it was all so new to me, and things were moving too fast. I wasn't against it, but I thought I should take my time, learn more about the Party. I finally joined a few months later. By then it was no big deal.

And I liked the people I met at the paper. I think the *Daily Worker* writers, on the whole, were among the least dogmatic people I encountered in the Party.

You know, there's something in the very nature of newspaper work, even on a Communist newspaper, that keeps you in touch with life. You're in contact with the real world, not isolated in an office all day. You get impatient with those self-serving press releases you just know are bullshit. After a while you get to be somewhat skeptical about all official pronouncements. I felt this especially when the Party went into its convulsions in 1956 after the Khrushchev revelations, when the *Daily Worker* was way out in front of the rest of the Party in calling for real change. It was a good try, too, even though it was doomed. Years later, when I worked a few years with an ad agency, I really missed newspaper people, and it was a great relief to go back to newspapering and newspaper people.

Those first weeks and months at the *Daily Worker* were exhilarating. Everything was new—for them and for me. I'd written sports for my high school paper. And I'd gotten a few stringer assignments from the old *Brook-*

lyn Eagle. Now I'm twenty-five years old and it's my first paid job as a full-time newspaperman. I hadn't been nervous writing for the weekend paper. But this was different.

All of a sudden I've got a whole page all my own six days a week. And a pretty free hand to do what I want with it. This was a big, full-sized page. Eight columns across, like the *New York Times*, but with fewer pages. And I've got to fill it up. There's no ads on that page. Resources are limited. Mostly a few young volunteers who come in and out. At the beginning, most times I'd write the lead story in a hurry without even a by-line. I'd listen to a Dodger or Yankee or Giant game on the radio and then I'd write the game story. I wouldn't put my name on a story like that.

We started in late September 1936, just before the World Series, which began first week of October those days. Yankees versus Giants. I remember my first headline: "Giant Power Threatens Yankees," in sixty-point railroad Gothic caps. I also remember thinking what fun it would have been if Cincinnati had won the National League pennant and the headline said, "Reds Power Threatens Yankees." But no one was gonna threaten the Yankees in 1936. They won in six. So much for Marxism in sports.

At the beginning I had a desk in a small room just off the traditional huge open city newsroom. I shared the space with Fred Ellis, a great guy, acerbic and fun-loving, who did the political cartoons. After a while I moved into the main newsroom because more and more they started calling on me to fill in whenever possible, like when someone had a day off. Do your sports work fast and be available for the city desk. Can you drop what you're doing and take this breaking story? We were always an undermanned newspaper. I had an enormous workload as a sportswriter. I could have spent all my days just filling the page without going to cover anything. But I felt impelled to show up at games. I had to get credentials. And to get fresh material on the page, firsthand stuff, interviews. There were times when I felt I had to be the hardest-working sportswriter in the United States.

Nothing reflected the Communist Party's new popular slogan "Communism Is Twentieth-Century Americanism" more than the *Daily Worker* sports section. Although Rodney frequently wrote and carried stories that had sports-related political overtones, it was still basically a sports page. Equally important, it was a page oriented to American sports. But old habits die hard.

In the period leading up to the launch of the *Daily Worker*'s sports section, a debate broke out over its focus. Rodney's position was that its main coverage should go to mainstream sports.

LR: If we were ever gonna be a paper beyond our narrow confines, I said to the volunteers and other staff members who were going to be writing for us, we'd have to begin acting as if we were already there. That meant we had to move into the sports arenas that most Americans are in.

One of our volunteer writers, Joe Smith, argued bitterly that we should concentrate on soccer, a scene he knew well. That's where Party people are, he said, and that's where our potential readers are—in the nationality groups. They're big soccer fans. I made the counterargument. I wasn't against following soccer, trade union sports meets, and the sports activities of progressive fraternal groups like the IWO. But in my mind those were secondary. I really wouldn't have been interested in being the sports editor if Joe's position had prevailed.

(Originally a split-off from the Workman's Circle, the IWO—the International Workers Order—was a left-wing counterpart to the many fraternal organizations characteristic of European immigrant groups in America. Organized principally along ethnic lines, it offered low-cost life and burial insurance to members. Many, including the IWO, had extensive sports programs and also operated children's summer camps.)

What Smith and some others had not yet grasped was that a major change in the Communist Party's demographics was already occurring. Not only was the Party growing, but the mostly Eastern European socialist-minded immigrants who made up the base of the Party in its formative years were rapidly becoming a minority. Replacing them was an influx of younger American-born men and women who were interested in popular culture and sports. Many were trade unionists who had been impacted by the Party's work in building the Congress of Industrial Organizations (CIO). Others were the children of immigrants more interested in becoming Americans than in preserving the culture and traditions of their parents. They grew up playing sports in the street and in schools and following professional sports. Sports weren't foreign to them. The long-awaited Americanization of the U.S. Communist Party was under way.

LR: I bristle at that phrase—the "Americanization" of the Party. It's the way some outsider would begin—as if we were all foreign-minded. I wasn't a foreign-minded kid. And I know a lot of other Communists who weren't; in fact, the whole generation that came into the party in the thirties. They didn't need "Americanization."

Irwin Silber: Maybe not. But the Party did. Don't you think when Earl Browder said, "Communism is twentieth-century Americanism," he was trying to broaden the Party and make it more an American institution?

LR: I don't have a problem when you put it that way.

Actually, in my early years as the *Daily Worker* sports editor, the older people used to come up to me all the time and say—often in a foreign accent—things like "I never read a sports page in my life until the *Daily Worker*, and now I read you all the time. It's really wonderful." And some young people too.

There was Rose Baron who ran the Workers Bookshop on East Thirteenth Street just downstairs from the *Daily Worker*. This was after we had started the daily sports page. She was one of those sturdy little petals of the movement who would go out on a rainy night to work for the election of Vito Marcantonio despite her rheumatism. One day she just suddenly came over to me bubbling all over and said, "Lester, I don't know from baseball. I don't know from football. But this is a wonderful thing you're doing. You're making Americans out of us." I was embarrassed, not only because it was an exaggeration but also because the process of "Americanization" involved so many cultural things besides sports.

But to talk about the "Americanization" of the Party without specifically relating it to that earlier immigrant generation is to echo the caricature of Communists as joyless people who don't live a full life, don't like sports, don't like movies. We were not like that. Not in the thirties. How could Communists have been, in many cases, the heart and guts of organizing the CIO, speaking to other workers, if they were that way? We weren't that way, which accounts for the passionately positive reception the sports section got. I'm not boasting. It's a fact that the sports section became the most popular part of the *Daily Worker.* I felt it. It vibrated back to me. I was the only one at the *Daily Worker* who regularly got tons of mail.

Mostly I wrote about professional baseball, boxing, and college sports. College basketball and football were big then—much more popular than the pros. Baseball got the most coverage. It was by far and truly our national pastime. If you were to ride around the streets in Brooklyn while the Dodgers were playing and a pickup truck passed you, it would be startling to hear anything coming out of the truck radio instead of Red Barber's voice. Baseball was the main American sport then, with no big competition. The World Series was a national event. In fact, I used to eat high off the hog in October.

Every night after World Series games—when the Series was still played in the daytime, as it should be—the host club in New York put on a fantastic feed for the sportswriters and their wives, as well as all the baseball bigwigs. The Yankees used the Grand Ballroom of the Biltmore Hotel. Especially during the lean depression years of the thirties, and with my *Daily Worker* salary, this was a spectacular eating and drinking orgy for me and my wife, Betty. And in those years, New York was the center of the baseball universe. Between 1936 and 1957—my years—the World Series was in New York fifteen times, ten of them between two New York teams. These lavish banquets were the social event of the year for the sports crowd in New York in October. The first one I went to, in 1937, Betty went out and spent $19 for a fancy dress to make the scene, an enormous sum for us in those days. But, hey, as we used to say, "Nothing's too good for the working class." Years after I left the sportswriting scene, I discovered that I had thrown away thousands of dollars when I cavalierly gave away the distinctive press pins working reporters got from each team in the series every year. Luckily I kept a few as souvenirs. Their worth goes up each year. Many are listed in a book like the auto Blue Book in the high hundreds.

Boxing was also big. How could it not be with Joe Louis and Henry Armstrong? We'd also have straight boxing stories. You wouldn't know they were in the *Daily Worker.* I'd speak to Billy Conn or Lou Nova or Buddy Baer or Jersey Joe Walcott. Joe Louis of course. Well, I shouldn't say straight stories as if we didn't have any social content and reflections. We went to the training camps, did prefight and postfight interviews, even covered the weigh-ins before big fights. We really covered boxing.

College football was our fall sport. The real choice I had to make was our winter sport. It was between basketball and ice hockey. Hockey filled the Garden just as much as college basketball did. New York had two hockey teams then, the Rangers and the Americans. Both for space and practical reasons, and the fact that I couldn't spend almost every night during the winter at the Garden, I had to decide between them. Actually it was not a hard decision. Basketball was the game most of our readers would identify with, not hockey. Who went to hockey games? I don't know. They weren't our readers. Sure, we had sports-minded guys who would follow the Rangers. But our readers came out of high schools that featured basketball, not hockey. Also, we were trying to build our circulation in the colleges. City College, NYU, to a lesser degree LIU [Long Island University] and St. John's. And as we built up our coverage, we'd send our features, interviews, analyses, and our all-city teams and such to the school papers, which often wound up on their bulletin boards. So basketball became our big winter sport.

What did we never cover? We never covered golf, auto racing, yachting, or horse racing except when we got a guy named Al after the war to pick winners. He was a big hit. We had readers who bet on the ponies. But we didn't cover horseracing as such. We didn't have big articles about who's gonna win the Kentucky Derby. Tennis was another sport we thought of as an upper-class, lily-white, waspy sport. We wrote about it, but minimally. Althea Gibson changed that in the 1950s.

We followed the seasons. At that time, the baseball season ended, then the football season began. Football season ended, basketball began. Only minor overlapping. Not the ridiculous stuff like today where they're still playing basketball in July. You had clear-cut seasons for each sport back then. One at a time, thank God. That helped us.

Fans Hail Idea of Buck Leonard Playing 1st Base for Yankees

Open Letter on Spirit of Lou Gehrig Is Well Received

By Nat Low

"Congratulations upon the campaign you started in today's Daily Worker to get the great Negro baseball star, Buck Leonard on the Yankees.

"There exists a greater opportunity today than ever before to break down the Jim Crow laws that have tainted our National Game.

"Now is the time to strike hard for Buck Leonard and all the other fine Negro baseball stars.

"Congratulations and the best of luck."

The above is the text of a phone call that came into the Daily Worker sport department yesterday, one of many which unanimously agreed with the "Open Letter to Joe McCarthy" which appeared yesterday.

Messages of congratulations and support came pouring into the office, all enthusiastic about the idea of getting Leonard, one of the greatest hitters in baseball, to play first base for the Yanks.

Fans pointed out that Leonard had hit some of the longest balls ever seen at the Yankee Stadium, and would fit right into the pattern of the Yank sluggers.

Most of the messages spoke of now to end Jim Crow not only in the great opportunity existing right baseball but everywhere else.

"The Joe Louis' and Dorie Millers are but mere examples of what the Negro people have to offer. While America is engaged in a life and death struggle against the Axis it would be crim-

Chapter 2

Growing Up in Brooklyn

B Y TRADITIONAL COMMUNIST PARTY STANDARDS, Lester Rodney was an unlikely choice as editor of the *Daily Worker*'s sports section. He had no previous ties to the Communist Party, invariably a precondition for anyone writing for the Party's newspaper. He didn't travel in left-wing, let alone Communist circles. He didn't come from a Communist family, nor did he have a track record supporting or participating in left-wing political activities.

Lester Rodney: I was in my twenties before I even knew what a Communist was. My father, who started out as a salesman for a silk factory in Paterson, New Jersey, and eventually got a small share of the business, was a staunch Republican. See what a little money will do? And he was active in local Republican politics. He wanted me to be a member of the Young Republican club and he even once arranged a date for me with the daughter of the club president. I remember when President Harding died in 1923. We had a big black-bordered photo of Harding in our front window with the words "We Mourn Our Loss Warren Gamaliel Harding" underneath. We were the only house in our block to do that. How many other people today know how to spell Harding's middle name? My mother never voted in her life and never even thought about politics. She was a convivial woman who thoroughly enjoyed life.

In later years, when she was at one of her card games with a group of women, someone asked her, "What ever became of that nice son of yours, Lester? What's he doing?" My mother said I was married and all that, and that I worked for the *Daily Worker*. Gasp, shock. "You mean he's a *Communist?*" My mother, startled, said, "It's okay, though. Lester explained to me that they were for good things, to help the people. And one thing about Lester, he never lies to me."

Most Communist Party members in the early 1930s were either immigrants or the first of their families to be born in America. Lester's parents, Isabel Cotton and Max Rodney, were both American-born, and their parents were part of an early wave of Jewish immigration to America from Europe in the 1860s.

LR: My mother's father, Harris Cotton, came from Manchester, England. One of the Yiddish British. He came here two years after the Civil War at age thirteen. I knew the old gentleman well up into my late teens. His wife, Amelia, my maternal grandmother, was from Vienna. My father's parents both came from somewhere in the Austro-Hungarian Empire. Their name was Rodstein—Meyer and Sarah. After a while our family name got circumcised to Rodney. I knew all four of my grandparents well.

Born April 17, 1911, in the Yorkville section of Manhattan in New York City, Lester was the third of four children. He had two older sisters, Mabel and Kate, and a younger brother, Ira, who was run over by a truck and killed when he was eleven years old. When Lester was six, his family moved to Brooklyn, where they shared a two-family home with relatives.

LR: One of the great memories of my life dates back to that move from the Bronx in 1917 when I was six. The moving van was loaded and about to leave when my mother said, "Why don't you ride with them?" . . . instead of the subway with the family. The moving men said sure, and I was perched with them on the high seat for the long ride through three boroughs, across bridges, down Broadway in Manhattan, a wonderland voyage of hours for a kid.

Four years later, as the family's fortunes prospered, the Rodneys bought their own home in the Bensonhurst section of Brooklyn. That comfortable existence—what today would be called upper-middle-class—came to a sudden end with the stock market crash of 1929 and the subsequent depression.

LR: My father lost his business in the '29 crash and became an old man overnight. We lost our house. My mother went to work operating a rooming house in Park Slope. Later on she opened a little hat shop in Newark. She had been a milliner as a young woman. I had gotten a partial track scholarship to Syracuse University but I had to drop it because we didn't have the money to cover the other half and I had to find work. Instead I took on odd jobs while trying to start a writing career.

One of my first jobs was serving summonses and drumming up business for my brother-in-law who was a lawyer. To tell the truth, I always thought it was a bit on the shady side. I'd go into lawyers' offices and ask them if they had any accident cases with certain insurance companies they were finding it difficult to settle with. I'd say, "We may be able to settle it for you." So I'd get an accident case that's languishing, they couldn't prove liability with London Guarantee or whatever insurance company. And I'd bring the cases to my brother-in-law and because he knew a lot of people on the inside, he'd wangle a settlement of a worthless case for maybe $200. I'd get 10 percent. After all, jobs were scarce and I had to make a living. I couldn't just sit around and write. . . .

I also did some chauffeuring. One of my aunts knew a rich family who needed a chauffeur to take their two kids to school and around the social scene. Would you believe I drove a sixteen-cylinder Cadillac—eight and eight? And I used to bring the car home and park it in front of our modest house. This big upper-class car parked overnight on 83rd Street in working-class Bensonhurst.

Then I started working summers as a lifeguard in a resort in Moodus, Connecticut. They threw me the lifeguard whistle and said, "While you're at it, take care of tennis." That was my introduction to the sport which has been the love of my life. I picked it up pretty fast. I never played in high school. We didn't even have tennis courts in New Utrecht.

Like most New York City kids my age, I was sports crazy. And for us, there was only one real sport—baseball. Sure, we played basketball, football, and other seasonal sports. But in the early 1920s, baseball commanded the attention and passion of young boys to a degree that's unknown today. It was truly *the* national sport. There weren't even radio broadcasts of the games then. You'd wait impatiently for the scores to appear on the front page of the afternoon papers—maybe two or three innings. All the games at Ebbets Field were played in the afternoon. For me and the other kids on my block in Bensonhurst, Ebbets Field was a magical place. If you just rode past it in the dead of winter in a car, you'd tingle with excitement, even though the place was closed and empty for months. And not just me. "Hey I walked on Bedford Avenue."

We'd hang around the local pool halls where they'd put up the scores inning by inning. When there was a home run they'd put a diamond around the box. And there would always be a huge crowd in front of the *Brooklyn Citizen* and the *Brooklyn Eagle* when the Dodgers were playing. The people would stand and wait until they put up the 0 or the 1 or whatever on a huge board hung outside the newspaper—and that's all, there was nothing else. They didn't have any machinery showing runners on the bases. That's what the fan interest was like back then.

How fanatical were we about baseball? When I was nine years old—this was in 1920—I skipped school one early October morning, got on my bike, and pedaled through much of Brooklyn from Bensonhurst to Ebbets Field in Flatbush—up Bay Parkway, Ocean Parkway, through Prospect Park to Flatbush Avenue to Empire Boulevard to the field. It was the first game of the World Series, Dodgers and Cleveland. The right-field exit gate, actually right-center-field, didn't quite reach the ground. So there was room for about six kids, lying flat on their stomachs on the Bedford Avenue sidewalk, to peer under it.

I got there early enough to be one of those six. All you could see was the centerfielder, second base, the pitcher, batter, and umpire. The rest you'd have to imagine or guess by the roar or groan of the crowd. I lay flat on my stomach for two hours or less—games were faster then—then back on my bike for the long trip home.

The Indians won. I even remember the score, 3–1. Stan Coveleski was the Cleveland pitcher. He was a spitball pitcher. That was legal then, and Rube Marquand pitched for Brooklyn. The Dodgers lost the Series and they didn't get to play in the World Series again 'til 1941, when they played the Yankees. And then I'd have to wait another fourteen years, 'til I was forty-four years old, to finally see the Dodgers win a World Series, in 1955.

I was always big on street sports, mostly after school. We didn't have things like Little League. We'd clear an empty lot of rocks and glass, level it out, form a team, and challenge other neighborhood teams. Hardball. But I also remember running out to catch passes in street football. I even played a little rough actual football without a helmet. Me and Gerald Ford. We even had a sort of league, playing football in the winter on the beach at Coney Island. We marked out the boundaries on the sand. It was slower running but sure easier on the body.

We even played a form of soccer in the street. Traffic was just an occasional nuisance in "rural" Brooklyn back then. And in hockey season, we'd have hockey sticks and a rubber heel for a puck and play it without ice and without skates. Just running. We'd have a net and goalie. I didn't swing a tennis racket until I was in my early twenties. A kid walking with a tennis racket on our street would have been jeered as a fairy.

But baseball has always been the dominant sport to me. The thing that stirs me. The artistry of it. Telling a friend, "You know, I'd rather see a Dodger-Philly game if they were in seventh place on a cloudy or drizzling day than see the best football game or the best tennis match." And I get impatient with people who say, "Oh, one-nothing, nothing happens." They don't know anything about baseball. They don't know the complex duel between the pitcher and the batter at the heart of the game. Well, a couple of the better announcers these days do get into that.

And I read sports sections omnivorously. It was about the only thing I read in the papers, just like any other dunce. My wife, Clare, and other educators think that youthful fascination with sports, and its attendant avid reading of the sports sections in newspapers, is hardly as negative as parents used to think. I guess it's the theory that anything that gets kids to read—never mind what, with the possible exception of comic books, which do not really have sustained reading and vocabulary building— is positive. Reading the sports section was far and away the most potent lure for kids who might not otherwise read outside school.

Lester's first sally into sports journalism came in his days at New Utrecht High School. The weekly school paper was called *NUHS*—pronounced "news"—an acronym for the school's name.

LR: I was intensely interested in New Utrecht's teams even before I ever played on any of them or ran track. But even then I wasn't happy with the almost childish way the kids wrote about sports. I knew I could do it better. So I went up to the newspaper office and offered to interview the basketball coach. And I got a prize quote out of him.

The team had just begun practice for the season and the coach wasn't very sanguine about his prospects. When I asked him, "How would you sum up your feelings about this squad?" he said, "Well, we're small, but we're slow." Great line. That's the way my story began. I had read sports articles and columns since I was about seven. And I had opinions about who was good and who wasn't.

I also played a lot of sports in high school. I was a good runner. We had the championship track-and-field team in the city for the four years I was there—1925 to 1929. We never lost a meet. Barney Hyman was the coach. We were just kids from the neighborhood. Bensonhurst and Borough Park. So why did we have the best track team year after year? They didn't recruit track stars from Brownsville or something. That didn't go on then. It was the coach. Any kid who came out for track was kept on the squad. He never said, "I'm sorry, you're not good enough. Try another sport." He worked with them and worked with them and some of them, amazingly, by their third year, began to be pretty good and produce. And that feeling about track, from a coach with that attitude, was at the heart of New Utrecht's supremacy. He'd walk down the hall sometimes and see a big kid, he'd say, "How'd you like to be a shot-put champion?"

Our teams were, I'd say, 85 percent Jewish, pretty much reflecting the neighborhood. The fastest sprinters, the best long-distance runners. I ran the middle distances. First I won the 600 novice, which was an event for people who had never won a medal. Then I ran the 880. I was on a two-mile relay—four guys running a half-mile each. That was at Franklin Field in Philly for the Penn Relays, the premium Eastern meet of all high schools. And we finished second.

I was fast, too. I could sprint, but not quite championship caliber, not quite that fast. But "quick" in sports. Then I played baseball for half a year in my senior year. They had a shortage of infielders. I was writing sports for the paper and someone asked me if I knew somebody who was a good ballplayer and hadn't bothered coming out. So I said, "I'm a pretty good infielder." I played second base. Some shortstop too. I hit over .300. If you make contact in high school baseball, and you can run, you get on base a lot.

I was smallish at 5'8½". I wore glasses already, which kept me off the basketball team until late the last season, when they began using eye-glass masks. I wasn't a starter on the basketball team. There were better players. I was like the eighth man.

If I had gone to day college I think I would have run track and played baseball. Not basketball. By then the teams were getting taller. Anyway, I got out of high school in '29 just when the whole world collapsed around us, and I was the man of the house. My father had a stroke after a while. Couldn't handle having "failed his family." He had no idea of the social context.

Even so, I kept playing. A group of us formed a club. We were right near Stillwell Avenue, so we called ourselves the Stillwell Athletic Club, or Stillwell AC. Just neighborhood kids, high school and early college age, and just working guys. There was a vacant lot on Stillwell Avenue that we converted into a baseball field. Empty lots like that were all over. It was semi-rural in much of Brooklyn at that time. We'd clean up the lot—rocks, glass, smooth it over—practice, and then we'd divide up into two teams if we had enough players.

After a while we played teams from other neighborhoods. Somebody who knew a kid with another team five miles away would call him, and he'd say, "How'd you like to play us?" and that's the way it evolved. We had a schedule of neighborhood teams. Our pitcher, Billy Renner, was the best athlete, so he became our captain. He'd say, "You. You're not big enough for first base. We need the big guy. You? You're slow as shit. You catch."

His big brother, Bricks Renner, worked as a bricklayer. He'd come out and coach us. He knew a lot about baseball. Bricks was in his mid- or late twenties. Working-class Irish family. We looked up to him. Bricks helped decide who played and the batting order.

We asked our parents for contributions to pay for baseballs, bases, other equipment. It was a fairly middle-class environment that I lived in before 1929, so parents would help out. Every kid had to have his own glove. Baseballs were a problem. You'd lose them. Or they'd go down a sewer. They were our biggest expense. In a Big League game, they throw baseballs out as soon as they get a little dirt on them. But we used very few. We'd get away with one or two balls a game. And one of them at the end might have black tape. We'd carry tape with us and if a ball got too badly scuffed, we'd tape it up. It became acceptable—a black-taped baseball in sandlot baseball. Not in semi-pro.

Bases. The semi-pros had regular bases. We improvised bases. We took some hard cardboard and put it in the exact spot and cut it to fit just the size of a base. It didn't protrude up. That's sandlot ball. Improvising on equipment, but the game itself was pretty good. The rules were the same. We had to have an umpire. We'd get volunteers to umpire. Kids who couldn't play well enough to play with us, but it was their neighborhood team and they'd come out and umpire. They could see. They could call balls and strikes.

In sandlot ball, as opposed to semi-pro, the umpire would stand behind the pitcher. Because he'd have to see the bases also. And also, it's kind of risky to be behind the plate without real good equipment. There was only one mask and the catcher had it. That's all he had. We often didn't even have chest protectors and shin guards.

Each team only needed a couple of bats. They didn't vary that much in weight. So a richer kid like me—my parents were comfortable before the depression killed us—had a bat. And another kid had a bat. And Bricks Renner, who was playing semi-pro ball then, got us some stuff. Helped us in creating the bases.

Irwin Silber: Were there any black baseball players on your team or any of the opposing teams?

LR: No. I was in a high school with ten thousand students and I don't remember a single black kid there. We're talking about Bensonhurst and Boro Park. Later on there were a few black kids, usually the children of parents who were working as servants or laborers or chauffeurs and lived in some pretty poor homes near there. Blacks were an abstraction to us. I didn't know anything. Sacco and Vanzetti happened when I was in school and I didn't have a clue. My parents were not socially conscious people. They'd say, "Let's go to the Chinks for dinner." And I used to sing along with other kids:

Hey you dirty little nigger
Does your mother know you're out,
With a hole in your britches
And your drawers sticking out?

For us, it had no connection to actual people. It was just the culture of the times that we grew up in.

Later on, I played some semi-pro ball. These were guys who worked and played ball just on weekends, mostly Sunday. Some of them were pretty good ballplayers, a few at a level comparable to lower or even middle minor leagues. They'd play against some team from the Bronx or New Jersey. Regular schedules. You'd pass the hat around and people would throw in change and an occasional dollar bill. We put on a good show.

And we'd split the gate. Everyone got paid. That's what made it "pro." It was "semi" because it wasn't really an organized league, although it wasn't completely haphazard. They did have schedules. And we did play once in Bushwick Field in Brooklyn, which was rented out to minor league teams. I made my way on to one of those neighborhood semi-pro teams for a couple of years. Shortstop. I was a reasonably good ballplayer, but never in my wildest dreams did I think that I was a potential Big Leaguer. I didn't have real power. But I suppose it helped me absorb knowledge of the game.

I was able to wangle a few stringer assignments for the old *Brooklyn Eagle*. But I never thought of sportswriting as a career. Not that I looked down on it. Sportswriting can be very good writing. It's actually produced many fine writers, like Ring Lardner, Heywood Broun, Gene Fowler.

As a kid, I had a kid's typical awe and reverence of sportswriters. I'd strain my eyes from under that gate to make out the press box behind and above home plate and fantasize being there writing or announcing the game on radio after that came in.

The day would come twenty years later when there'd be an overflow crowd, let's say the Dodgers playing the Giants on a Sunday at Ebbets Field, and people milling around, "You got a ticket? You got a ticket?" Some starting to leave in disappointment. They only held 34,000 people there. And I'd stroll through like Moses parting the Red Sea with my magic Baseball Writer's card and walk in to the best seat in the house and pick up some roast beef and beer on the way—all on the house. The press box at Ebbets Field.

IS: A dream come true?

LR: At that age you can fantasize about something without thinking that it will really happen. When I did become a sportswriter, it unified me with that young boy, especially since I was a Dodger rooter all those years. So you can imagine the superunity in me later as a Communist when the Dodgers were the first to take a black player. It completely united me. And it wouldn't have been the same if Cleveland or some other team had been the first.

WEATHER
Partly
Cloudy,
Mild

Daily Worker

★★
Edition

Vol. XXIII, No. 55   New York, Tuesday, March 5, 1946   (12 Pages) Price 5 Cents

ANTI-SOVIET SCARE REVIVED IN CANADA

———— See Page 3 ————

Call National Parley to Form Win-Peace Body

—See Page 3

Robinson Snappy At Bat in Florida

Phone Strike Thursday

—See Back Page

3 POWERS TO SPAIN: EASE FRANCO OUT

—See Page 3

QUILL

Quill Scores

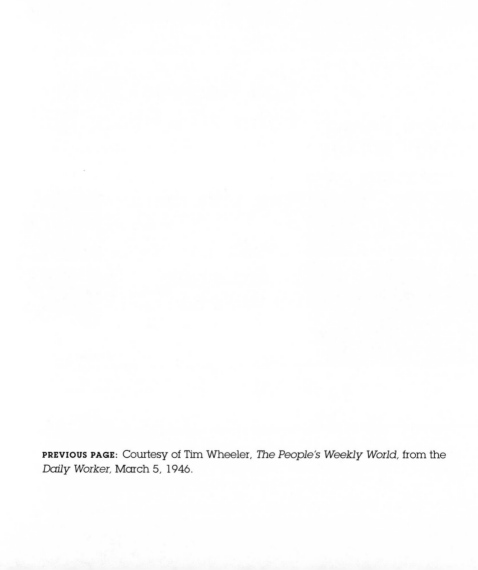

Chapter 3

A Communist in the Press Box?

W HEN THE *DAILY WORKER* SPORTS PAGE was launched in 1936, the famous syndicated liberal columnist and one-time sportswriter Heywood Broun, struck by the seeming incongruity of the event, commented: "The *Daily Worker* has begun a sports section. It will be interesting to observe what happens, because, so far as I know, you can't class-angle a box score."

It didn't take long for Broun and others to find out what would make the *Daily Worker* sports section unusual. In addition to well-written, knowledgeable reports on major sporting events, Rodney was alert to the human side of sports—including topics most papers would barely, if at all, touch. Some of these did have a class angle—such as the time Walter O. Briggs, the owner of the Detroit Tigers, fired their star catcher and manager, Mickey Cochrane.

Managers are regularly fired by team owners, but Cochrane's case was special. When he took over as manager, the Tigers were at best a mediocre ball club. Under his leadership, the team won the American League pennant in 1934 and the World Series in 1935. In 1936 and 1937, they finished second to the peerless Yankees. Concurrently playing and managing, Cochrane suffered a life-threatening injury when he was hit by a beanball during a crucial series with the Yankees in 1937. Nevertheless, in the middle of the 1938 season, when the Tigers were in third place, Briggs fired Cochrane.

Outraged, Rodney wrote a blistering column denouncing baseball owners in general and Briggs in particular. Apparently Broun, like many others in the sports community, read Rodney regularly, because the columnist came up with a typically ironic piece of his own. He wrote:

The *Daily Worker* has gone to bat upon the case of Mickey Cochrane of the Tigers. I picked up a copy of this radical sheet by mistake in the subway yesterday. My eyes are not what they used to be, and I swear I thought that some absent-minded royalist had mislaid his *Herald-Tribune*. When I got a good look at the abandoned paper and discovered its identity I was minded to toss it back upon the floor before it could enmesh me in subversive activities. But the ride was long and the day was hot, so I thought, "I'll just look at the sports page. There can't be any harm in that."

I remembered that the *Worker* had a sports page because when the innovation was introduced some years ago a newspaper wit [Broun himself, actually] remarked, "I suppose those Reds will try to class angle the box score." He was joking, naturally, because a hit is a hit and an error is an error under any economic system whatever.

The sports page featured a column, "On the Scoreboard," by Lester Rodney with a picture of a ball-player in one column measure, just above the fold. In its physical appearance this was just like the makeup of the most patriotic papers in the land, and so, heedlessly, I plunged into the text.

Imagine my surprise and horror to discover that the baseball expert of the *Worker* was using the summary dismissal of Mickey Cochrane as a pretext to agitate against the sanctity of private property and question the gratitude of big league magnates.

"It's a thankless task, this working for millionaire owners like Briggs and Wrigley, who sit in their front offices and play with the jobs of their men as the whim strikes them," whined this outside sportswriter who would evidently tear down the Bill of Rights. "It reminds me of the Redfield cartoon where two dowagers are reclining on a lawn and one of them yawns, 'Let's fire a butler. I'm bored to death.'"

By now, of course, I had my warning, but just out of a kind of mocking curiosity I plunged ahead to see what kind of garbled tale the radical would cook up in his attack on a prominent businessman like Mr. Briggs, who makes [auto] bodies.

According to Rodney, of the *Worker,* Mickey Cochrane took a laggard team in 1934 and won a pennant. The next season he added a World Series victory, and in 1936 and 1937 he brought his team home in second place behind the rampaging Yankees. In the latter year he kept on catching while he was sick and he was beaned and almost killed in a crucial series with the Yankees. Now he is tossed out without notice. Mr. Briggs builds bodies, and maybe he finds it difficult to distinguish between a dented fender and a ball player with a fractured skull. Scrap iron is scrap iron in men or materials.

But hold on! What's happening? Those last two sentences weren't in the *Worker* at all. I made them up right out of my own head. That's what propaganda will do to you if you don't watch it.

Abashed and repentant at being taken in by the smooth words of Rodney the Red, I jumped out at the next Subway station and procured a copy of the *New York Times.* To my surprise I found that his facts were correct. It was only his implications which were wrong. John Kieran in the *Times* stated the sound position which every rooter should take.

"The Detroit ball club," he wrote, "is the property of Mr. Walter O. Briggs, the big body man, and nobody should tell him how to run his business. He hired Gordon Stanley Cochrane. He fired Gordon Stanley Cochrane. That's his business." And to that I am sure that everybody who believes in Thomas Jefferson will say, "Amen."

It is disheartening to learn that when Cochrane was asked if he intended to come back as a baseball manager, he said, "If these things can happen to you, then that kind of job is not for me."

> Where's his gratitude? When he lay at the door of death after his skull was fractured in a ball game, Mr. Briggs paid all his hospital bills. (*New York World-Telegram*, August 10, 1938)

But it took some time before Rodney gained entry to the press box.

LR: My first breakthrough came with basketball. But unless you were willing to pay your way in and just sit in the stands, you had to be a member of the Basketball Writers Association. But it wasn't just a matter of coverage. I wanted to establish that the *Daily Worker* was a legitimate newspaper with a legitimate sports section. Ned Irish was the big muck-a-muck then. He ran Madison Square Garden and he decided who qualified for the press box. So I sent him clippings of my articles covering CCNY [City College of New York], St. John's, Manhattan, Fordham, LIU, and NYU at the Garden and sometimes at their gyms. Finally he said, "Enough!" After that I got invited to all the meetings of the Basketball Writers. We met for lunch every Monday at the famous Mama Leone's restaurant, the writers and the coaches, *La Dolce Vita*.

Baseball was harder to crack. The first thing I did was write to the secretary of the Baseball Writers' Association (BBWA) of America. I told him the *Daily Worker* had started a sports section and I was covering baseball and wanted to be a member. They wrote back and said, in effect, "You'd better get a track record." It took a year before I was admitted as a working professional for a regular sports section. They wanted to see that we were really covering sports and not just writing "Communist propaganda," I suppose. Up 'til then, all I could get was a pass letting me in the park to see the game, but I couldn't go on the field or in the clubhouse. Or eat the pregame roast beef. So I didn't have one-on-one interviews with players for a while, at least not on the field or in the clubhouse. But you didn't have to be a member of the BBWA to go to the Hotel Biltmore when the Cleveland Indians were in town and chat with the manager or the players. I'd say, "I'm a baseball writer, New York *Daily Worker*," and they'd talk to me. They never said, "Let's see your card." So I wasn't completely shut out.

The Communist thing rarely came up. Most ballplayers weren't sure what the *Daily Worker* was. Maybe they thought it was a trade union paper. After a while, when I got the credentials to browse around the field and clubhouses, they all got to know me as a sportswriter.

Of course, the other sportswriters knew the *Daily Worker* was a Communist newspaper. So I got a certain amount of razzing, but for the most part it wasn't hostile. I remember one guy saying, "Does Joe Stalin know about this?" Some typical kidding around of newspaper people. But, of course, they were also curious. The *Daily Worker* went to every paper in the city, nine major dailies, so they began looking at what we did with sports. And after a while I began to hear things from some of them. Not so much in the press box but when I met them outside in training camps and at the Newspaper Guild bar. The Guild was a very big thing then.

I remember Dick Young of the *Daily News* saying something like "I hate the guts of the Commies and what they stand for but if they were all like you . . ." Then one day he pulls me aside and says, "Here's something I can't get into the *Daily News* but I'd damn well like to see in print." I don't remember what it was. But it was interesting that he saw the *Daily Worker* as someplace where you could "get it into print." Like we were the conscience of the trade.

Once in a while I'd have a dialogue with a well-meaning guy like Harold Rosenthal of the *Herald Tribune*. He'd say, "Aren't you restricted in what you can write on the *Daily Worker*? Don't the Commissars check you out?" And I'd say, "The funny thing is, it so happens I'm not restricted. Mostly because there's a lot of ignorance about sports and they're grateful to have a page they won't have to edit. I can do things a lot of you guys can't. I can belt big advertisers, automobile manufacturers, or tobacco companies. Like Briggs who owned the Detroit Tigers. You guys can't write anything about the ban against Negro players. I can do that." So just the fact of my presence opened up that kind of chat with some of the writers.

Another writer I'd call a generally liberal guy who would lean toward the Loyalists in the Spanish civil war but not much more than that. Later on, he'd probably be taken aback by McCarthyism. He came to me one day and said, "You know, I probably believe in many of the same things you do. Not communism. But you're an intelligent guy. You write good stuff. How do you explain all the statues of Stalin over there? Like a god. What's that got to do with what you say is communism? Where the people are equal." Twenty years later I would have said, "Yeah, that's pretty stupid." But at the time—and this is really embarrassing—I said, "What you don't understand is the role Stalin played in that country. How grateful the people are to him because they got rid of the czar, they opened the country up to everybody and so on and so forth. Sure, they probably overdo it. But he doesn't order all that. They want to do that."

Some of them were real characters. Like Howard Cosell. He was a young guy just breaking into the field, when I was a veteran sportswriter. A lot of what people said about him was true; he was an insufferable egotist with a self-righteous demeanor. But I also knew the Howard Cosell who was unafraid to break taboos on the air and was a helluva innovative broadcaster. He would show up in the press boxes—mostly boxing and football—but he followed all the big-time sports.

I admired him as a guy who didn't abide by the carefully laid down rules. You don't say this. You don't say that. He was very good. And he was always top-notch on what was still the race question. He was a real wonderful interpreter of Muhammad Ali. I remember him raising hell with sportswriters. About the jokes and the sneering when, as Cassius Clay, he changed his name to Muhammad Ali. He'd say, "Who the hell are they to tell somebody they can't change their name? America is full of people who changed their names." Stuff like that.

He'd say, "Did you have immigrant parents? You never met a Hungarian who changed his name?" He'd say, "What about Mark Twain? That wasn't his name. It was Samuel Clemens. Who says you can't change your name? Muhammad Ali wanted to establish a new identity. He considered Cassius Clay a slave name." He brought things like that up. He liked the *Daily Worker*, our sports coverage, not our politics.

But there were some guys who really had it in for me, like Dan Daniel of the *World-Telegram*. He hated the idea of a Communist in the press box. This was in the thirties. He had a special venom about it, as though his father had suffered because of Communists or something.

Then there was Jimmy Cannon, the sports columnist of the *New York Post*. He took after me. He attacked me in one of his columns for injecting a class angle into some sports piece I'd written. This was after the war. I remember he said something about "Some young snotnose named Lester Rodney . . ." And I shot back, "I'm not that young that I didn't spend thirty-two months in the Pacific." Anyhow, everybody figured that we're on the verge of coming to blows. And I even wrote—I was so mad—"If Mr. Cannon has anything further to say in a personal way I'll be at my usual ringside seat at the Friday-night fights at Madison Square Garden." Silly stuff like that.

He never would have attacked me physically. He was a paunchy guy and I was in much better shape than him. I'd have decked him. It's a good thing it never happened. I always felt completely uninhibited writing about things other papers and other writers said where social issues were involved, which wasn't usual in the trade.

Another guy I had a couple of run-ins with was Milton Gross of the *New York Post.* For one thing, he was always making cracks about the age of the black ballplayers. He once claimed Jackie Robinson was older than he actually was, and Jackie was furious. I know because I was in the dugout with Jackie when he read Gross's piece. He called it a straight-out lie.

Why was Jackie so mad? Because when you make a player out to be older than he really is, you're playing the owners' game. They use it to hold down players' salaries, and there was already plenty of differentiation in pay scales between black and white players. And Gross never speculated about white players' ages. I mean he covered the Yankees and never "discovered" that Tommy Henrich, for instance, was three years older than he was listed at, which he laughingly revealed when he retired.

Another thing was Gross's posturing about the big basketball scandals of the early fifties, when he demanded that all the players involved in the fix should be thrown in jail. That righteous hypocrite bastard. The *Post* ran the gambling odds on college basketball every day. CCNY five and a half over Bradley, like that, encouraging the atmosphere of gambling around college sports. Now he wants them to go to jail, the kids who see all this going on around them and who shave points to win by less than the gamblers' predicted margins, which were obligingly published in the *Post.* They're playing for nothing. Gross was one guy who never spoke to me.

He'd turn his back and walk past me. Not even a "Good morning, Les." So there was that overt animosity.

On another level, a couple of the "gentlemen" of the *Times*, John Drebinger and Roscoe McGowan. They were correct. They'd say, "Good morning." But they'd never have even a casual conversation with me for years, unlike most of the writers.

But, in general, I got along pretty well with the other writers. . . . They got a kick just out of my being around. Newspapermen like the offbeat. I wasn't there as a Communist, but as a sportswriter. They knew where I stood politically, but I didn't preach to them. You know, in all my years as a sportswriter nobody ever raised the question whether a Communist should be allowed in the press box—not even in the McCarthy years during the fifties. Because they knew me. I'm a fellow working sportswriter and knowledgeable. At the end when I left, the baseball writers voted me honorary lifetime membership in the Baseball Writers' Association. That's usual—but it's not automatic. They vote on it. It's a magic card, automatic free entry into any baseball game and press box in the country. Kind of nice to have. Even after I retired, by the way, I was still asked to vote on players for the Hall of Fame.

The main thing is, I was one of the guys.

And here's something most people probably don't know. The New York basketball writers had their own team, and I was on it.

IS: Where did you play?

LR: Madison Square Garden.

IS: C'mon.

LR: We played between halves of one of the games at the Garden. They used to have doubleheaders for the college teams. Maybe they'd have a Philadelphia night, say NYU against Temple and St. John's against Villanova. So we'd have a game between New York writers and Philadelphia writers. Just fifteen minutes. The fans loved it. Our coach was Everett Morris, the basketball writer of the *Herald-Tribune*.

He put me on the starting team. I grew up playing playground basketball and I was still a pretty good shot. Plus I was comparatively young for a sportswriter, so I could run up and down the floor.

The fans loved it. All these funny-looking guys, some bald and pot-bellied, playing basketball. I remember once some Villanova fan threw a dead fish on to the floor during our game. They probably had it in case of a bad call against their team.

Lester was also a regular performer in the Baseball Writers' annual dinner and show. Written and produced by the writers themselves, the show lampooned the game and targeted the stuffed shirts around it with scathing and often scatological parodies to popular songs.

Rodney attended most of the sportswriters' functions. One of these, in 1940, was a reception for two Finnish athletes. This was during the period of the Russo-Finnish War, and a prominent attendee was ex-president Herbert Hoover. One of the writers thought it would be a lark to bring Hoover and Rodney together. Here's the way Bob Considine, the top sportswriter for the Hearst newspaper chain, reported the moment in the next day's paper:

Mr. Hoover Meets Mr. Rodney

Among the sportswriters at the welcome-here whiskey and conversation party for Paavo Nurmi and Taisto Maki the other day was Lester Rodney, sports editor of the *Daily Worker,* the Communist Daily. Harold Conrad of the *Brooklyn Eagle* was talking to [former president] Herbert Hoover, head of the Finnish Relief Fund, when he noticed Rodney at the Scotch trough, ordering some of that capitalistic old hooch.

"Mr. Hoover," Conrad said, "I want you to meet the gentleman from the *Daily Worker.*" He steered the ex-president over and introduced him.

"Your paper has been belting my brains out lately," Hoover said to Rodney with a nervous laugh.

Rodney shrugged. "Because you're helping the Finns, I guess."

"You forget this," Hoover told him with a slight rise in choler. "In 1923, when Russia was starving, I raised $75 million for its people."

"They must have been White Russians," Rodney replied. (*New York Daily Mirror,* Feb. 5, 1940)

Rodney is quick to say that he had a free hand in editing the *Daily Worker*'s sports section. And by and large he did. But there were times, he acknowledges, when something he wrote evoked some "serious questions," even "grave questions, comrade" from one of the Party's higher-ups.

One instance occurred in 1947 when the Barbell Club, the national organization of America's weight lifters, sent a letter to the *Daily Worker* sports page complaining about some comments in the Soviet press that they felt were demeaning to their members. Their complaint was that the magazine *Soviet Sports* had belittled the results of an international meet in Philadelphia on the grounds that it was unrepresentative in terms of worldwide participation. What the Soviets were really saying, since they were the main rivals to the United States in weightlifting, was that they had not been in the meet. In response, the Americans pointed out that they had invited the Russians to attend and compete, all expenses paid, and that after a considerable delay, the Soviets had declined to attend for "technical reasons." They also suggested that maybe the Russians were afraid of losing since the Americans had beaten them a year earlier at a meet in Paris. A copy of this response was sent to the *Daily Worker,* with a request that the paper run it.

Rodney decided to air the weight lifters' grievance and wrote a column about it, saying that the evidence of the invitation, the disappointing reply, and the subsequent article in the Soviet magazine certainly suggested a lack of reciprocal cordiality by the Russians. "Our very capable grunt and lift men, the best in the world on recent performances," he wrote, "have a legitimate beef against having their victory run down by invited non-participants, and we're happy to air it."

He also noted that international rudeness was not exclusive to the Russians. The year before, some Soviet musicians and dancers had been invited to the United States by some American cultural groups. On arrival, they were confronted by the Justice Department, insisting they sign statements calling themselves "foreign agents." Outraged, the Russians said, "The hell with it," and went home. "Would an American group take that kind of malarkey from the Soviet Union or any other country?" asked Rodney. "I don't think so. I hope not" (*Daily Worker*, November 5, 1947).

Inevitably, Rodney's column came to the attention of someone in the Party hierarchy, and shortly thereafter he was visited by Jack Stachel, one of the Party's main ideologists. As Rodney recalls:

LR: Stachel's manner was mild, sort of more in sorrow than in anger. Like, you don't put it quite that way, comrade, that the Soviet magazine was cockeyed wrong and unsportsmanlike. But if the tone was temperate, the message was clear. The Soviet Union can do no wrong—not in the pages of the *Daily Worker*, anyway. I didn't back down and nothing more was made of it.

Asked whether there were any other incidents involving the Russians, Rodney offers an outlook significantly at odds with some of the stereotypes of American Communists.

LR: I only had one direct contact with the Russians as a *Daily Worker* writer. One day Morris Childs—he was the editor, then—says to me, "There's a Russian guy here who says he's active in Soviet sports. He wants to talk to you." So Morris brings him in. It turns out, the guy wanted some advice—he assumed I was more brilliant than I am—on the best tactics to use when the Russian basketball team takes on the American team in the Olympics. Fast break or slow the ball down and make it a half-court game? Use their height in rebounding against the athleticism of the Americans? Not to get into a running game with them? He wanted my opinion on all that.

I said, "You may not believe this but I'll tell you anyway. I'm an American. And even though the Russians are my socialist brothers and I fight for peace between our two countries, I'm pulling for the Americans to win. But I'll tell you something else. You can't run with the Americans and beat them, and you're not going to beat them in the half-court either, because they're too good." And when I covered the Olympics or wrote about other Olympics that I wasn't at, I always made it clear that I'm rooting for America. I also focused on interviews with Americans. The fucking Russians, you couldn't interview them anyhow. They walled them off. The athletes themselves, if you caught them outside their compound, were pleasant guys and kidded around like Americans. But you couldn't arrange an interview with them. They acted fearful.

Another time I caught some flack from a Party official was for a column I wrote about a young woman who had tried out for the Class B Harrisburg, Pennsylvania, minor league baseball team. The team had actually signed her—Mrs. Eleanor Engle, a local twenty-four-year-old stenographer. She was an infielder and went through one pregame workout but never played in a game. The manager said he wouldn't use her, and the minor league "czar," name of Trautman, denounced the playing of a woman on a league baseball team as a "travesty." I don't know if signing Mrs. Engle was just a publicity stunt to boost attendance or what. But it seemed clear enough to me that Mrs. Engle herself was ready to play and never got the chance.

I wrote that whether or not she would have been good enough to play minor league ball, the thing was used as a pretext for sneering at women in sports by sportswriters, most of whom would have fallen on their faces if they whirled through the infield drill as Mrs. Engle did. I also pointed to the remarkable strides being made by women in sports when they do get a chance to compete with reasonably equal facilities and training, and wound up saying, "Mrs. Engle or any other woman should be entitled to get a chance if they rate it, and should be permitted to go as far as their abilities take them without having to take the derision of typewriter athletes who couldn't carry their gloves." And "three cheers for her try."

But I had one paragraph in that column for which I caught hell from Betty Gannett, another ideological watchdog. "It could be that women may never be good enough to play Big League baseball, though I wouldn't bet against it. But there *are* questions of physiology involved, of sheer muscular strength, leg and arm muscular drive."

Well, the next morning Betty Gannett storms into my office gripping the offending column and says something like "How can a Communist sportswriter say that women aren't capable of doing things men can do?" She had a few other choice remarks, but that was the gist of it. What I should have said, I guess—but I didn't at the time—was that the real fight should be for equal funding for women's sports in high school and college rather than campaigning for women to get into the men's game where they'd quickly be outclassed. We didn't think that way back then.

That was 1952 and women have come a long way in sports since then, but I think I would still write that same paragraph today if someone asked me if I thought women would ever play Big League baseball. And I guess Betty Gannett, who certainly was coming from sincere feelings about discrimination against women in real life but ignorance about sports, would still get mad about it.

In its heyday, contrary to popular belief, the *Daily Worker* often opened its pages to rather intense debates, usually on ideological rather than political questions. Rodney went out of his way to generate such discussions. Early in 1954, for instance, the *Daily Worker* sports section was fixated on a running debate involving Rodney and a number of readers over the political and (occasionally) literary merits of Mark Harris's baseball novel, *The Southpaw.* On other occasions, battles royal raged among readers about the ideological content of movies and plays.

Perhaps the most intense debate was between Rodney and Dr. Howard Selsam, a Marxist philosophy professor, on the question of "Baseball and Ethics." Director of the Party-run Jefferson School, Selsam was generally considered the authority on philosophical questions. His book *Marxism and Ethics* was an attempt at spelling out a code of Communist ethics that would prevail in a socialist society.

LR: Some time back in the fifties I got into a discussion with a French comrade who was an athlete. He was curious to know more about baseball and I was doing my best to explain the game to him. And at some point we got into the question of what happens when a player slides home and the umpire calls him safe but the player knows he was out.

So I say, then he's safe. And the Frenchman—I forget his name—says, "But shouldn't the player immediately say, 'Oh no, I wish I was safe, but I was out.'" So I say, "Are you crazy? I could never get words like that out of my mouth. You play to win. And if the umpire misses the call, that's it. Nobody would. A preacher's son playing baseball wouldn't say, 'Oh no, I was out.'" Then he says, "But that's dishonest." And I say, "No. That's baseball."

Well, I was always looking for provocative topics that would get the readers involved. So I decided this would make a good column. That's when Selsam got into it. He sent me a long letter, which I decided to publish in the *Daily Worker*.

I don't remember it word for word, but it was something like "That's the way everything is under capitalism. And that wouldn't happen under socialism."

> The question is not "should the player report truthfully to the umpire?" [Selsam wrote,] but rather, "How is it that this great game has become so commercialized and corrupted and so played to win at any cost that all other considerations are thrown to the winds? Our sports simply reflect the prevailing morality of the imperialists." (*Daily Worker*, April 24, 1952)

IS: I would have told him to lighten up. The whole idea that this was a question of ethics or morality is just silly. The situation you describe predates capitalism and, in my opinion, will be a part of baseball as long as the game is played. It's part of the game's internal logic. The game depends on the umpire making the call. A player can't override that call, whether for selfish or benevolent reasons. It would undermine the game. Umpires will make mistakes and the only recourse is that the mistakes will generally even out.

LR: You think it would be the same under socialism?

IS: That's what really pisses me off about Selsam's comment. It reflects the hubris of the Communist movement in those days. Selsam thinks he *knows* what every aspect of life will be like under socialism. But nobody knows that. And yes, if baseball will still be played in a socialist society, I imagine its internal logic would be pretty much what it is now. Sure, there'll be changes—and not just in baseball, of course. But they might not be the ones you or me or Dr. Selsam think. Were there any repercussions from this debate?

LR: We got a lot of letters from readers pro and con. But I think the Party leaders had other things on their mind at the time.

While these incidents tell us something about the ideological mind-set of many Party leaders and members, they do not address the question of censorship in its most common form: self-censorship. For the most part, journalists pretty much know what the parameters are for what they can and can't say in print. Rodney was no exception.

LR: Self-censorship? Sure. That happened from time to time. Fans used to ask me about Willie Mays, who was certainly one of the great ballplayers of all time. You know, if a white guy comes into the Big Leagues and he chases women, is happy-go-lucky, and he laughs like hell, well, he's just your average apolitical American ballplayer. And if you ask him any kind of serious question, that's what he'd say. "I'm just a ballplayer." That's the way Willie Mays was, which doesn't mean that he didn't know he was black and that he knew what he owed guys like Robinson and Campanella. He never did anything bad. He never sucked up to the whites, and he was proud, but he was just a ballplayer. Campy never thought too much of him because Willie would never say anything with content. I don't think he ever had too many serious thoughts in his head. Now, if I'd put that in the *Daily Worker*, Ben Davis [a prominent black Party functionary] probably would have come down on me with a lecture like "Is that the kind of image we want to project about a black hero?"

The one I really wrestled with involved Paul Richards, the manager of the Chicago White Sox. He was from Waxahachie, Texas, and a former Big League catcher. I was talking to him once in the clubhouse, and in the midst of some discussion about the treatment of black players, he said something like "You know, we white Southerners, when we get rid of the poison, we're more natural about white and black." That took me by surprise. Both the assertion and his acknowledgment of the "poison." When I asked him why that was, he said, "Well, you know, we talk alike and we're a little slower and we've had more natural contact with them as kids, and the northern whites, they often worry about are they gonna say the right thing to a Negro ballplayer. We don't worry about that. We kid with them."

After that I looked for signs of what Richards said when I went into the dressing rooms. I know who's from the South and who isn't. The results were mixed. I was willing to cede to Richards, who was from Texas. His point, by the way, was not that earth-shattering. There's a cultural affinity. Kids in southern towns often played together. And they have a manner of speech that's similar. And a way of kidding around. The northern whites would be afraid to walk over and clap a black guy on the shoulder and say, "Hey! Here it is in black and white." The southern whites could kid around with their Negro teammates in a more natural way. I saw enough of that to make me feel that Richards was on to something. And southern whites were thrown into this so they had to react one way or another. Some of them remained virulently racist, like Dixie Walker, though even ol' Dixie had to mute that and just play ball in '47. The only evident thing was that he never waited at home plate to congratulate Jackie after he hit a home run with Dixie on base.

"Look around the dugout of mixed teams," Richards said to me. "Who kids around in the shower, splashing each other or making funny remarks, personal remarks? Southern whites with the blacks. And the blacks know them as back-home brothers, once they're rid of the poison."

Asked whether he might have held back from writing about that because people in the Party might see it as a concession to racists, Rodney said:

LR: That resonates a little with me. If I didn't, it would be because I was a little chicken. Because it could be misinterpreted. Like, are you insulting every northern liberal? Or are you deifying a southern racist just because he good-naturedly says a word or two to somebody he plays with? Still, Richards was making a very interesting point. And remember, he always put in that very important qualification—"once you get rid of the poison."

But the biggest story, the one that more than any other gave the *Daily Worker* sports section its distinctive quality and, ultimately, begrudging recognition, was its crusade to break the color line in major league baseball.

PAIGE ASKS TEST FOR NEGRO STARS

Brilliant Hurler Challenges World Series Winners to Game

Confident That Negro Players Could Show Big League Caliber—Tells of Trimming Major Leaguers Consistently on Coast—Players, Fans Want Negro Stars—Fan Vote Would Show Up Jim-Crow, He Tells 'Daily'

By Lester Rodney

"Let the winners of the World's Series play us just one game at the Yankee Stadium —and if we don't beat them before a packed house they don't have to pay us!"

That was the challenge thrown yesterday by Satchell Paige, brilliant Negro pitcher, at the unwritten Jim Crow restriction that keeps him and other Negro ballplayers from their rightful place in America's National Pastime.

Paige didn't make that statement boastfully. It was made with a quiet confidence backed by the records.

Satchell Paige Asks American Sportsmanship

Satchell Paige, famous Negro pitcher, makes the following three propositions to big league baseball in order to establish the point as to whether Negro players are good enough for the big leagues and whether the fans want them.

1. —His Negro all-star team will play the winners of the World's Series at the Yankee Stadium and if they don't beat them, won't ask any money—despite the fact that the house would be sure to be packed.

2. —He will join any big league club next year at his own expense until he had proven his worth as a pitching star—and if he doesn't prove his worth will forget the whole thing.

3. —Let there be a vote cast by all baseball fans entering big league ball parks as to whether they want Negro players in the game or not.

"No all-star team of major leaguers has ever beaten a Negro team on the Pacific Coast in after the season games." he told me at his room in the Olga Hotel in Harlem.

"How many times have you beaten them out there Satchell?" I asked.

He smiled. "I don't remember exactly—but they never beat me in four years trying. And they had some ball players trying. Joe DiMaggio, Charley Gehringer, Dizzy Dean, Pepper Martin, Babe Herman and others." Seriously he added, "There must be something wrong somewhere. Must be just a

never be tolerated. We toured the state from one end to the other and you should have heard the crowds cheer us.

"They said we couldn't go into Texas and we did. Now the same people are telling us that the people don't want us in the big leagues. . . ."

"Another phony bugaboo they used was that Negro pitchers would be wild and might skull a white player, causing trouble. Well, in all the years we've been playing, no Negro pitcher has ever hit a white player with a ball. We've shown what control really is!"

LAUDS 'DAILY' CAMPAIGN

I asked Paige if he had been aware of the drive launched last spring by the Daily and Sunday Worker to have the Brooklyn Dodgers give him a trial.

"Yes," he answered. "I was out in Puerto Rico then, and heard about it. That was really starting something. When you keep talking about the issue and press-ing it, it just is a question of time

Chapter 4

"Jim Crow Must Go!" (Part 1): The *Daily Worker*'s Campaign to Break the Color Line in Organized Baseball

IN HIS 1997 BIOGRAPHY OF JACKIE ROBINSON, Arnold Rampersad, discussing the campaign to end the color line in baseball, writes:

> The most vigorous efforts came from the Communist press, including picketing, petitions and unrelenting pressure for about ten years in the *Daily Worker,* notably from Lester Rodney and Bill Mardo. (Rampersad 1997, 120)

When Lester Rodney launched the *Daily Worker*'s crusade to desegregate organized baseball in 1936, his was a lonely voice. Most fans who filled the major-league ballparks at the time were barely—if at all—aware that the game was lily-white. That was just the way things were in those days. Nor did they learn from the sports pages of their daily newspapers about the color line rigidly enforced by the club owners and the whole baseball establishment. Few were even aware of the existence of a band of skilled, vibrant black ballplayers with the ability to play in the Big Leagues.

Lester Rodney: Search the sports pages of our great newspapers in the mid-thirties and you'll occasionally come across brief items about a game between the Negro League Kansas City Monarchs and the Baltimore Elite Giants, but never a mention that these players were barred from advancing to the major or even the minor leagues. No incredulous editorials blasting this un-American discrimination, no investigative articles listing the qualified and overqualified black players, no queries addressed to the commissioner, the league presidents, the team owners, the managers, and the white players. The conscience of American journalism on baseball's apartheid ban, sorry to say, was not in the hands of America's major daily newspapers.

How much American baseball fans missed because scores of talented earlier African American ballplayers never got a chance to show their stuff in the Big Leagues can never be fully calculated. They missed seeing the prime years of the wondrous Satchel Paige, called by Dizzy Dean "a better pitcher than I am, ever was, or ever will be." They missed seeing Paige's battery mate, Josh Gibson, fabulous as both hitter and catcher, of whom Hall of Fame pitcher Walter Johnson said:

> There is a catcher that any big league club would like to buy for $200,000. They call him "Hoot" Gibson and he can do everything. He hits that ball a mile and he catches so easy he might just as well be in a rocking chair. Throws like a rocket. Bill Dickey isn't as good a catcher. (*Daily Worker,* April 15, 1939)

There were others: John Henry Lloyd, a shortstop known as the "black (Honus) Wagner," evoking the response from the all-time, all-star shortstop, "I am honored to have John Lloyd called the Black Wagner. It is a privilege to have been compared with him" (Peterson 1970, 74); Charlie Grant, a turn-of-the-century second baseman so good, famed manager John McGraw tried to smuggle him onto the Baltimore Orioles as an Indian; Cuban-born Jose Mendez, called the "Black Matty" after Christy Mathewson, perhaps the greatest pitcher of his era; and "Cool Papa" Bell, Oscar

Charleston, Judy Johnson, Buck Leonard, Rube Foster, Ray Dandridge, and scores of others (all now in the Baseball Hall of Fame).

None of these athletes could play in "organized baseball"—so called because the various professional leagues that term embraced were under the jurisdiction of a uniform structure and set of regulations put in place by the owners of the major- and minor-league teams and enforced by the commissioner of baseball, who was selected by them.

It is not as though the worth of these African American athletes was unknown to the baseball establishment. Many a Big League manager knew but wouldn't say publicly that there were at least several players of major-league caliber in the Negro Leagues they would be willing to bring to their clubs if the team owners would allow them to. Most owners knew it as well. But, as the "bible" of Big League baseball, the *Sporting News,* freely acknowledged in 1923, organized baseball had a "tacit understanding that a player of Ethiopian descent is ineligible." That "understanding" prevailed for another twenty-two years.

Professional baseball had not always been segregated. Baseball historian Jules Tygiel estimates that "as many as two dozen blacks played on teams in the professional leagues" in the 1880s (Tygiel 1993, 13). But at its inception in 1876, the National League, which quickly became the dominant force in organized baseball, instituted and generally enforced a whites-only policy. That was also the year in which the federal government abandoned the policy of post–Civil War Reconstruction that had greatly expanded the rights of the newly freed slaves in the South. The end of Reconstruction ushered in an era in which racial segregation was accorded official authorization in virtually every aspect of life—not just in the South but throughout the country. The Civil Rights Act of 1875, which had legislated equal treatment in public facilities, was declared unconstitutional by the Supreme Court, which subsequently (in 1896) ruled, "Laws permitting, and even requiring, their separation in places where they are liable to be brought into contact do not necessarily imply inferiority of either race to the other" (*Plessy v. Ferguson;* this ruling was not overturned until 1954).

Baseball did not escape this racist onslaught. Led by subsequent Hall-of-Famer "Cap" Anson, with the at least tacit and often the overt support of most white players, the crusade to drive blacks out of organized baseball gradually succeeded. By 1899 it was complete. From then on, even the *fact* of blacks who played baseball at a major-league level was rarely mentioned by sportswriters for the major newspapers and magazines of the day.

Until Branch Rickey signed Jackie Robinson to a Brooklyn Dodgers organization contract in 1945, baseball's color line was largely unaddressed by the mainstream sports media, while being vigorously denied by the baseball hierarchy. Even while racial barriers were eroding in other sports as a result of the breakthroughs of Jesse Owens and his fellow black stars at the 1936 Berlin Olympics and the accomplishments of Joe Louis and Henry Armstrong in the boxing ring, "organized" baseball remained lily-white.

In 1933, the weekly *Pittsburgh Courier,* the largest-circulation black newspaper in America, ran a groundbreaking four-month series on racial discrimination in baseball. Using the title a "Big League Symposium," the *Courier* solicited comments from a host of baseball executives on the subject. All heatedly denied the existence of a color line, and the paper barely addressed the subject for the next five years.

There were a few notable and occasional exceptions to this curtain of silence. In 1931, Westbrook Pegler, writing in the *Chicago Tribune,* took baseball to task for excluding blacks. How could it be considered the national pastime, he asked, if it would not allow Negroes to participate? Two years later, Heywood Broun, one-time sportswriter and nationally syndicated columnist, used the occasion of the annual sportswriters' dinner to remind his audience that Paul Robeson had won a spot on the "mythical All-American" football team while playing for Rutgers, and that American blacks had won honors representing the United States in the Olympics.

Baseball's response to all this—as it would be for another dozen years—was simply to deny the charge that blacks were excluded from the organized sport. Thus, in 1933, National League president John A. Heydler would say with a straight face, "Beyond the fundamental requirement that a major-league player must have unique ability and good character and habits, I do not recall one instance where baseball has allowed either race, creed or color to enter into its selection of players" (Peterson 1970, 175). Of course, Heydler's carefully phrased caveats—his own inability to "recall" an instance of discrimination and the qualifications of "good character and habits"—provided a convenient escape hatch should an instance of overt discrimination be found.

In 1936, however, the substance and tenor of the scattered, unorganized protests against the color line accelerated markedly when the *Daily Worker* brought Lester Rodney on as editor of its newly initiated daily sports page.

It all began with a dramatic announcement in the paper's pages on August 13, 1936:

Outlawed by Baseball!

The Crime of the Big Leagues!

The newspapers have carefully hushed it up!

One of the most sordid stories in American sports!

Though they win laurels for America in the Olympics—though they have proven themselves outstanding baseball stars—Negroes have been placed beyond the pale of the American and National Leagues.

Read the truth about this carefully laid conspiracy.

Beginning next Sunday, the *Sunday Worker* will rip the veil from the "Crime of the Big Leagues"—mentioning names, giving facts, sparing none of the most sacred figures in baseball officialdom.

The promised exposé dominated the *Daily Worker*'s Sunday sports section for the next three weeks. Under a front-page banner headline, "Fans Ask End of Jim Crow Baseball," an unsigned editorial by Lester Rodney blasted "the un-American . . . [and] invisible barrier of race prejudice [that] keeps the Negro ball players on the sidelines. Fans, it's up to you. Tell the big league magnates that you're sick of the poor pitching in the American League. You want to see Satchel Paige out there on the mound. You're tired of a flop team in Boston, of the silly Brooklyn Dodgers, of the inept Phillies and the semi-pro Athletics. . . . Demand better ball. Demand Americanism in baseball, equal opportunities for Negro and white. Demand the end of Jim Crow baseball!" (*Daily Worker,* August 16, 1936).

The direct appeal to fans to place demands before baseball's owners and top officials was a harbinger of the campaign the *Daily Worker* would wage over the next decade, a campaign that would see picket lines at major-league ballparks and that would, a few years later, gather several million signatures on petitions to Baseball Commissioner Kenesaw Mountain Landis calling for an end to the color line.

A week later, the *Daily Worker* gave a further hint of what was to come in the years ahead with a report by writer Ted Benson on a confrontation with National League president Ford Frick, himself a former sportswriter. "Is there anything in baseball," Benson asked Frick, "to prevent an owner who has 100 percent control of his club from employing Negro ball players to represent him in the big leagues?"

Somewhat taken aback by the unexpected directness of the question— especially since it had been posed by a white sportswriter—Frick for the first time went on record as saying that there "was no rule" barring blacks. Then, tactically retreating—and clearly invoking a planned script—Frick repeated word for word 1933 National League president John A. Heydler's statement: "Beyond the fundamental requirement that a major-league player must have unique ability and good character and habits, I do not recall one instance where baseball has allowed either race, creed or color to enter into its selection of players"—to which he added, "The particular hypothetical question which you submit, however, indirectly involves all clubs of the League and it is not within the province or the authority of the League president to express an official opinion in the matter" (*Daily Worker,* August 23, 1936).

LR: The idea of the interview was to knock out the alibi of the club owners that it wasn't up to them. So the question was "Is there anything in writing about Negroes not being able to play in Big League baseball?" He must have anticipated we were going to ask him something like that so he probably consulted his lawyer, who I'm sure told him, "Whatever you say, don't say there's something written about this." And there probably wasn't. It was a "gentlemen's agreement."

But when we got from him the fact that there was no written ban, that enabled us to put the club owners on the spot. So then we began questioning the Big League magnates, most of whom wouldn't talk to us, but not all. We got several replies, most of them evasive. They'd say things like "My stand on democracy is well known" and "It's not up to me," or imply that the players would never stand for it.

When Rodney had Ted Benson go on to query club owners on the issue, Tom Yawkey, owner of the Boston Red Sox, dismissed the question by saying he'd "never given any thought to the matter." Eddie Brannick, secretary of the New York Giants, claiming "no bigotry or prejudice toward anyone," asked Benson, "What do you want to bring this up for?" Ed Barrow of the Yankees refused comment, while Philip Wrigley, owner of the Chicago Cubs, and William Benswanger, owner of the Pittsburgh Pirates, were both "out of town" and unavailable. (A few years later, Benswanger, after a similar query by Rodney, would be the first owner to respond favorably.) In the same August 23 issue, Fred Farrell, sportswriter for the *Daily Worker*'s West Coast counterpart, *The People's World,* explored the records of outstanding black players who, he argued, could make any Big League team.

A week later, the *Sunday Worker* carried a page of letters from fans who were overwhelmingly in favor of ending the ban. From then on, the campaign against Jim Crow in baseball became the hallmark of the *Daily Worker* sports section.

LR: We never had what you might call a plan for the campaign. But a strategy did evolve.

First was simply to raise hell about the color ban and get it into the public consciousness. Except for the black weeklies, which had limited impact, it just wasn't being talked about then.

Second, we set out to popularize the black stars and document that they could compete on the Big League level.

Third, shoot down the notion that the white players and managers wouldn't stand for it by directly putting the question to them.

Fourth, we immediately put the league presidents and the commissioner on the spot by challenging them to say whether there was an official ban, which they denied, of course.

But maybe the most important was to generate fan participation in the campaign.

Our biggest asset, though, was that the time was right. Black athletes had stolen the show at the 1936 Olympics in Berlin, especially Jesse Owens, who won four or five gold medals. And Hitler had made such a big deal about his Aryan athletes and was so embarrassed he wouldn't even shake the hands of the American blacks. This was all over the newspapers, which had these marvelous pictures of black medal winners draped with the American flag. And Joe Louis was on his way to the heavyweight title, the first time there'd be a black heavyweight champion in more than twenty years. So it was a good time to say, "Why not in baseball?"

At the same time, I felt that if we were to succeed I had to establish our credentials as an American sports section, not as a paper whose only interest in sports was to grind an ideological ax on this one issue. I didn't think what we had to say about the color line would carry much weight with the new readers we were trying to attract, as well as ballplayers and managers, unless we had demonstrated our commitment to the sport as sport. Nevertheless, right from the start we began doing things that none of the other papers were doing. When the Negro Leagues played in New York, we'd cover them and highlight players we thought were good enough for the Big Leagues. You could call that part of a campaign to familiarize our readers with black players and to break down the silence. How many people except other ballplayers and managers knew there were black players good enough to play in the Big Leagues? The other papers, like the *Times* and the *Post*, might have briefly reported on a Negro League game, but if Satchel Paige pitched a shutout or even if Josh Gibson hit the longest home run ever at Yankee Stadium, they'd never say, "Why isn't this guy playing for a major-league team?" They didn't even note that Paige beat the top Big Leaguers consistently in postseason exhibition games on the West Coast.

One can only marvel at the tenacity and patience of the Negro League players. Some would voice disgust and frustration at the ban. But underneath it all there was an extraordinary élan and life force around the Negro Leagues. A sense of casual and playful camaraderie. High spirits. They sure didn't look or act like downtrodden victims. The movie *Bingo Long and the Traveling All-Stars* caught a little of that.

On the other hand, the quality of play was very uneven. You'd see players like Satch and Josh Gibson and Buck Leonard whose game screamed "Big League superstar!" Others had quite ordinary talents, like minor leaguers with possible Big League potential. Of course, most of these guys never had the intensive, highly organized technical coaching from early on that their white contemporaries did. But there was a looser feeling, more fooling around and showmanship than in the Bigs. It was part of their selling point; crowds came to expect entertaining style, and that could negatively impact the overall caliber of play.

And the playing conditions left a lot to be desired, though that also varied. As you might expect, playing conditions in Big League stadiums weren't too bad. But Roy Campanella, who, unlike Robinson, was a real product of Negro League baseball, starting at age fifteen, had some wild stories to tell. Doubleheaders, for instance. We think of a doubleheader as playing a game, resting, then playing the second game on the same field. Not in the Negro Leagues, though. Roy told me:

"We'd finish an afternoon game and pile right into the old bus, no showers and change of uniforms, and bump along maybe one hundred or two hundred miles or more to the next game. We'd eat sandwiches in the bus. In those days, you couldn't count on stopping at some roadside restaurant and being served—even at the back door. A pit stop to use a bathroom could be a big adventure. When we got to the ballpark for the second game of the doubleheader, we'd pile out of the bus and shake the stiffness with just a little warm-up before the night game."

The best players, the ones who knew they were good enough or thought they were good enough to play in the Bigs, certainly fantasized about it. After all, it's one thing to enjoy what you're doing where you're doing it, be high-spirited and appreciated and all that, yet anyone who makes his living with a particular talent wants to show that talent where the biggest spotlight is, not to mention the biggest money. Would someone who knew he was a world-class pianist be content to stay in Podunk? When the ban was ended, you didn't hear any of the black players saying, "I think I'd rather stay in the Negro Leagues, it's more fun."

Most of the owners in both organized baseball and the Negro Leagues opposed desegregation. The Big League muck-a-mucks, when they deigned to talk about it, claimed the players would all be against it and that there'd be riots in the stands and on the field. But their real concern was that if the color line was broken, black fans would flood the ballparks and drive the white fans away. The Negro League owners, of course, knew that desegregation would inevitably make their franchises defunct. Some of them even spread stories that Satchel Paige preferred staying where he was, where he was making good money and was an established star.

LR: That was one big fat myth, with more than a little racist overtone. When I interviewed him in '37, Satch was already thirty-one, and I remember him saying, "I don't think they can keep us out much longer." He was wrong. It was eleven more long years before Satch, probably the best pitcher in the game, would break in as a forty-two-year-old rookie. It was a damn outrageous tragedy, and America has gotten off the hook rather lightly for it.

Shortly after becoming a member of the Baseball Writers' Association, which gave him access to the playing field, the dugout, and the dressing rooms as well as the press box, Rodney began buttonholing managers, asking them about the color line. The first manager he tackled was Burleigh Grimes of the Brooklyn Dodgers.

LR: That was in 1937 at Ebbets Field. I'd been covering the Dodgers all that summer so Burleigh knew who I was. And I think I can fairly say he respected me as a writer by this time because he knew I didn't sensationalize things. On this particular day I saw Burleigh out in left field, where he was probably working with the left fielder or something. So I strolled out there to chat with him.

We started talking about the game and who was going to pitch that day. Baseball chatter. And at one point I ask him, "How're things going for the team?" It wasn't a very good team then in 1937. It finished sixth in an eight-team league. And he says, "Frankly, I could use another pitcher and just one good hitter. But we're doing the best we can." He was a former Big League pitcher himself. So I say—and I remember these were my exact words—"Burleigh, how would you like to put a Dodger uniform on Satchel Paige and Josh Gibson?" Well, he looks at me like I'd just hit him over the head with a club. You just didn't talk about those things then. He stops for a minute. And then he begins to talk to me, patiently, like a father to a child. You know, this was more than sixty years ago, so these weren't his exact words. But almost.

"Lester," he says, "you're wasting your time. This'll never happen. Just think about the trains in the South. Think about the hotels. Think about the restaurants. How could it happen? It'll never happen." So I say, "Do you know some of the good black ballplayers?" And he says, "Of course I do. We all do. I know how good they are. But let's talk about something else. First, it's never going to happen. And I don't wanna talk any more about it."

"Burleigh," I say. "Can I at least write, 'I know how good they are—Burleigh Grimes?' I'm not saying you'll—"

Now he's almost livid. "No, no!" he says. "I'm not gonna stick my neck out!"

"I won't say you're in favor of it or anything like that—just 'I know how good they are.'"

"No, no." He didn't want to be the first.

Even the most die-hard racists had to grudgingly acknowledge that Paige and Gibson were two black players who could walk right onto a major-league team. It would be almost impossible for any baseball fan who never saw them play to know how good Paige and Gibson were. Not just the best black players. To me, Josh Gibson was the best catcher, period. Number-one catcher on any all-time, all-star team. I wasn't the only sportswriter who knew that. He was the best catcher this country ever produced. He tore up the Negro Leagues. But he knew there was no future for him in the Big Leagues and he got sloppy. He knew he was the best and he was bitter. He drank. It happened too late for him. By the time Jackie broke the color line, Josh was past his peak. But he was awesome. You talk about an all-time, all-star team, Josh Gibson towers over even Johnny Bench, the definitive Big League catcher, and Roy Campanella, who was certainly right behind Bench, and Bill Dickey of the Yankees.

Josh was no less than a right-handed-hitting Babe Ruth. Maybe more. And as good as Bench defensively. Can you imagine that? Yet it wouldn't be right to think of Gibson and these other guys only as unhappy victims. They weren't crushed people. Their games were a joy to watch and they were fun guys. But they weren't able to do what they did best in the place where that was on display and where they could get paid big. In the Bigs. So it did eat away at a man like Josh, who knew he was the very best. All these great ballplayers you never heard of—Smoky Joe Williams, possibly a better pitcher than Paige; Cool Papa Bell, the greatest centerfielder, as good or better than Willie Mays. Not just for them, but for Americans generally. Baseball history, which is certainly part of American history, would have been so different.

Even players or sportswriters who said there weren't any black players good enough to play in the major leagues would concede, "Well, maybe Satchel Paige." Satch was a genuine phenomenon. As a pitcher, he came close to being the mythical figure everyone talked about. Was he the greatest pitcher ever? Hard to say. At the very least, he certainly would have been right up there with Mathewson, Walter Johnson, Cy Young, Lefty Grove, Sandy Koufax, Carl Hubbell, Bob Feller, Bob Gibson, you name them. And Satch knew it. I once asked him how many games he thought he would win if he pitched in the Bigs. This was when he was in his prime, of course. "Thirty to thirty-five a season," he said matter-of-factly. I believed it. He was used to pitching an incredible amount of innings on short rest.

There were white fans who didn't know the name of another Negro League player who had heard about Satchel Paige, even though very few of them ever saw him pitch. Every time there was a rumor that some Big League team might be getting ready to bring on a black player, it inevitably focused on Satch. There was something of a stir in 1937, before the season even began, when the Dodgers were said to be considering hiring him. They'd gotten a lot of flack in Brooklyn, which we had a lot to do with. We had a lot of readers in Brooklyn, and they started writing to the Dodger management, especially since the Dodgers were consistently in the second division and their loyal legion of die-hard fans would have loved the prospect of anyone who could improve them. At one point they seemed to be on the verge. And then suddenly they chickened out. I'm sure there was a lot of pressure on them from the league and from the other owners. This was ten years before Jackie Robinson.

Later that year, when Satch was in town with the Kansas City Monarchs, I called him for an interview, and he said, "Sure, come to my hotel." He was at the Olga Hotel in Harlem, which is no longer there. It was well known. I remember taking the subway up to Harlem. It was on 137th Street, I think, just off Lenox Avenue. It looked like an old brownstone, but it was an old beat-up hotel. Anyway, I get there and he's alone in this room and his legs are sticking out off the end of the bed. Satch was about 6' 4" and they didn't have beds long enough. There was nobody else there. No agent. He knew I was from the *Daily Worker*. He knew my face because I had covered Negro League games and chatted with players. He was also aware of our campaign and even mentioned that he had read about it while playing in Puerto Rico.

The thing is, I hardly had to bring up the question of why he wasn't pitching in the Big Leagues. He was busting with that. While we talked he began to come up with ideas. Why don't they have a poll? Every Big League fan going into a game next year, just ask them yes or no, do you want colored players in the Big Leagues. But he also had prepared one biggie in his mind beforehand. "Let the winners of the World Series play an all-star Negro team just one game at Yankee Stadium," he says, "and if we don't beat them before a packed house they don't have to pay us a dime!"

"Can I print that?" I ask.

"Absolutely." He wanted this in the newspapers, but he hadn't gotten anywhere because the papers weren't paying any attention to him. He was an embarrassment to them. Like a bad conscience. How does somebody who works for a paper that doesn't mention the fact that blacks are banned interview Satchel Paige and come out with this challenge? He can't. But Satch knew that we would.

So I say to him, "What makes you so sure you'll win?" And he replies, "We've been playing teams of major-league all-stars after the regular season in California for four years and they haven't beaten me yet. And they had some ballplayers trying. Joe DiMaggio, Charley Gehringer, Dizzy Dean, Pepper Martin, Billy Herman. . . . Must be just a few men who don't want us to play Big League ball. The players are okay and the crowds are with us. Just let them take a vote of the fans whether they want us in the game. I've been all over the country and I know it would be one hundred to one in favor of such a game. Yankee Stadium couldn't hold the fans who'd come out for that game."

We played this up big. He loved it. He wanted ten copies. It created a stir. I mean, here was the most famous black player in the country challenging the ban publicly for the first time. The challenge was never accepted, of course. And none of the other papers carried it. That doesn't mean the other sportswriters and the baseball establishment didn't know about it. It was a minor sensation. And it certainly didn't hurt our reputation in Harlem as being the paper that was for blacks in baseball. I think that had something to do with Ben Davis [a prominent black Communist] being elected to the New York City Council. Adam Clayton Powell knew what we did. He talked about the campaign.

Just before I left I said to him—he was thirty-one then—"Satch, this may not make you feel any better, but I remember Dazzy Vance (who was a great Dodger pitcher, Hall-of-Famer), he first came into his own in his thirties. He knocked around 'til then. He hit his peak at thirty-four." And Satch says, "I'll be happy to get my break at thirty-four. I don't think they can keep us out that long."

(Satchel Paige finally did get his break—not at the age of thirty-four, but when his greatest years were behind him. Bill Veeck of the Cleveland Indians signed Satch in mid-season of the summer of 1948, almost eleven years after the interview. Even then, he amassed a 6–1 record in about a third of the season while helping Cleveland to its first pennant in almost thirty years.)

LR: Part of the stereotype the sportswriters pinned on Satch was that he was something of a clown without a serious thought in his head. In fact, Satchel Paige was a wonderful showman. Sure, he was made out as a Stepin Fetchit type content to "play with his own." But the black fans knew he was putting on a show. And they loved it. To paraphrase Shakespeare, there was always a method to his clowning. It brought paying customers into the ballpark. And he had real baseball intelligence.

In one of our conversations, he told me how, in 1949, a year after he had broken in with Cleveland, he was facing a very dangerous hitter—one of the great hitters—I think it was Johnny Mize, who was then a Yankee. It was in a critical game situation with the bases full.

"No way I was gonna let that guy take three swings at me," says Satch, who was then forty-three. "You know what I did? I deliberately threw three balls. They didn't look like intentional balls. Just missed by a few inches." He had that control. So it was 3 and 0. In that situation, he figured correctly that Yankee manager Bucky Harris would tell Mize to lay off the next two pitches because they needed the run. Satch's next two pitches were called strikes. So then he needed only one pitch to get Mize out. And he did. Only Satchel Paige could have done that. Only he would have had the confidence and the control.

He used to put a dime on a little stick and someone would hold it up at home plate before the game started in the old Negro Leagues, and he'd knock the dime right off with his first pitch. He called in his outfield sometimes. That was one of his most famous stunts. He'd wave them in and tell them to sit down. He knew he could keep the batter from hitting the ball into the outfield. But he only did that when he knew exactly who he was facing. And that was in his prime years.

All this happened less than a year after we began the campaign. 1937 was also the year Joe DiMaggio spoke up. A group of us were standing around with Joe in the stadium. This was Joe's second year as a Big Leaguer. And one reporter—I forget who it was—asks him who was the best pitcher he ever faced. Nobody was thinking of black players. DiMaggio stuns everybody by saying without hesitation, "Satchel Paige." He had played against Satch in a few postseason exhibition games in California. Joe didn't make a big deal out of it either. He didn't say, "I'm against discrimination." He was a very aloof guy, as everyone knows by now, though more so later on. But in that case he answered a question honestly and he had no compunctions about it. He knew Paige was black and that blacks were banned when he said that. We had a huge headline the next day. The other papers never mentioned it.

The campaign continued to accelerate in 1938. More papers were confronting Big League magnates on segregation. Sam Lacey, sports editor of the *Washington Herald,* a black paper, managed to get a remarkable concession out of Clark Griffith, owner of the Washington Senators. "There are very few big league owners," Griffith told Lacey, "who are not aware of the fact that the time is not far off when colored baseball players will take their places beside those of other races in the major leagues" (Tygiel 1993, 32). Although Griffith went on to list all the "difficulties" this prospect faced, if nothing else, his statement raised expectations that the color line would be broken, thereby heightening the campaign's momentum.

For the first time, the Communist Party's annual May Day parade in New York City featured banners calling for an end to Jim Crow in baseball. At a time when this annual event drew tens of thousands of marchers—many of them young sports lovers from the new CIO unions—and even larger numbers of spectators, the parade through the heart of Manhattan became a vehicle for broadening public consciousness of the campaign. (Baseball and basketball teams from the Fur Workers', Meat-Cutters', and Ladies' Garment Workers' unions also marched in that year's May Day parade, reflecting the transformation brought about in Communist circles by the new Popular Front policy and the influence of what had become the *Daily Worker*'s extremely popular sports section, now several pages long.)

Also in 1938, scores of Young Communist League members began fanning out to ballparks, in New York and elsewhere, with leaflets highlighting the remarks of ballplayers and sportswriters on baseball's racial barrier.

An incident that summer added fuel to the campaign. Asked during a dugout interview aired over a Chicago radio station what he did in the off-season, Jake Powell, an outfielder with the New York Yankees, replied that he was a policeman in Dayton, Ohio, and that his favorite activity was "beating niggers over the head and throwing them in jail" (WGN Chicago, July 29, 1938).

Five years earlier, the baseball establishment would have laughed it off. This time, however, there was a huge popular uproar from baseball fans and black organizations demanding Powell's indefinite suspension, which Baseball Commissioner Landis couldn't ignore. But his response—a slap-on-the-wrist ten-day suspension—served to underscore the hypocrisy of baseball's oft-stated principle that "a major-league player must have unique ability and good character." The more telling punishment for Powell was that his idea of a "funny" remark turned into another nail in Jim Crow's coffin.

But 1939 was the year the campaign gained the momentum with which it continued from then on. That year the *Pittsburgh Courier* jumped into the campaign in a big way. The *Courier*'s reawakened attention to the issue was due principally to Wendell Smith, who had started covering sports for the paper the year before. Smith heralded the *Courier*'s new commitment early in 1939 when he wrote:

> In the past five years this form of sporting segregation has been revealed to the public by the press of the nation. Such celebrated writers as Jimmy Powers, Lloyd Lewis, Shirley Povich, Bill Corum and Dan Parker have seen fit to champion the cause of the Negro player. Courageous writers like those mentioned and the ever-fighting Negro press with the *Pittsburgh Courier* in the vanguard, have laid the question squarely before the officials of major league baseball. (*Pittsburgh Courier,* February 15, 1939)

Rodney and the *Daily Worker* were never mentioned.

Smith's omission and the events that followed immediately thereafter suggest that he may have been given some encouragement by the baseball establishment itself, which clearly was unhappy at the fact that the Communist *Daily Worker* had gained prominence as the foremost crusader on the issue. At the very least, baseball's hierarchy could reasonably expect that the generally conservative *Courier* would be somewhat less confrontational than the *Daily Worker.*

An exclusive interview granted Smith by National League President Frick a few days later adds credence to this possibility. In it, Frick no longer hid behind his legalistic dodge to the *Daily Worker* two years earlier when he had declared that there was "no rule" barring black players. (It was already an open secret by then that the color line was held in place by a "gentlemen's agreement" rather than a piece of paper which could prove embarrassing if ever uncovered.) This time Frick admitted that "We have not used them [black players] . . . because we feel that the general public has not been educated to the point where they will accept them on the same standard as they do the white players. . . . The time is near when Negro players will be starring on big league teams. . . . I cannot name any particular day or year, but assure you that when the people ask for the inclusion of your players we will use them. I do not think the time is far off and with constant crusading by the press of both races it is bound to come. However, you must keep fighting" (*Pittsburgh Courier,* February 25, 1939).

Amazing advice coming from one of the bastions holding the Jim Crow system in place. Equally amazing, American League president Will Harridge said virtually the same thing in an interview he gave Wendell Smith a short time later, concluding that baseball would "open the now barred gates in five years—or less" (*Pittsburgh Courier,* August 12, 1939). Harridge also criticized New York Giants manager Bill Terry for telling Smith that while he knew "as well as everybody else does, that there are a number of Negroes who have the ability to play in the major leagues," still he didn't "think Negroes will ever be admitted in the majors." (Giants stars Carl Hubbell and Mel Ott publicly registered their disagreement with Terry. Typically, only the *Daily Worker* and the black press reported it.) Harridge went on to tell Smith that "the reaction of American League managers and players—when they appeared in *The Courier*—would be more liberal and optimistic."

Four months after the Ford Frick Interview, Smith launched a series of eight consecutive articles on the color line in the *Courier*'s pages. In it he interviewed forty players and eight managers in what the *Courier* headlined as "The Most Exclusive, Startling and Revealing Expose of the Attitude of the Major League Players and Managers Themselves Ever Written" (*Pittsburgh Courier,* July 15, 1939).

In 1937, Brooklyn Dodgers' manager Burleigh Grimes had refused to let the *Daily Worker* quote him to the effect that he thought some black players were of Big League quality, saying he didn't want to stick his neck out. But two years later, every National League manager except Bill Terry of the Giants cooperated fully in Smith's series of interviews. (The series was apparently limited to the National League because the *Courier* was based in a National League city and the interviews could be conducted as each team came through town.) One after another they came: Bill McKechnie of the Cincinnati Reds; James (Doc) Prothro of the Philadelphia Phillies; Leo Durocher of the Brooklyn Dodgers; Ray Blades of the St. Louis Cardinals; Casey Stengel, then of the Boston Bees (the Boston Braves of that era were so bad that they changed their name to the Bees in an effort to boost sagging attendance—it didn't help); Pie Traynor of the Pittsburgh Pirates; Gabby Hartnett of the Chicago Cubs. To a man they echoed Frick: each had seen black players who could play at a major-league level; integration will happen when the fans are ready for it. Similar sentiments were expressed by, among others, Ernie Lombardi, Mel Ott, Carl Hubbell, Johnny Vandermeer, Bucky Walters, Al Simmons, Hans Wagner, Paul and Lloyd Waner, Arky Vaughn, Augie Galan, Dizzy Dean, Paul Dean, and Pepper Martin.

Clearly, there had been a shift in the baseball establishment's strategy. Although the magnates and league officials were not prepared to drop their policy, they shifted the blame to (white) "fans" and white players who "weren't ready" for the change.

The *Daily Worker* greeted Smith's series with open arms. A phone call from Rodney congratulating Smith on his initiative led to an informal agreement whereby each paper could reprint the other's stories on the campaign. The first article focusing on Bill McKechnie and the Cincinnati Reds was immediately reprinted by the *Daily Worker,* with Rodney enthusing in a separate column, "What you see on this page today is going to bust Jim Crow right out of American baseball. It may take another year and it may not, but discrimination in our national pastime is through. The last excuse for it is now forever blasted by the players and managers themselves. . . . *The Pittsburgh Courier* is to be congratulated for making this vital contribution" (*Daily Worker,* July 23, 1939). Rodney also blasted the attempt to blame white fans and ballplayers for the color bar, pointing to statements by numerous ballplayers and fan turnouts for postseason exhibition games between Negro League and major-league all-star teams.

Over the next two months, the *Daily Worker* reprinted—in whole or in part—every single installment of Smith's *Courier* series. It was the only daily newspaper in America to report on the *Courier*'s groundbreaking series and the outpouring of anti-segregation statements by ballplayers. As the series wound down, Wendell Smith wrote to Rodney:

> I take this opportunity to congratulate you and the *Daily Worker* for the way you have joined with us on the current series concerning Negro players in the major leagues, as well as all your past great efforts in this respect. The public seems to like the series very much and we feel that our efforts have not been in vain. In the future, perhaps we can work out something similar to the present series together too. In the meantime, I wish you the best of luck and admire you and your liberal attitude. (*Daily Worker,* August 20, 1939)

Unfortunately, but undoubtedly in keeping with the times and the generally conservative views of his paper—and possibly in deference to the cooperation he was getting from the baseball establishment—Smith's admiration for Rodney's and the *Daily Worker*'s efforts did not find their way into the *Courier*'s own pages.

But Smith was hardly alone. Even the hint of a baseball color line had long been heatedly denied in those days—let alone that the Communists were actively campaigning against it. Nevertheless, tacit acknowledgment of the growing impact of the *Daily Worker*'s campaign against the color line came from the baseball establishment itself. In a move reminiscent of charges by the defeated Confederates after the Civil War that northern "carpetbaggers" were stirring up otherwise happy-go-lucky "nigras," defenders of baseball's racial status quo argued there would be no problem with the racial state of baseball if it weren't for outside "agitators" who, in the words of the *Sporting News,*

> have sought to force Negro players on the big leagues, not because it would help the game but because it gives them a chance to thrust themselves into the limelight as great crusaders in the guise of democracy. . . . Some colored people are not looking at the question from the broader point of view, or for the ultimate good of either the race or the individuals in it. They ought to concede their own people are now protected and that nothing is served by allowing agitators to make an issue of a question on which both sides prefer to be let alone. (Peterson 1970, 179)

The same theme was struck by the erratic, flamboyant, and notoriously inebriated Larry MacPhail, then president of the Brooklyn Dodgers, who would later, when no longer with the Dodgers, become the mainstay of the owners' attempts to stem the integration tide. "The discussion of the problem," he declared, "has been contaminated by charges of racial discrimination—most of it vicious propaganda—circulated by professional agitators who do not know what they are talking about" (Peterson 1970, 179).

While reprinting and highlighting the *Courier*'s initiative, the *Daily Worker* was making big news of its own that year in New York.

LR: In 1939, I thought the great fight was being won. That was the year I got my first favorable comment from an owner, when William Benswanger of the Pittsburgh Pirates wrote back to my usual question about the color line saying, "I don't see why it wouldn't be the same as having black musicians." Coming from an owner, that was a breakthrough statement.

That's what enabled Leo Durocher to speak out in my interview which appeared in the *Daily Worker.* I put the same question to Leo that I put to Burleigh Grimes two years earlier. But Leo was very different from Burleigh, who was a marginal manager. Leo was a cocky guy. Scrappy. More confident. And sophisticated. He felt this thing coming, I'm sure. And what he said was, "Hell, yes! I'd sign them in a minute if I got permission from the big shots."

Later, in 1942, when I was inducted into the army, the *Daily News*, then the largest circulation of any newspaper in the United States, had an article by Hy Turkin, who wrote:

> A casual remark made by Leo Durocher to Lester Rodney, Sports Editor of the *Daily Worker*, now in the Army, may do more for his place in history than all his shortstopping and managing histrionics. He said that he would hire Black players and this is like the tail of the tornado that has overwhelmed Judge Landis with two million signatures and threatens the democratization of our national pastime. (N.Y. *Daily News*, July 21, 1942)

The *Herald-Tribune* had something like that but snottier. They had some patrician guys there. Their article was something like "Before he went to the army, Lester Rodney of the *Daily Worker* dragged up the old red herring about Jim Crow in baseball and produced a quote from Leo Durocher that's now created a lot of agitation." That was the tone of it.

There was also a big step up in our petition campaign that year. Members of the Young Communist League fanned out everywhere with petitions—the Big League ballparks, the Negro League games, busy street corners. They'd go up to people and ask, "Would you sign a petition to give Negro ballplayers a chance to play in the Big Leagues?" And they got pretty good responses. We had a goal of one hundred thousand signatures that year and we went way beyond it. That's part of the almost 2 million signatures that eventually wound up on Landis's desk.

Although Rodney coordinated the campaign, the underlying foundation for it was the Communist Party and the various institutions it set up.

LR: The actual implementation was in the hands of a middle level of Communist Party leadership who were baseball fans and some of the leading people in the YCL, the live ones like Gil Green and Carl Ross, whose political imaginations could grasp the implications of the campaign. They were the ones who went to the Party sections near Ebbets Field to get them involved. I didn't organize the petition campaigns. The YCL clubs did. We reported it and stimulated it.

Pete Cacchione—he was the Communist city councilman from Brooklyn —also got into it in a big way. The top Party leaders would give me an occasional pat on the back, but they had other things on their minds. But did I ever sit down with Earl Browder, William Z. Foster, Ben Davis, who would have ideas on how to map out the campaign? No. Nothing like that.

Our people in the trade unions really pushed the campaign. The NMU [National Maritime Union], District 65, a huge union, mostly young workers, with left leadership. The Furriers. It came as a big shock to a lot of trade unionists that blacks weren't allowed in baseball. They weren't that much different from the general population that way. We had to educate them to the fact that there were black players good enough to play in the Big Leagues. Many of them had never even heard of Satchel Paige. The overwhelming culture back then was still accepting of discrimination. Hey, we went into the Second World War two years later with a segregated army and navy. Whether people accepted it easily or uneasily, very few did anything about it. I'm sure black trade unionists were more conscious of baseball's discrimination. But they too were facing the prevailing culture of accepting what was. This is why the campaign took ten damn years to win.

Politically conscious blacks were aware of what we were doing. I remember one Negro League game between the Homestead Grays and the Philadelphia All-Stars where a score of YCLers displayed blowups of *Daily Worker* articles on the campaign while circulating the petitions. They got signatures as fast as giving away free hot dogs. This was before the ball game, and I was hanging around with some of them when a guy comes up to us, signs a petition, and says, "That's a wonderful campaign your paper is carrying on, and it's getting results. You're doing a great job." It was A. Philip Randolph, head of the Brotherhood of Sleeping Car Porters, who wasn't overly friendly to the Communists [quoted in the *Daily Worker*, August 7, 1939]. Inside the stadium a few of the YCLers spot Josh Gibson in the Grays' dugout. He signs a petition and says, "Like to get up there."

YCL members were also out in full force at ballparks elsewhere, collecting thousands of signatures in Philadelphia, Chicago, Detroit, Cleveland, and Washington, D.C. Back in New York, bands of young Communists made their way to crowded New York beaches and parks in the summer heat, getting additional hundreds of signatures on their petitions.

In the spring of 1939, the campaign penetrated the halls of the New York state legislature when State Senator Charles Perry from Harlem introduced a resolution originally drafted by *Daily Worker* writer Mike Singer, the paper's Albany correspondent, that read:

> The legislature of the State of New York has from time to time enacted legislation designed to prevent racial discrimination in the various branches of the government as well as in private industry and labor unions and . . . there are in the United States many baseball players whose skill is equal to or surpasses that of many now playing in the many leagues of organized baseball but who are prevented from seeking or finding employment therein. . . . This discrimination is against the expressed intention of the State of New York. (*Daily Worker,* May 21, 1939)

The resolution was forwarded to Commissioner Landis and the respective presidents of the National and American Leagues—Ford Frick and Will Harridge. While not binding on anyone, the resolution foreshadowed legal steps in New York and elsewhere that would make local teams liable for enforcing the whites-only policy of the leagues.

Also in 1939, but unacknowledged at the time—and since—the *Daily Worker* became the first paper in the country to tout Jackie Robinson, then a student at Pasadena Junior College in California, as a major-league prospect. Dave Farrell, a writer for the *People's World,* the weekly West Coast Communist newspaper, wrote a column that subsequently appeared in the *Daily Worker:*

> Of the many fine Negro ball players I've seen in recent years, Jackie Robinson strikes me as having the best chance to cut the

buck in organized ball. . . . He's a corking fielder, a darned good
hitter and a helluva guy with a bunt. But it isn't until you've seen
him on the bases that you realize what a tootsie he is. His extraordinary speed will drive pitchers crazy and balk them to death.
(*Daily Worker,* October 4, 1939)

In 1940, the momentum generated in 1939 kept picking up steam. Now
other papers and groups, not just the *Daily Worker,* were getting into it. A
major step was taken when the New York Trade Union Athletic Association (TUAA) threw its full weight into the campaign. The TUAA had been
formed the year before by thirty or so unions in the New York area. Although left-wing unions had taken the initiative to set it up, the TUAA attracted the interest of many other unions as well.

Its main function was to organize sports programs for union members.
They set up leagues in baseball, basketball, track, soccer, and other sports
and helped the unions popularize participation in sports for their members.
There'd never been anything on that scale for the unions. It was very professional.

A year later, the TUAA had grown to fifty-six American Federation of
Labor (AFL), Congress of Industrial Organizations (CIO), and independent unions with a combined membership of more than three hundred thousand. The membership included transport workers, office workers, auto
workers, cleaners and dyers, telephone workers, wholesale and warehouse
workers, building service workers, furriers, and government workers,
among others.

In 1940, their second year, the TUAA announced a campaign to get 1
million signatures on petitions to break the color line in baseball, and they
launched a Committee to End Jim Crow in Baseball, which actually became the spearhead of the campaign.

LR: Although initiated by the TUAA, the Committee to End Jim Crow in
Baseball was open to any organization that wanted to join the campaign.
One of the first was a group of thirteen New York metropolitan-area college
sports editors from NYU, CCNY, Columbia University, Brooklyn College, St.

John's, and others who met in a conference April 16, 1940, to map out a plan of action. Their initiative probably had something to do with the fact that the *Daily Worker* had won a sizable readership on New York's college campuses through its intensive coverage of college basketball. Among those addressing the gathering were Dan Burley, sports editor of the *Amsterdam News,* and Milton Gross, a sportswriter for the *New York Post.* Jimmy Powers and Dan Parker of the *Daily Mirror* also joined the committee.

The TUAA was also given permission by the New York World's Fair—a huge tourist attraction that year—to take over the World's Fair Stadium on two successive Sundays in June and July for a big labor sports carnival. The theme for the first day (June 30) was "Peace and Progress for Labor," but for the second (July 7) it was "Ending of Jim Crow in Baseball." The program for the latter included four baseball games between racially mixed teams. Petitions circulated by the Committee to End Jim Crow in Baseball accumulated more than ten thousand signatures in the two days. Left-wing congressman Vito Marcantonio was one of the speakers at a ceremonial program that evening.

The widening scope of the campaign was reflected in the fact that while the Communist Party was a strong presence in many unions in those years, and Communists were heavily involved in all these events, genuine enthusiasm for the campaign was now shown by large numbers of people who had nothing to do with the Communist Party.

Some significant breakthroughs also occurred in the press. Wendell Smith's series in the *Pittsburgh Courier* had stimulated other black sportswriters to speak up more forcefully; and while most of the big-city daily press continued to tiptoe around the issue of baseball's color line, a few other papers began to mention it. None of them, however, editorialized against the ban. But where once a curtain of silence had pretty much reigned, some columnists began speaking up. Typical was a piece by Jimmy Powers of the New York *Daily News* written in the form of a "Memo to Bill Terry," manager of the Giants. Terry was the one National League manager who had told Wendell Smith the color line would never be broken. Powers wrote:

Memo to Bill Terry: Bill, what's the use of trying to kid yourself—
you just ain't got a team this year. You may say you haven't the
money, or front office cooperation, or material. This may be true.
But do you know what you can—and should—do? Draft the best
colored stars in America!

Get yourself a batch of Satchel Paiges, Josh Gibsons and other
truly great ball-busters. You'd find the Polo Grounds jammed with
new and enthusiastic rooters. . . . Bill, you can make yourself the
biggest man in baseball and I mean big. There is absolutely no law
on your books barring a decent, hard-working athlete simply because his skin is a shade darker than his brother's. . . . You've got a
pennant at your finger-tips. (Jimmy Powers, N.Y. *Daily News,* February 23, 1940)

Needless to say, the *Daily Worker* reprinted Powers's "memo" the next day.

A few months later, the *Philadelphia Record* made essentially the same
point to the owners and managers of the perennially dismal Phillies and
Athletics. Drawing heavily on the work done by the *Daily Worker* and the
Pittsburgh Courier, the article declared:

The Athletics and Phillies can be pennant contenders—not next
year or the year after or five years from now—but immediately. Experienced players are available who could strengthen the A's shaky
pitching staff, give the Phillies the batting punch they need. These
players could make potential champions out of any of the other
also-rans in either major league. . . . But they are Negroes, and organized baseball says they can't come in. . . . But no vote is ever
taken on the subject, no manager or owner dares defy the Jim Crow
tradition which in the past has been the most inflexible unwritten
law in the game. (*Philadelphia Record,* May 14, 1940)

Later that year, articles along the same lines appeared in the *Saturday
Evening Post* and *Colliers.* These were followed by a series in the *Chicago
Daily News* highlighting the career of Satchel Paige, whom the author
called "probably the most remarkable pitcher in the history of baseball."

LR: Something else was happening. You could feel the impact of the campaign against baseball Jim Crow on other sports—in football, for example. A handful of African Americans had made it onto otherwise white college teams immediately after World War I. Paul Robeson was the best known, at Rutgers. He was an end. I did some research on him, going back to the way he was covered by the New York papers during his college days. Mind-blowing! I'd never read such tributes to an athlete on a purely athletic basis. You could tell, the sportswriters couldn't believe their eyes. They'd write things like "This giant roamed effortlessly and took the place of three men in opening holes on the offense. He was a raging tiger on defense. And then he ran down the field and caught forward passes with one hand." No one had ever seen a football player like this guy.

Paul Robeson was named to Walter Camp's official All-American team in 1918, the only black player so honored in those years. But in the political climate of the Red Scare in the 1950s, his name was removed from the team, resulting in the incongruous depiction of the 1918 team as having a ten-man roster. Having thus protected America from the perils of communism, the football establishment maintained this farce for forty-five years until, finally, Robeson's name was restored to the record books in 1995.

LR: Modern-day professional football didn't find its niche until 1933, when the National Football League [NFL] came into being. Before then pro football had been a pretty haphazard thing. But the NFL also copied baseball and had its own color line. In 1939, the hands-down standout in college football was Kenny Washington, a black halfback with UCLA and a heck of a baseball player too. He was passed over for the All-American team and for the NFL draft that took place early the next year. Things like this had happened before, of course, but again, except for the *Daily Worker* and some of the black papers, no one blinked an eye. That's the way things were. But the mood in the country was changing; and in sports it was changing especially because of all the activity around baseball Jim Crow. You could see this early in 1940, just after all the breakthroughs of the year before, when a sports broadcaster by the name of Sam Balter spoke out about discrimination in professional football on his nationally syndicated radio program. We got a transcript and ran it in the *Daily Worker.* No one else considered it news.

> Open letter to Mr. Carl Storck, president of the National Football League, and to the owners and coaches of that circuit:
>
> No one else will say this. At least nobody has so far. . . . But this weekend, when you gentlemen convened at your annual meeting, you established a precedent that seemed to be so deliberate that it calls for an open statement of policy.
>
> You gathered together and you selected the 1939 college football players to play in your circuit next year. . . . You chose a lot of fine football players . . . until you were scratching fairly mediocre players. . . . [But] nobody chose Kenny Washington, the leading collegiate ground-gainer of the 1939 season, the 6-foot, 195-pound halfback who has been the heart and soul of his team all season and piloted that team to an undefeated season. Everyone who has seen him agrees he is not only the best football player on the Pacific coast this season, but the best of at least the last ten years . . . a player who has reduced to absurdity all the All-American teams selected this year because they did not include him. . . .
>
> You have scouts—you know this better than I do—you know their unanimous reports; he would be the greatest sensation in pro league history with any one of your ball clubs. He was Number One on all your lists. None of you chose him. [You know why—] Mr. Washington is black. (Sam Balter, "Inside Sports"; full text in *Daily Worker,* January 14, 1940)

Also "overlooked" was Washington's teammate Jackie Robinson, probably the second-best black college football player in the country.

Over the next few years, as the "End Jim Crow in Baseball" campaign grew in scope and intensity, the baseball establishment was caught in a dilemma. Having disavowed the existence of any rule barring black players, and having acknowledged that more than a few black players were of major-league caliber, the owners and league officials could not simply go on blatantly stonewalling the growing clamor to end the obvious segregation of the game. Once again the baseball hierarchy shifted ground, hoping to defuse the campaign by making some verbal or token concessions to popular demand while keeping the lid on any real changes.

Where once no major-league club would even consider offering a try-out to a black player, mounting pressure to maintain an image of fairness led to some awkward and cruel confrontations. Pressured by the *Daily Worker,* the Pittsburgh Pirates offered Roy Campanella a look-see. But when owner William Benswanger was unable to discourage Campanella with a host of conditions, the tryout was summarily cancelled.

Later, in 1945, the Boston Red Sox, under pressure from a member of the city council, grudgingly agreed to give three black players a tryout: Sam Jethroe, later a star center fielder for the Boston Braves; Marvin Williams, an infielder with the Philadelphia Stars of the Negro Leagues, who never made it to the majors; and a one-time four-letter college all-star from UCLA, recently discharged from the army, named Jackie Robinson. Of the three, Robinson was easily the standout, peppering Boston's Green Monster left-field wall with screaming line drives and hitting several shots over it. Red Sox manager Joe Cronin (watching from a secluded spot) and the club's chief scout, Hugh Duffy, also got a good look at Robinson's speed on the bases and his fielding skills. "What a ballplayer," said Duffy. "Too bad he's the wrong color" (Rampersad 1997, 120). Later Cronin admitted to the city councilman, who had also attended, "If I had that guy on this club, we'd be a world-beater." But Cronin never pushed owner Tom Yawkey to sign Robinson. The tryout was a sham. The Red Sox would remain lily-white until 1959. They were the last team to integrate.

LR: After the 1941 season, I thought a breakthrough was pretty close, a year or two at the most. But I also felt we had to keep up the pressure. At first we targeted the owners, after Frick said it was up to them. And in one sense it was. But it would have been impossible in those days for any individual owner to buck the rest of the establishment. So we decided to raise the heat on Landis.

The commissioner of baseball, Judge Kenesaw Mountain Landis, was not just the public face of organized baseball. He was a very powerful commissioner, the first of his kind. And a racist—shrewd, but a stone racist.

> Few Americans of the era matched his esteem and popularity. Yet Landis did not warrant this reputation. He brought to baseball a disdain for law and due process characteristic of his judicial career. A "grandstand judge" who won fame in controversial cases like . . . the wartime trials of IWW [Industrial Workers of the World] leaders, Landis often acted arbitrarily, and higher courts overruled his decisions with "startling frequency," according to one analyst. . . . Most contemporaries agreed that he adamantly opposed desegregation. (Tygiel 1993, 31)

LR: We had always pointed to Landis as the one who had the authority to end the color line. But now we really put the spotlight on him. The war was on and blacks were being sent overseas and were among the casualties. So I decided to write Landis an open letter using that as a theme. We ran it under the headline "Time for Stalling Is Over, Judge Landis." This was about a month before I was drafted.

> Judge Kenesaw Landis
> Commissioner of Baseball
> 333 North Michigan Ave.
> Chicago, Illinois
>
> Negro soldiers and sailors are among those beloved heroes of the American people who have already died for the preservation of this country and everything this country stands for—yes, including the great game of baseball.
> So this letter isn't going to mince words.
> You may file this away without comment as you already have done to the petitions of more than a million American baseball fans. You may ignore it as you have ignored the clear statements of the men who play our National Pastime and the men who manage the teams. You may refuse to acknowledge and answer it as

you have refused to acknowledge and answer scores of sports columns and editorials in newspapers throughout the country—from the Coast through Chicago, Philadelphia, New York and down to Louisville and countless smaller cities.

Yes, you may ignore this. But at least this is going to name the central fact for all to know.

You, the self-proclaimed "Czar" of baseball, are the man responsible for keeping Jim Crow in our national pastime. You are the one who, by your silence, is maintaining a relic of the slave market long repudiated in other American sports. You are the one refusing to say the word which would do more to justify baseball's existence in this year of war than any other single thing. You are the one who is blocking the step which would put baseball in line with the rest of the country, with the United States Government itself.

There can no longer be any excuse for your silence, Judge Landis. It is a silence that hurts the war effort. You were quick enough to speak up when many Jewish fans asked for the moving back of the World Series opening by one day to avoid conflict with the biggest Jewish holiday of the year . . . quick to answer with a sneering refusal. You certainly made it clear then that you were the one with the final authority in baseball. You certainly didn't evade any responsibility then.

America is against discrimination, Judge Landis.

There never was a greater ovation in America's greatest indoor sports arena than that which arose two months ago when Wendell Willkie, standing in the middle of the Madison Square Garden ring, turned to Joe Louis and said: "How can anyone looking at the wonderful example of this great American think in terms of discrimination for reasons of race, color or creed?"

Dorie Miller, who manned a machine gun at Pearl Harbor when he might have stayed below deck, has been honored by a grateful people. The President of our country has called for an end to discrimination in all jobs.

Your position as big man in our National Pastime carries a much greater responsibility this year than ever before and you can't meet it with your silence. The temper of the worker who goes to the ball games is not one to tolerate discrimination against 13 million Americans in this year of the grim fight against the biggest Jim Crower of them all—Adolf Hitler.

You haven't a leg to stand on. Everybody knows there are many Negro players capable of starring in the big leagues. There was a poll of big league managers and players a couple of years ago and everybody but Bill Terry agreed that Negro players belonged in the big leagues. Terry is not a manager any more, and new manager Mel Ott, who hails from Gretna, Louisiana, is one of the players who paid tribute to the great Negro stars.

Bill McKechnie, manager of the Cincinnati Reds, set the tone for all the managers when he said: "I could name at least 20 Negro players who belong in the big leagues and I'd love to have some of them on the Reds if given permission."

If given YOUR permission, Judge Landis.

Manager Jimmy Dykes of the Chicago White Sox this spring was forced to tell two fine young Negro applicants for a tryout at the Pasadena training camp: "I know you're good and I'd love to have you. So would the rest of the boys and every other manager in the big leagues I'm sure. But it's not up to us."

It's up to YOU, Judge Landis.

Leo Durocher, manager of the Brooklyn Dodgers who were shut out in Havana this spring by a Negro pitcher has said: "I wouldn't hesitate a minute to sign up some of those great colored players if I got the OK."

Your OK, Judge Landis.

That's the sentiment of player, manager and fan.

The *Louisville Courier Journal* of a month ago, entering the nationwide demand for the end of Jim Crow in our National Pastime, said: "Baseball, in this war, should set an example of democracy. What about it, Mr. Landis?"

Yes, what about it, Mr. Landis?

The American people are waiting for you. You're holding up the works.

And the first casualty lists have been published.

Yours,

Lester Rodney

Sports Editor, *Daily Worker*

(Published in the *Daily Worker*, May 6, 1942)

After that we kept blasting away at Landis every chance we got. "Can You Read, Judge Landis?" "Can You Hear, Judge Landis?" and "Can You Talk, Judge Landis?" in huge headlines. One time I noticed the attendance figures for a game between the Kansas City Monarchs and a team of former Big League All-Stars at Wrigley Field in Chicago. So out of curiosity, I checked the attendance of the White Sox–Detroit doubleheader being played in Chicago the same day. Well, the Monarchs–All-Star game, with Satchel Paige pitching, had outdrawn the White Sox–Tigers doubleheader by more than ten thousand fans. We turned that into a "Can You Count, Judge Landis?" piece. All these ran with our biggest headline type, above the masthead.

Landis was clearly nettled by the *Daily Worker*'s focus on him. A few months later, he called in Leo Durocher for a little "chat" after a *Daily News* article recalling that Leo had told Rodney he would be ready to hire black players if he got the okay. Right after that, Landis held a press conference in which he finally said, "There is no rule, formal or otherwise," barring black players from Big League baseball (July 17, 1942; cited in Tygiel 1993, 30).

Rodney was in the army by then and his somewhat naive replacement, Nat Low, got carried away, hailing Landis's statement as "a great victory" and crediting Landis with having "struck a mighty blow for unity and democracy."

Landis struck his "mighty blow" for democracy on July 16, 1942. A year and a half later, organized baseball remained lily-white. Increasingly impatient, a group representing the Negro Publishers Association requested a place on the agenda of the annual meeting of baseball club owners. Landis, as usual, presided over the gathering and granted the request. But at the last minute, the publisher of the *Chicago Defender* arranged to have Paul Robeson, then at the height of his artistic career and playing in his much-heralded production of *Othello* on Broadway, attend and be the delegation's spokesperson.

The ever-wily Landis quickly rose to the occasion by introducing Robeson to the assembled magnates in highly salutary terms and then declaring:

I want to make it clear that there is not, never has been, and as long as I am connected with baseball, there never will be any agreement among the teams or between any two teams preventing Negroes from participating in organized baseball. (Judge Kenesaw Mountain Landis, December 3, 1943; cited in Falkner 1995, 111)

Robeson responded:

The time has come that you must change your attitude toward Negroes. . . . I come here as an American and former athlete. I urge you to decide favorably on this request and that action be taken this very season. . . . The American people will commend you for this action which reflects the best in the American spirit. (Foner 1978, 151)

According to all reports, Robeson's twenty-minute impassioned speech was greeted with lengthy applause by the owners, who then adjourned to a closed session. Afterward Landis slightly amplified on his earlier position, saying, "Each club is entitled to employ Negro players to any and all extents it desires. The matter is solely for each club's decision without any restriction whatsoever."

Years later, a Freedom of Information Act request revealed the fact that the FBI had monitored the meeting. A report to J. Edgar Hoover stated, "Pressure is being exerted for the purpose of lifting the ban upon Negro players participating in organized ball. . . . All of these individuals have been reliably reported as members of the Communist Party" (*Sports Jones,* August 24, 2001).

Once again, Nat Low greeted Landis's statement with more enthusiasm than it deserved. All Landis had really done was get himself off the hook and put the responsibility for segregation back on the owners. Despite all the fine words and the applause for Paul Robeson, the 1944 season came and went without the slightest indication that the color line would be crossed. What made the owners' stubbornness particularly ironic was that with so many Big Leaguers off to war, teams were signing white players of mediocre talent—even including a one-armed outfielder—while ignoring known black stars of the Negro Leagues.

But then, shortly after the 1944 season was over, something happened that would change the internal political dynamics of organized baseball forever. Judge Landis died of a totally unexpected heart attack. Although the significance of this event for organized baseball, and especially for its Jim Crow norm, was not immediately apparent, there could be little doubt that an era had come to an end.

When Landis became commissioner in 1921, baseball was in deep trouble. The Black Sox scandal of 1919 had cast a shadow over the game. As rumors of other possible scandals proliferated, attendance at ballparks fell off sharply. The owners were at odds with each other on policy matters and unable to speak with a single voice. The one thing they finally agreed on was the need for a strong hand at the tiller—a high commissioner of organized baseball who would bring law and order and respectability back to the national pastime. So they brought in Landis, a federal court judge, and gave him what amounted to absolute authority over the game. And he used it. The owners liked to portray Landis as a benevolent dictator, tough but fair. He was even known as the "czar" of baseball.

From the owners' point of view, Landis exceeded all expectations. He imposed a discipline on them that made it next to impossible for any owner to break ranks—not just on the color line but on any significant issue that might come up. Nor did he hesitate to discipline or suspend "trouble-makers" who stepped out of line.

A few months after Landis's death, the owners named a new commissioner, Kentucky senator A. B. "Happy" Chandler. Proponents of integration groaned. Kentucky was a segregated state, and Chandler, a former governor, had never given any indication of dissatisfaction with the status quo. In fact, that was probably a consideration in his choice.

By then, New York Yankees president Larry MacPhail, by virtue of being head of baseball's richest and most powerful franchise, had become the dominant figure in baseball's inner councils. Although nominally in favor of integration, MacPhail had actually become its most die-hard opponent. In a letter to Chandler shortly after his installation, MacPhail advised the new commissioner that the race question had become "increasingly serious and acute. . . . The three New York clubs are in a critical position right now. We can't stick our heads in the sand and ignore the problem. If we do, we will have colored players in the minor leagues in 1945 and in the major leagues shortly thereafter" (Chandler Papers, cited in Tygiel 1993, 42).

JUDGE LANDIS?

n be ended this year,

nt Negro and white
ormed to call on Judge

this matter their own
who pay the freight at
rking and fighting for
nal unity against Hit-

spoken out against this
sportsmanship—at least

teams and don't for a
a union game. They
in our national pastime.
rking and fighting to-
gether. What a lift it
take part in the mighty
row in the tremendously

ime is ripe. Delegations
to Judge Landis. Pour
st discrimination today.
er count for more than
f the country has spoken
all—immediately.
ake him talk up. Com-
ons. He's at 33 North

THE STARS COULD ONLY GET TWO HITS OF SATCHEL PAIGE IN SEVEN INNINGS OF TRYING. WHY DOES YOUR SILENCE KEEP HIM AND OTHER NEGRO STARS FROM TAKING HIS RIGHTFUL PLACE IN OUR NATIONAL PASTIME AT A TIME WHEN WE ARE AT WAR AND NEGRO AND WHITE ARE FIGHTING AND DYING TOGETHER TO END HITLERISM?

*   *   *

CAN YOU HEAR, JUDGE LANDIS? The thirty thousand fans cheered Paige and the other Negro stars plenty loud enough to be heard at your nearby office at 333 North Michigan Ave.

*   *   *

CAN YOU READ, JUDGE LANDIS? Jimmy Dykes, manager of the Chicago White Sox, told Jackie Robinson, young Negro shortstop star:

"I'D LOVE TO HAVE YOU ON MY TEAM AND SO WOULD ALL THE OTHER BIG LEAGUE MANAGERS. BUT IT'S NOT UP TO US. GET AFTER LANDIS."

Larry MacPhail, president of the Brooklyn Dodgers, told the Daily Worker: "THE MATTER IS PRIMARILY IN THE HANDS OF JUDGE LANDIS."

President Benswanger of the Pittsburgh Pirates, yes, a magnate, told the Daily Worker: "I don't see why Negroes shouldn't be allowed in baseball to make their contributions as they do in music and literature. I would be in favor of it if the question came up."

*   *   *

CAN YOU TALK, JUDGE LANDIS? A million fans sent you their signatures on petitions, big league managers, players, fans, sports writers have asked for the end of Jim Crow in baseball. You haven't said a single word yet. SPEAK UP, JUDGE LANDIS!

Chapter 5

"Jim Crow Must Go!" (Part 2): And the Walls Came (Slowly) Tumbling Down

O
NE LATE AUTUMN DAY IN 1945, Sgt. Lester Rodney, stationed with the Fifty-second Field Hospital on a remote island in the South Pacific, received a cablegram from Nat Low in New York.

Lester Rodney: I'll never forget that day. It was pretty unusual for anyone to get a cable, especially an enlisted man, so the first thing I thought was that someone in my family had died. But it was from Nat Low.

> Congratulations. Dodgers yesterday signed Jackie Robinson for Montreal farm. You did it!

Well, I was stunned and elated at the same time. I didn't even mind Nat's exaggeration that "I" did it. I had been away almost three years and had no idea of what had gone on. It was also frustrating. How do you express your feelings to someone not just about Jackie Robinson but the role of the *Daily Worker* and the Communist Party in the whole thing when they're totally unprepared to think of you that way?

But there was one guy in our outfit who was a Communist. Howard Loucks, a big, tough, rangy guy whose ancestors went generations back in America. He was born in southern Colorado and worked in the lead mines. Became a union organizer. We had a great talk about it. Hey, what are the odds on two CP members in an outfit of 176 men?

Earlier that year, the New York state legislature had passed the Ives-Quinn Anti-Discrimination Act, which made discrimination in employment because of race, creed, or color unlawful. Faced with a rapidly growing black population (the result of the huge migration northward of blacks out of the South during the war), the continuing agitation by the Communist Party (two of its leaders had been elected to the New York City Council), and the substantial electoral clout of the left-wing American Labor Party, the legislature saw the political handwriting on the wall and passed the measure overwhelmingly.

The new law did not mention baseball specifically, but this time Nat Low got it right, declaring in the *Daily Worker* that the unprecedented law "heralds the end of Jim Crow in baseball, not only in New York State, but in all states and all baseball leagues" (*Daily Worker,* March 7, 1945). Low's point was that even though the law applied only to New York, it set a basis for at least one of the three New York teams to break the color line; and once that barrier was breached, it would be impossible for other teams not to follow suit. (Low was right, but as with the Supreme Court's ruling on school integration, it would take a lot longer before that actually happened.)

Two months later, another body blow was delivered to the color line in baseball when, much to everyone's surprise, the new baseball commissioner, Happy Chandler, gave striking evidence that he would not be a Landis clone on the race issue. In an interview with United Press (UP) reporter Walter Byers, Chandler declared, "I believe Negroes should have a chance like everyone else. The arrangements are yet to be worked out, but I believe that this is a free country and everybody should have a chance to play its favorite pastime" (*Daily Worker,* May 5, 1945).

Chandler's statement went significantly beyond previous comments by Landis, Frick, and Harridge, but many—including the *Daily Worker* and much of the black press—were far from convinced. "Actions, Mr. Chandler, speak much louder than words," wrote Nat Low (*Daily Worker,* May 5, 1945).

One person who could read the handwriting on the wall was Branch Rickey. The Dodgers president had recognized for some time that the integration of baseball could not be stopped indefinitely; and whatever personal sentiments may also have motivated him, the man who had virtually invented baseball's farm system for the St. Louis Cardinals understood that the first team to sign black ballplayers would gain a decided edge over all its rivals.

Rickey had been planning to sign a black player for some time. He had said so to the team's owners and sent scouts out to evaluate potential black Dodgers. Chandler's statement was a signal that the new commissioner would lend his authority to the move—or at least wouldn't oppose it. And so, sometime in the summer of 1945, Rickey took the fateful step, breaking ranks with the other owners, and started signing black players for the Brooklyn Dodgers organization. His first move, on October 24, 1945, was to sign Jackie Robinson to a contract with the Dodgers' Montreal International League farm team. A few months later, Rickey signed Roy Campanella and Don Newcombe to the Dodgers' AA Nashua (New Hampshire) club.

For the *Daily Worker,* Robinson's signing was front-page news. Nat Low saw it as pointing "the way to the complete integration of the Negro people in all fields of endeavor." Mike Gold wrote:

> It may have more of an effect than even the singing of Marian Anderson or Paul Robeson. And if this great medieval fortress of Jim-crowism has been breached, let all good Americans know that the Communists were the first to start the fight. . . . I hope this lesson will teach America that the Communists are useful citizens who form the core of a healthy democracy. (*Daily Worker,* October 26, 1945)

Public reaction, in general, was either favorable or at least not antagonistic. Most of the major metropolitan dailies were cautiously supportive and relatively low-key. All treated it solely as a sports story. While noting that Robinson was the first black player in organized baseball in modern times, few mentioned the color bar that had, up until then, excluded blacks. By and large, the black press hailed the breakthrough and highlighted Branch Rickey's role in bringing it about. Neither the big-city dailies nor the black papers mentioned the role of the *Daily Worker* in the decade-long struggle for baseball's integration.

But not everyone was happy with the news. One of the bitterest of the diehards was Judge William Bramham, commissioner of minor-league baseball, who complained in undisguised fury clearly directed at Branch Rickey:

> It is those of the carpetbagger stripe of the white race, under the guise of helping but in truth using the Negro for their own selfish interests, who retard the race. (Quoted in Rampersad 1997, 130)

> The Negro is making rapid strides in baseball, as well as in other lines of endeavor. They have their own form of player contracts and, as I understand it, their organizations are well officered and are financially successful. Why should we raid their ranks, grab a player and put him, his baseball associates, and his race in a position that will inevitably prove harmful? (Quoted in Peterson 1970, 191)

A good number of Negro League team owners—many of whom were white—likewise opposed integration, because it would obviously undermine their own business interests.

Bramham's suddenly discovered and hitherto undisclosed concern for the welfare of black athletes and the Negro baseball leagues was quickly echoed by others in the press as well as the baseball establishment. "We live happier with segregation in athletics as well as all other activities," commented sportswriter Bud Seifert for the Spartansburg, South Carolina, *Herald-Journal,* a sentiment expressed in one form or another by most southern sportswriters. And *Atlanta Journal* sportswriter Ed Danforth declared, "The only menace to peace between the races is the carpetbagger white press and agitators in the Negro press who capitalize on racial issues" (Tygiel 1993, 74).

Opposition to Robinson in organized baseball was not, however, limited to southern sportswriters. Baseball's "bible," the *Sporting News,* in keeping with its cozy relationship with the game's magnates, had long been a staunch opponent of integration, a position it reiterated regularly. Shortly before Robinson's signing, as pressure to break the color line was mounting, it solemnly declared, "There is not a single Negro player with major league possibilities." Consistent to the bitter end, *Sporting News* greeted the signing in typically surly fashion, saying that Robinson's "baseball abilities, were he white, would make him eligible for a trial with, let us say, the Brooklyn Dodger Class C farm at Newport News, if he were six years younger" (Peterson 1970, 193).

Joe Williams of the *New York World-Telegram* was so locked into the prevailing racial stereotypes as to claim there were no black players good enough for the majors, never had been, and probably never would be. According to Williams, "Blacks have been kept out of big league ball because they are, as a race, very poor ballplayers" (Golenbock 1984, 144). Jimmy Powers of the *Daily News,* who had previously spoken out a few times against the color line, dismissed Robinson as a "1001–1 shot to make the grade" (Tygiel 1993, 76), while Roscoe McGowan of the *New York Times,* who covered the Dodgers, doubted he would make the Royals, let alone the Dodgers (Rampersad 1997, 143).

That such comments did not speak well for the abilities of these judges of baseball talent quickly became obvious. Robinson's first game for Montreal came on Opening Day, April 19, 1946, at Roosevelt Field in Jersey City against the Jersey City Giants. A larger-than-sellout crowd, including a large number of blacks—many coming from Philadelphia, Baltimore, and even more distant points to witness the history-making occasion—thronged the stadium. It was, wrote Bill Mardo, who covered the game for the *Daily Worker,*

> one of the most sensational debuts any ball player ever made in any ball game. Robinson dazzled a capacity crowd by collecting four hits in five times at bat, one of which was a savage 335-foot liner

over the left field wall; drove in four runs; scored four times; stole two bases; set up a speedy double play; faultlessly handled six chances with but one wild throw to mar his work afield; and put on one of the most amazing exhibitions of base-running to be seen in this Jersey ball park in many, many years. One word—Robinson—was on everybody's lips as they excitedly filed out of the ball park . . . and Jackie Robinson was cheered all the way to the dugout. (*Daily Worker,* April 19, 1946)

Robinson, wrote Joe Bostic of the Harlem-based *Amsterdam News*, "did everything but help the ushers seat the crowd" (Tygiel 1993, 7).

But it wasn't all cheers as the Royals and their new star made their way through the rest of the International League.

LR: Jackie's year in Montreal was a horror in many ways. Rachel Robinson wrote about the unimaginable tensions as the team traveled around to different cities in the league. The worst were Baltimore and Louisville. And it wasn't just Robinson. Black fans came out in unprecedented numbers when Montreal was in town. And in these cities, where segregation codes were taken for granted, blacks made up a fairly high percentage of the population. I guess some white fans felt they were getting a glimpse into the future when they saw the large numbers of black fans who came out. They felt "their niggers" were getting uppity and they could easily imagine —with good reason—that the segregationist stability of more than half a century was now in trouble.

It was much better in Montreal. Canada had less racism than the United States, and Montreal's French Canadian majority took to Robinson. But neither the city nor the team was immune from racist garbage. Clay Hopper, the Royals manager, was from Greenwood, Mississippi, in the Deep South. He was a decent enough guy, though certainly reflective of his time and place, and treated Robinson fairly. And once Jackie Robinson began tearing up the league, Hopper was ecstatic about having him.

But at first, he was hardly pleased at the prospect of managing a team with a black player, telling Rickey, "Don't do this to me." Black sportswriter Carl Rowan tells the story of Rickey and Hopper watching a preseason

game when Robinson made a sensational catch that Rickey sponta-
neously said was a "superhuman play." Hopper just shook his head and
said, "Mr. Rickey. Do you really think a nigger is a human being?" (Tygiel
1993, 104).

By season's end, however, Hopper had changed his language and
general comportment toward Robinson for the respectful better. He later
said Robinson's advent made him a better person. Hopper's change says
something about how the everyday reality of Jackie Robinson impacted
on people who had been conditioned to racist thinking.

Of course, the early Hopper wasn't the only racist the Royals encountered. After one game in Baltimore won by the Royals, a mob of frustrated
white fans surrounded the clubhouse where the Montreal players were
changing and started yelling, "Come out of there, Robinson, you nigger
son of a bitch, we'll getcha" (Falkner 1995, 139). Robinson hadn't even
played in the game. Fortunately, two Montreal players stayed in the clubhouse with Robinson until the mob eventually gave up and dispersed.

Opposing players injected a strong note of racism into the usual bench
jockeying. In Syracuse, opposing team players threw a black cat out on the
field while Robinson was kneeling in the on-deck circle, taunting him with
shouts of "nigger pussy." Others staged watermelon-eating displays.

Robinson led the league in a telling statistic: most times hit by a
pitcher. According to Jules Tygiel, Larry MacPhail admitted that he had
ordered pitchers for the Newark Bears (a Yankees farm team) deliberately
to throw at Robinson, and that one International League manager stated, "I
offered to buy a suit of clothes for any pitcher on our club who knocks
him down" (Tygiel 1993, 133). Other players went out of their way to spike
him or engineer collisions. As a result, injuries kept Robinson sidelined
for several weeks during the season.

Outwardly, Robinson maintained a stoic composure; but in fact, says
Falkner, "he was coming apart at the seams." With Robinson having trouble eating and sleeping and frequent bouts of nausea, a physician finally
told him he was suffering from "nervous exhaustion."

After a five-day rest, Robinson was back in uniform and—much to the
embarrassment of the savants who had dismissed his chances—proceeded

to tear up the International League. He won the league hitting title with a .349 batting average and wound up with the highest fielding percentage in the league while stealing forty bases, batting in 66 runs, and scoring 113 runs. He was the main reason Montreal won the pennant by eighteen and a half games. And as if that weren't enough, he led his team to victory over the Louisville Colonels in the Little World Series with a .400 batting average.

Meanwhile, Roy Campanella and Don Newcombe, signed by Rickey a few months after Robinson, were doing the same at Nashua. Campanella, who was already an outstanding defensive catcher, led the team for the season with fourteen home runs and ninety-six runs batted in while amassing a .290 average. Voted the league's Most Valuable Player, he was also a unanimous choice for all-league catcher. Newcombe, a big, 6'4" pitcher and a strong hitter, finished the season with a 2.21 earned run average and a 14–4 record. Nashua went on to win the league championship, beating out the first-place Lynn Red Sox, with Newcombe pitching and winning two of the four games. Afterward, the Lynn general manager complained to Nashua general manager Buzzie Bavasi, "If it wasn't for them niggers, you wouldn't have beat us" (Tygiel 1993, 151).

Robinson's spectacular accomplishments, together with those of Campanella and Newcombe, were the handwriting on the wall for the die-hard defenders of baseball's color line. The claim that black ball players were inherently unqualified to play at the major league level could no longer be credibly advanced to save baseball's "whites only" preserve. *Sporting News* continued to defend segregation, arguing that "the use of mixed teams in baseball would benefit neither the Negro nor white professional game because of the possibility of unpleasant incidents" (August 6, 1946). Tommy Thomas, manager of the Baltimore Orioles, took a different and somewhat franker tack. Tacitly acknowledging the ability of blacks, Thomas warned his players that if "you let him [Jackie Robinson] in … they'll all be coming in now. You'll all be out of a job" (Tygiel 1993, 129).

The likelihood that Robinson would be wearing a Dodger uniform in 1947 was a prospect all the owners, with the obvious exception of Branch

Rickey, found unnerving. Integration was now staring them in the face. Largely engineered by Larry MacPhail, who had left the Dodgers to become president of the New York Yankees, the magnates and their satraps gathered in a top-secret meeting in August 1946. According to Chandler, all the other owners adamantly opposed Rickey and condemned him for breaking ranks. But the assembled tycoons of the national pastime were so alarmed at the possibility the report would leak out that they collected every copy of it at the meeting's close. When Branch Rickey subsequently asked to get a copy, he was told that all copies had been destroyed.

It was difficult for many people at the time to understand the magnates' reluctance. The prevailing view among liberal-minded whites was that racism emanated from the culture of uneducated, poor southern whites, not well-educated, wealthy Northerners. And since allowing blacks into organized baseball would clearly bring a vast upsurge of African American fans into the ballparks, the owners would be all for it. So why were the magnates pursuing a policy that was seemingly contrary to their own financial interests?

The answer came out years later, after Robinson had broken the racial ban and other teams had started signing black players, when MacPhail's secret report was finally revealed. In it, MacPhail warned the owners and league officials, "However well-intentioned, the use of Negro players would hazard all the physical properties of baseball." Noting that Robinson's one year at Montreal had sparked a "tremendous increase" in black attendance, MacPhail cautioned the moguls that such a development was really not in the owners' best interest. "The percentage of Negro attendance at some games at Newark and Baltimore was in excess of 50%," he reported, and "a situation might be presented, if Negroes participate in Major League games, in which the preponderance of Negro attendance in parks such as Yankee Stadium, the Polo Grounds and Comiskey Park could conceivably threaten the value of Major League franchises owned by these clubs" (Tygiel 1993, 85).

But Rickey persisted. With Chandler making it clear he would not use the powers of his office to block him, Rickey brought Robinson up to the Dodgers just before the 1947 season began.

LR: The actual notification came during a game between Montreal and the Dodgers at Ebbets Field on April 10, 1947, five days before the season opener, while Robinson was still with the Royals. It was only an exhibition game, but because the word had already leaked out, the press box was jammed. It was the sixth inning and Robinson was at bat, when Arthur Mann, Rickey's assistant, brings out a bunch of sheets of paper that he hands to each of us. Then he takes the press box microphone and he says, "The Brooklyn Dodgers announce that they have purchased the contract of Jackie Roosevelt Robinson from the Montreal Royals." And wow! Everybody jumps for the phones. And three writers—Dick Young of the *Daily News*, Jim Becker of the Associated Press, and one other guy, I forget who—come over to me and say something like "Well you guys can take a lot of credit for this."

But the truly historic moment was Opening Day. That's when Jackie's name in the starting lineup actually entered the official records of organized baseball.

I had often wondered what that day would be like. I guess I imagined it would be formally treated like a tremendous event. No one quite knew what would happen. A wall doesn't come tumbling down immediately with the first breach. Partly because the media and the Dodgers themselves played it so cautiously and routinely, and also maybe because Rickey, in his big daddy way, asked Brooklyn's black population to play it cool. There wasn't even a full house at Ebbets Field that day. There was even a suggestion of apprehension. Remember, this is more than a decade before the great Civil Rights movement.

Jackie Robinson's first official appearance in a Dodger uniform came on Opening Day, April 15, 1947, in a game with the Boston Braves. In his column for the *Daily* Worker that day, Lester Rodney wrote:

> It's hard this Opening Day to write straight baseball and not stop to mention the wonderful fact of Jackie Robinson. You tell yourself it shouldn't be especially wonderful in America, no more wonderful for instance than Negro soldiers being with us on the way overseas through submarine infested waters in 1943.

The mainstream New York dailies were far more restrained. Principal attention in the city's sports pages was focused on the impact of Dodgers manager Leo Durocher's one-year suspension from baseball a week earlier and on the usual hoopla of Opening Day. On the fiftieth anniversary of Robinson's major-league debut, the *New York* Times looked back on how those papers—including the *Daily Worker* (!) and the *Times* itself—recorded the event:

> The *Herald Tribune* led its sports section with Joe McCarthy's rejection of [Branch] Rickey's offer to manage the team. The Robinson story was buried in a preview of the season, after news that "Gladys Gooden will accompany herself at the organ as she sings the national anthem."
>
> In the *Daily News,* Dick Young noted Robinson in the 17th paragraph of his story, in a reference to where he should hit in the Brooklyn lineup.
>
> The *Brooklyn Eagle* made no mention of Robinson that day.
>
> The *New York Times* "deemed the history-making event less important than the expectation of 50,000 fans at Yankee Stadium, Durocher's suspension, the Braves-Dodgers pitching matchup, and John Cashmore, the Brooklyn Borough President, throwing out the first ball." Rounding up the day's highlights, *Times* sportswriter Louis Effrat wrote, "The first of his race to make the grade since 1884, Robinson will cover first base for Brooklyn." (*New York Times,* April 13, 1997)

In all fairness, however, it should be noted that most of the papers had run sizable stories a few days earlier when the Dodgers announced that Robinson would be brought up from Montreal.

LR: When I left the *Daily Worker* in 1942 to go into the army, I was sure a black player would be in the Big Leagues soon. But I didn't think Jackie would be the first. There were better, more proven candidates. Paige was up in his thirties and Josh Gibson was in decline. But there were players in their prime and ready, like Buck Leonard, a great first baseman. Or Campanella, who was a standout as a catcher, the toughest position in base-ball. Then there was a wonderful third baseman, Ray Dandridge. He was so good that years later, in 1951, when he was thirty-six, the Giants picked him up for their Minneapolis farm team in the top minors, where he hit .369. I guess he didn't qualify for Rickey in the forties because he was un-educated and spoke like a southern farm hand. In other words, like a great many of the white Big Leaguers. And in Rickey's way of thinking, that kind of guy couldn't be the first. Rickey's choice of Robinson was espe-cially surprising because Jackie was known as a militant. He had been court-martialed in the army for refusing to sit in the back of a bus in Texas.

But Jackie was probably the only college man among the possible can-didates. Rickey always used to say he was looking for a particular kind of ballplayer—educated, articulate, intelligent—and I'm sure his scouting re-ports told him that Jackie had the stuff. In a way, it also may have been because Jackie was a militant. To Rickey that meant that Robinson would fully appreciate the social and historical significance of the move and know what he was in for. "You're gonna be called nigger," he told Jackie. "Pitchers are gonna throw at your head. They'll spit at you. You'll be as-saulted mentally and maybe even physically. I want you to imagine that and I want you to tell me you're not gonna fight back for two years." Rickey figured that Robinson was smart enough to understand why he had to lay low.

I've often been asked how I felt about that. My view was, if it's okay with Robinson, then it's not the thing you make an issue about. Apparently Jackie—this proud, aggressive guy—was willing to do this. If you criticize this, you're implicitly saying this guy is an Uncle Tom. I never really thought about whether I was right or wrong on this. Ben Davis was always aggressive on anything smacking of a racist attitude. But he never came to me and said, "How come you allow this plantation owner to order Jackie Robinson how he should behave?" or something like that.

And let's face it: there would have been one incident after another. Anyone called Jackie a nigger, he'd challenge and they'd fight. There'd probably have been a series of incidents that could have muddied the whole thing. So it never entered my mind to publicly make an issue out of that in the *Daily Worker*. And you gotta remember the context of the times.

Here's the first black ballplayer in our national pastime, a historic American event. Today everyone sees it that way. But April 15, 1947—no message from the president of the United States, Harry Truman. Did that occur to anybody? Not a word. How come? A year later, after the deed was done, Truman was on easier ground. That's how big baseball was. Then he felt he could desegregate the army. What a difference a year makes, and Jackie made much of that difference. That's no overstatement.

Rickey did meet with the black civic and church leaders in Brooklyn before Jackie's debut and asked them to diplomatically make it known to their congregations to "behave themselves." The big white papa thing. Still, a retroactive look at the context of the times and Rickey's purpose might induce a more charitable view.

Branch Rickey was much more complex than we Communists made him out to be at the time. He could be pompous, arrogant, and egocentric. Modesty was definitely not his strong point. Months after the breakthrough with Jackie, Rickey had a picture of Abraham Lincoln on the wall behind his desk. Once having done it, for whatever motives—and they weren't all religious—he began to fancy himself as the Great Emancipator. But Rickey wasn't just a calculating businessman; neither was he the saint his public relations team promoted. But it was Rickey who pulled the trigger when the others wouldn't, and looking back fifty years later, I have no reason to doubt the sincerity of his religion-based feelings against discrimination.

Rickey's favorite story was of how, early in the century, when he was coaching the Ohio Wesleyan baseball team, he had a black ballplayer, Charley Thomas, on his team. They were playing Notre Dame in South Bend. But when the team went to their hotel, the manager refused to register Thomas. Then, according to Rickey, he convinced the manager to put a cot in Rickey's room so that Thomas could stay there. In those days, a hotel would bar blacks unless they were traveling with a white person as a servant. When he went up to bed, said Rickey, he saw Thomas sobbing bitterly while rubbing his hands as though trying to get the color off. That incident, he said, stuck in his memory and, later on, as a Christian, he couldn't rest until he found a black player for the Big Leagues (Tygiel 1993, 51).

LR: At the LIU [Long Island University] conference in '97 commemorating the fiftieth anniversary of Jackie coming to the Dodgers, Bill Mardo asked where was Rickey in all the years after that incident. When you were a big executive with the St. Louis Cardinals, says Bill, the good black players were right under your nose coming into the St. Louis ballpark when the Cards were out of town. So where were you looking? In Istanbul? The *Village Voice* loved that. They called it a breath of fresh air.

I mentioned that a few years ago to Harold Rosenthal, who was the *New York Herald-Tribune*'s baseball reporter starting a few years after the Robinson breakthrough. We corresponded regularly after we both retired, until he died. And he said, "Branch Rickey was in St. Louis and he wasn't about to stick his neck out. He would've had his head handed to him."

Mardo had a telling point, but there's more to it than that. Rickey was also part of the culture of his time. And he was much shrewder than the other magnates. He knew during the war he could do in Brooklyn what he couldn't have done in St. Louis. He knew that by signing Robinson he and the Dodgers would benefit both in the standings—which gets translated into money—and in fan appeal—which also translates into money. You could see he was gleeful about the fact that nobody else was doing it and left it all to him. You could say he was smart enough and bold enough to seize the moment and take credit for what had become inevitable.

Of course, it always rankled me that he never acknowledged the role of the *Daily Worker* in all this. But he was a big anti-Communist and he hated the idea of us getting credit for anything—especially for breaking the color line. He didn't want anyone to think that he had succumbed to pressure from the Reds.

Still, for all the posturing and self-serving sanctimony, Branch Rickey deserves credit for being the one who actually made the big move. That wasn't easy to do, although maybe an even tougher test came later. The thing I give Rickey the most credit for by far was the way he acted after he made the decision, whenever there was an attempt to sabotage it.

First, he had to deal with Dixie Walker, the star of the Dodgers and the team's most popular player going into the '47 season. Walker was a southern racist to the core. He'd say things like "It's the Commies who want to break down the [color] lines." He was the one who started an anti-Robinson petition among the Dodger players, asking Rickey not to bring Jackie up from Montreal. He was actually surprised at how many Dodgers refused, especially fellow Southerner Pee Wee Reese, who was from Kentucky.

If Robinson came up, Walker said, he wanted to be traded. He finally agreed to stay but said it would be his last year with the Dodgers. During the season, Walker avoided the traditional handshake at home plate any time Jackie hit a homer. Otherwise he kept his feelings to himself. Then, after the Dodgers won the pennant in '47, he let it be known that he'd changed his mind and would now be willing to stay. I guess the extra World Series money had something to do with that. But Rickey remembered and traded Walker to Pittsburgh before the 1948 season began.

Kirby Higbe, who said the same thing, was traded immediately. And when Carl Furillo said before the '47 season, "I ain't gonna play with no niggers!" Rickey snapped back, "You don't want to play with no niggers? Then you can go back to Pennsylvania and pound railroad ties for $15 a week. You'll never set foot on a Big League baseball field again." Carl played. They all played.

There was also some talk of teams threatening to strike if Robinson was on the field. But the only time that ever amounted to anything was in 1947 by a group of St. Louis Cardinal players. Ford Frick, to his credit, let them know that anyone who wouldn't take the field against another team on racial grounds would be out of baseball. Frick had a strange history in all this, blowing hot and cold with the wind.

According to *New York Herald-Tribune* sportswriter Stanley Woodward, Frick told the Cardinal team:

> If you do this you will be suspended from the league. You will find that the friends you think you have in the press box will not support you, that you will be outcasts. I do not care if half the league strikes. Those who do will encounter quick retribution. All will be suspended, and I don't care if it wrecks the National League for five years. This is the United States of America and one citizen has

as much right to play as another. The National League will go down the line with Robinson whatever the consequences. You will find if you go through with your intention that you have been guilty of complete madness. (Tygiel 1993, 186)

LR: The other magnates all had it in for Rickey. I remember once him telling a group of sportswriters, "Off the record, guys, everybody who runs a team doesn't like what I did. And they can go to . . . heck!" (I never heard him curse, not so much as a "damn." And he didn't drink. We called him "Branch, the NonAlcoholic Rickey.") "But if they think they're gonna make me change my mind, or if they think they can confine this to Jackie Robinson and that it'll die out with Jackie, they've got another think coming."

Even after Rickey defied them, most owners still hoped to keep baseball white. Now their strategy was to keep integration confined to the Dodgers, while hoping Robinson would flop and bring the "experiment" to an end. Jackie settled that dream pretty quickly. Still, you couldn't say the fight had been won until other teams began doing the same thing. So we told our readers to get after the fifteen magnates who were still holding out.

But now you have an X factor—Bill Veeck, president of the Cleveland Indians. He's the guy who took the next big step. Four months after the Dodgers brought up Robinson, Veeck created a major sensation and, in effect, ended the attempt to keep democracy from spreading by bringing in a young, untried, twenty-two-year-old black player, Larry Doby.

Actually, we may have had a little something to do with that too, because after Jackie came in, we kept mentioning other black players we thought had major-league potential, and Doby was one of them. We saw him a lot because he played for the Newark Black Eagles right across the river from New York. So we began harping on Doby. Also Monte Irvin, Doby's teammate at Newark. [The Giants brought Irvin up in 1949.] When Veeck brought Doby directly up to Cleveland, he was consciously declaring that desegregation wouldn't be confined to the National League. It was a sensational move. But Doby was overwhelmed. He had a terrible first year with Cleveland. He played first base, though he had played second base at Newark. He batted .156 in the twenty-nine games he played.

They easily could have dropped him. But Veeck didn't want to give up. He asked Lou Boudreau, Cleveland's playing manager, and Lou said, "This guy's gonna be a good hitter but he's pressing. Let's move him to the outfield. He's young and fast." So that's what they did, and the next year—this was 1948—he was a key guy in pushing the Indians to the pennant and World Series championship, the last Cleveland won.

That same year, '48, Veeck made another dramatic move, signing Satchel Paige in mid-season. That was a wonderful thing for Veeck to do, considering Satch was forty-two by then. When they were talking about bringing him up, Boudreau put on a catcher's mitt and he told Veeck, "Let me catch him and I'll tell you whether we should bring him up or not." Satch threw a few and Boudreau turned to Veeck and said, "Bring him up. He'll help us." And he did. Paige won six and lost one in less than half a season. He had one shutout. He drew a record-breaking crowd to Comiskey Park when they played the White Sox. But he was a little over the hill and uneven. He didn't have a great World Series. Still, he was a good relief pitcher for four more years.

Bill Veeck was an American original. He lost part of his leg during the war. He was a fan's owner. He said, "You know these 'nights' they have for a big star, or someone who's retiring. How about a night for a fan?" So he came up with this idea where the one-thousandth guy to go through a particular turnstile, they'd stop him and pull him aside. Well, number one thousand was a guy named Joe Early. So they had a big Joe Early night. Joe was just an ordinary working guy. And they brought him out on the field looking kind of bewildered and gave him a car and so on. And Veeck said, "That's the way we feel about fans. Why should all the big shots who already have cars get another one?" That gives you a clue.

Then there was the time he brought a midget up to the Big Leagues. That was in 1951, when Veeck had just moved to the St. Louis Browns. In those years the Browns were a perennial last-place team. Attendance was way down. There's a doubleheader with the Tigers coming up in St. Louis, and it's going to be a big American League fiftieth-anniversary celebration. So Veeck dreams up this stunt of hiring a midget, Eddie Gaedel, and actually signs him to a St. Louis Browns contract.

Between games there's a big show. Acrobats. Antique cars. And at the very end, they bring out a giant anniversary cake. Suddenly the cake busts open and out jumps Eddie, in a Browns uniform wearing the number ⅛. Eddie's all of 3'7". Oh yeah, and Happy Chandler, the lord high commissioner of baseball, is in the stands for the occasion.

Anyway, the game starts, and in the bottom of the first Eddie comes out of the dugout swinging a miniature bat and is announced as a pinch hitter for the leadoff man. Red Rolfe, the former Yankee, is the manager of the Tigers, and he comes charging out on the field to protest. But Veeck had prepared the way and the Browns' manager, Zack Taylor, produces a copy of the signed contract that had been registered in the league offices the day before. So the umpire rules that Eddie can bat.

The Detroit pitcher, of course, gets completely rattled and can't find the tiny strike zone. Eddie walks on four pitches. That's why you'll find in the official records the name Edward Carl Gaedel, one at-bat as a Big Leaguer. That's because as soon as Eddie got to first base, they sent in a pinch runner. The next day, American League president Will Harridge banned midgets from baseball. It was only good as a gag once.

Another first, Veeck set up a huge nursery in the Cleveland stadium and staffed it with professional child-care nurses. Any mother who wanted to catch a ball game could drop her kid off there for the duration of the game absolutely free. I saw the place. It was a kid's wonderland. "You know something," Veeck told me, "when we started that, I was just thinking of making it easy for the mothers to come out to the game. I never had in mind what a wonderful thing it would be just to have youngsters of different colors and creeds playing together naturally."

That was Veeck. He had that great touch of fun and irreverence. Plus a social conscience.

He was a great showman—and a loose cannon. That's the way the owners looked at him. They were horrified when he took on Doby. But he didn't give a shit for them. He was rich, scion of a wealthy family. He wasn't an aloof office guy. He never even dressed like one, a shirtsleeve guy before that became common. He'd come down on the field and he'd talk baseball with Paige, and Satch would talk about the old days of barn-storming and busing and all that. I guess you could call him a populist.

Veeck caught some flack after signing Doby. One letter, apparently, got his goat. It wasn't one of those "Goddamn you for signing a nigger" letters. It was more like, does Cleveland really need this, and won't this muddy the waters, and it'll hurt the blacks as well as the whites. That kind of thing. So he wrote back to the guy, answering him point by point, and he gave the letter and his answer to the *Cleveland Plain Dealer*. Gordon Cobbledick, their top baseball writer, ran it. One of our readers in Cleveland sent me the clipping. And we reproduced the exchange. Veeck appreciated that. Next time he saw me he said something like "Glad you put that in your paper in New York." And I said something like "Well the *Times* wasn't gonna do it."

He's my odds-on favorite baseball magnate. Along with his intelligence and humanity, he would have had my vote any time for baseball commissioner.

Veeck's signing of Satch made possible what was, for me at least, one of the great dramatic moments in baseball history. This was in '49, Satch's second year. A big game. The Indians and the Yankees are battling it out for the pennant and Early Wynn, one of Cleveland's aces, is pitching with a 4–1 lead. In the eighth inning, Rizzuto and Henrich lead off with hard-hit singles—Phil going to third—and DiMaggio walks up to the plate. First and third, nobody out, and DiMaggio up. Boudreau, who's playing third now, calls time, walks to the mound, takes the ball from Wynn, and waves his right hand out to left center field where the Cleveland bullpen is. The little iron fence in left field opens and out walks Satchel Paige, jacket over his shoulder and glove in hand.

Sitting there in the press box, I can't help but think back to that moment eleven years before, when a reporter asks a young Joe DiMaggio who was the best pitcher he had ever faced, and Joe says, "Satchel Paige." Now eleven years later they face each other again—not in a postseason exhibition game but at a crucial moment of a pennant race.

There's always an air of drama in the changing of a pitcher. It's a piece of theater, a pause in the action, the exit of a central performer, and the entrance of a lone, newly important figure who walks in toward the middle of the diamond with measured steps and looms larger and larger as he comes. And here's the first black guy to come walking out of that Yankee Stadium bullpen. All the infielders are at the mound. And here's Satchel Paige coming in to pitch to Joe DiMaggio with nobody out and runners on first and third, before fifty-five thousand roaring fans. A home run ties the score. A single scores one leaving two on and nobody out with the potential winning run at the plate. DiMaggio has singled in his last two at bats. It's one of those Yankee situations, the kind where people have that feeling and say later they just knew the Yanks were going to break through and win.

Paige hands his jacket to the Cleveland batboy and takes his warm-up tosses. The ump bends down and ceremoniously brushes off the plate, puts his mask back on, and DiMaggio steps in.

In the anemic make-believe that passes for baseball movies—except maybe *Bull Durham*—DiMaggio would either hit a home run or strike out. But Hollywood drama is never the ebb and flow of real life. In real life this night, the forty-two-year-old Satch couldn't quite keep DiMag from connecting solidly, but he does keep Joe from doing much damage. Paige slips through two quick called strikes on the corners and now, ahead of the hitter, makes Joe hit the pitch he wants him to hit. It's a long, soaring fly caught in deep left center field. The run scores from third, but it's one big out. Pitching with his typical infinite care, Satch then disposes of the next two batters on routine flies to the opposite field, away from their power, and finishes the ninth by getting three more batters in a row. Twice, as he whips the ball around the corners, never giving the hitter anything good, he goes behind 3–1, and each time he chokes off Yankee hopes for a walk, coming in with a beautiful low curve for strike two and then getting his man. A big win for Cleveland, although the Yanks go on to win the pennant.

In the press box after the last out, a New York writer, I forget who, says, "Imagine, at his age. He must have been the greatest pitcher of all time." Another guy says, "I suppose he really was."

After Brooklyn and Cleveland broke the color line, the New York Giants were next, bringing up Monte Irvin and Henry Thompson in '49. Irvin was a great outfielder for the Giants, a key star in their pennants of '51 and

'54. Thompson was a competent journeyman infielder for years. Then came the Boston Braves with Sammy Jethroe in '50, and one by one the other teams got smart and joined America. The Yankees had signed a few black players to their minor-league farm teams but didn't bring any of them up to the Bigs until 1955, eight years after Jackie went to the Dodgers, when they brought up Elston Howard, a very good catcher.

The Yankee top management had some real sons-of-bitches. George Weiss, the general manager, was an out-and-out racist. Every sportswriter knew it. When he was asked, "How about the Yankees getting a colored ballplayer?" he said, "You really want one of them in our pinstripes?" You know, this mystique of the Yankee pinstripes. They created that image. That's a part of it. But it went deeper than that. They also were saying, in effect, we can prove that you don't need blacks by being the best team and all-white. And they were for a while. But why? Because they were the big power with all the money, and they could go out and get the pick of the best white players. It was like Notre Dame getting all the best Catholic football players. They fished out Joe DiMaggio. He was a free agent. Anybody could have signed him. But they made the most attractive offer. They had the inducement of the Big City and almost a guarantee of added World Series money. The richest team concentrating a good percentage of the best available white players, naturally you could seem to prove a point that you don't need blacks.

The *Daily Worker* directed a lot of the campaign during the early fifties at the Yankees just because they were the Yankees, the down-the-nose team. Besides, most of our readers were in New York. So we hammered them. We ran columns and angry reader letters and reported on available players in their own Kansas City affiliate. We forced them to respond in mealy-mouthed ways. But they stalled for a long time.

Because of their stubborn refusal to bring any black players on their roster, the Yankees blew a chance to sign Willie Mays back in 1949. Joe Press, who was president of the Bushwick Club in the Negro Leagues, regularly used to recommend outstanding prospects from the Negro Leagues to the Yankees, all of whom were turned down. In 1949 he strongly recommended Willie Mays, then playing for the Birmingham Barons. The

Yankees passed—as did the Red Sox—and a year later Willie was signed by the Giants.

LR: It wasn't easy for those first black players in the majors. It was toughest of all on Jackie Robinson. That first year was grueling for him. Incident after incident of harassment, even physical assaults.

There was a shortstop on the Chicago Cubs, Lenny Merullo. One time he pretended that Robinson had tried to spike him when he slid into second. Merullo jumped on Jackie and began to pummel him, knowing that Robinson was under the no-fight-back restraint. Other players and the umps had to pull him off. Another time, Enos Slaughter of the Cards went out of his way to come down at Jackie's heel at first base. Everybody saw him veer to do it. He could have severed Robinson's Achilles tendon and put him out for a year. The Phillies, who were managed by the notorious racist Ben Chapman, were among the worst. They would yell all kinds of racist taunts when Jackie was at bat and then razz white Dodgers with gibes like "Is he gonna fuck your sister tonight?" Encouraged by the players, some fans would yell, "Goddamn nigger," like it was one word.

And it wasn't easy going for Jackie even on the Dodgers. Nothing overt like with Merullo or Slaughter. And certainly not the obscenities. But sometimes the racist conditioning would come out. Once, during a rain delay, Jackie was sitting in on a card game and Hugh Casey the relief pitcher gets a hand he likes. He walks over to Robinson and says, "Let me rub your head for good luck." I didn't see that, but Robinson told it to Roger Kahn, who wrote about it.

Jackie just sits there while Casey says to the other players, "Where I come from, it's good luck to rub a nigger's head." That's the kind of thing Jackie went through quietly even with the Dodgers in '47. There were probably other incidents of that kind, though not as crude.

Some umpires—not all of them, to be sure—also vented their racist feelings, although in slightly more subtle ways. To begin with, they were all white. It would be another twenty years before there was a breakthrough on that front. A lot of them were also from the South, and they weren't used to having blacks talk back to them. And some of them would just freak out if Jackie or Campy said things that would have gone right by the boards if a white player had said them.

Things got especially tense from 1949 on, when the real Jackie Robinson was finally allowed to stand up. Aggressive and vocal, the kind of athlete he was at Pasadena City College and UCLA, the kind of man he'd been in the Jim Crow army—this was a Jackie Robinson few whites had seen. And he immediately ran into the double standard. White players with the same qualities—Durocher, Eddie Stanky, Billy Martin, the old Cardinal Gashouse Gang—were invariably seen as tough, scrappy competitors, winners. But the first black player was termed shrill and irritating.

Once Jackie got thrown out in a crucial series in St. Louis when Ump Bill Stewart called ball four on a close 3–2 pitch by Don Newcombe to Enos Slaughter, then immediately ejected Jackie for a silent, body English sign of disagreement, a wince. The Dodgers lost that game 1–0. Can you imagine Stewart looking to get Robinson's reaction and—bang! just like that— "You're out of here!" Unimaginable. A little later that same year, I saw Ralph Houk of the Yankees, who was catching that day, wheel on Ump Bill Grieve at the Stadium and go berserk. He actually laid his hand on the ump, cursing him. They had to pull him away. He wasn't ejected. Important game, you understand, and Yankee catcher Yogi Berra was on the injured list. Talk about double standards.

And the top officials of baseball made it worse. Before the 1950 season even began, National League president Ford Frick, in a completely unprecedented announcement, picked one player, Jackie Robinson, to publicly warn against rough baserunning. So what do you expect? In a game that season, Ump Jocko Conlan calls a third strike against Robinson, who walks away silently. Conlan turns and calls out, "It was right over the plate!" Jackie takes the bait, whirls, and disagrees. Out of the game. Out with him go two batting streaks—hit safely in sixteen straight games, reached base in fifty-five straight. Nobody in the press box could remember an umpire so blatantly provoking a player into ejection.

Robinson wasn't the only one. Campanella got it too. In '52, Frank Dascoli, a motorcycle cop in the off-season—not that there's anything wrong with that, but maybe he was working on his racial profiling—was another umpire looking for a pretext to bounce a black player. In one close play at the plate, Dascoli called the runner safe, and all Campanella said, in his usual mild way, was "But I had the plate blocked." Dascoli immediately jerks his thumb up in the air and yells, "You're out of here!" And then, naturally, the Dodger bench got on Dascoli's case. So Warren Giles, the president of the National League at that time, who had previously run a Jim Crow team at Cincinnati, publicly criticized the Dodgers. He mentioned just one name, "Jackie Robinson was particularly objectionable." There was only one Dodger identified by Dascoli and thrown out of the game, a white pitcher named Johnny van Cuyk. The next time Robinson crossed paths with Giles, he brought this up and Giles replied, "You were hollering, weren't you?" Even Charlie Dressen, the Dodger manager, a real establishment guy, was moved to say angrily that Jackie, while up there with the good bench jockeys, never used objectionable language or brought in anything personal or racial, whatever.

So for Jackie there was no great sigh of relief like "We did it, now I can relax and just be a ballplayer."

Joe Louis (LEFT) and Paul Robeson

Satchel Paige shortly after being signed
to the Cleveland Indians by Bill Veeck

Lester Rodney
(LEFT) chatting
with Red Rolfe,
New York Yan-
kees third base-
man

May Day paraders (1947) welcoming Jackie Robinson to the Dodgers

Members of United Wholesale and Warehouse Workers Union (CIO) marching in May Day Parade (circa 1940)

Pete Cacchione (ABOVE), first Communist elected to New York City Council (1941)

Ben Davis (LEFT), a Communist elected to New York City Council in 1942, together with Communist Councilman Pete Cacchione pushed legislation to end racial discrimination in baseball

Clyde Sukeforth (LEFT), Brooklyn Dodger scout who first signed Jackie Robinson; Jackie Robinson; Branch Rickey. (Reprinted with special permission of King Features Syndicate.)

Nat Low, *Daily Worker* sports editor (LEFT), and Joe Bostic, *People's Voice* sports editor, accompany two black ball-players—Dave (Showboat) Thomas and Terry McDuffie—to a Brooklyn Dodgers tryout in Bear Mountain, 1945

Cartoon in *Daily Worker* (May 6, 1942) aimed at Baseball Commissioner Judge Kenesaw Mountain Landis

Lester Rodney at the Long Beach *Independent Press-Telegram* (late sixties)

Ford Frick (LEFT), President National League; Judge Kenesaw Mountain Landis, Commissioner of Baseball; Will Harridge, President of American League (1937)

Demonstrators protesting baseball discrimination are arrested in Detroit

Joe DiMaggio in San Francisco Seals uniform, shortly before signing with New York Yankees

Earl Browder (ABOVE), General Secretary of U.S. Communist Party, 1932–1945

William Z. Foster, Chairman
of the U.S. Communist Party,
1932–1957

Clarence Hathaway, editor of
the *Daily Worker*, in 1936

A Dance to Lester Rodney (Jules Feiffer). Courtesy of Jules Feiffer.

BASEBALL HAD SOMETHING TO DO WITH THAT 9-0 SCORE

By LESTER RODNEY

DID BASEBALL have anything to do with the historic Supreme Court decision calling for the ending of school jimcrow in our land? A lot of ballplayers, Negro and white, think so. If you were to ask the game's greatest catcher, Roy Campanella (a member of the executive board of the N.Y. NAACP) he'd give it as his frank opinion that baseball was the most important groundbreaker for democracy below the Mason-Dixon Line. "All I know," says Roy, "is that the ballclubs going down there and travelling together and playing together and living together were the first all the time. Baseball had to be the greatest teacher of democracy when you look at it."

Take one Southern city and the difference the breaking of baseball jimcrow made. In 1946, Jackie Robinson was a rookie with Montreal; first Negro signed to a job in organized baseball. The parent Brooklyn Dodgers and Montreal were scheduled for their usual exhibition games in Southern cities. When they got to Jacksonville, Fla., they found the gates of the ballpark locked. The city fathers forbade the game.

That was 1946. Now jump to 1953, not long as history goes, but seven years after Robinson, Doby and the other Negro stars started to take their place in our national pastime. The same Jacksonville, Fla.—a ceremony at home plate of the very same ballpark. Hank Aaron of the local Jacksonville team is receiving a trophy as the "Most Valuable" player in the old Sally League, comprising cities like Jacksonville, Savannah, Montgomery, Macon, Columbus and Augusta. Hank Aaron, the player with "Jacksonville" across the chest of his uniform, the one being honored, is a Negro.

there was a deep roar of greeting. Then some booing began in the white stands. Then a third thing happened, clapping in the white stands, and finally about half the white fans stood up clapping to disasociate themselves from the booers. Imagine that tumultuos moment if you can. Who were those who stood up and clapped? Were they Southerners who the next day woke up entirely changed and began fighting jimcrow? That, of course, is silly. But they were typical. white Southerners looking at baseball players on a ballfield with its concept of fair play, and their latent feelings of sportsmanship were challenged directly, even though in a limited context. They reacted.

Who will dare estimate the meaning of the Dodgers vs. the Atlanta Crackers that night in Georgia, or flatly state that it had no part in the greater victories to come—and still to come.

⋆

'Not in Memphis, Or New Orleans'

CITY after city in the South became the scene of these exhibition games, and now it was the Indians, Giants, White Sox, the Braves in addition to the Dodg-

There was a little Hollywoodish scene for a moment as the flustered clerk said excuse me and went in to confer with someone else .Then he came back and said "Sign here, Mr. Doby," and that was that. As Joe Gordon had said, Doby was with the team, wasn't he? You gonna fight the Cleveland Indians?

The Santa Rita Hotel down in Tucson, Ariz., where the Indians train, did "fight the Cleveland Indians" for two years and the Negro players had to stay separate from their teammates. With the help of a vigorous educational campaign by the local Civil Rights Congress, which found fertile soil among the sports minded populace, the Santa Rita was finally forced to open its doors

⋆

Joe Louis and an Alabama GI

OF COURSE baseball is not the only sport which gets an assist in the successful attacks on jimcrow ideology. How about Joe Louis? How many sports conscious young Southern men, weaned on the heart and justification of racism, the notion that Negroes are inferior to whites, couldn't fully resolve the elementary conflict caused by Joe Louis, a Negro, knocking out the best white fighters? THAT'S superiority, not inferiority.

In my outfit in World War II, a guy from Alabama, fascinated by the discovery that I was a

Chapter 6

The Impact of Baseball's Integration

T HOSE WHO OPPOSED breaking baseball's color line were right about one thing: integration would not only have a profound impact on the game itself, it would be a turning point in sports as a whole and a precursor to deep social change in American society at large. What many feared, however, Rodney embraced as part of a broader vision of an America ultimately free of its racist legacy. But even among those who supported the campaign, few could imagine the actual impact the integration of the national pastime would have on the prevailing Jim Crow norms.

Lester Rodney: The end of the color line in baseball thoroughly transformed an institution that was watched and followed by more Americans than anything else, bar none. Not that it happened overnight. And not that there weren't still battles to be won after the big breakthrough. But within a few years, the world of baseball was turned upside down so far as race was concerned. And Jackie Robinson was the lightning rod. He wasn't about to make it easy for whites with any racial prejudice—conscious or otherwise.

Even during those two years when he couldn't fight back, Robinson projected a sense of self-confidence in his ability and his right to be where he was that challenged every tenet of white supremacy. Someone else might have eased into that role in a way that may have made whites feel comfortable. Jackie didn't. He made them feel uncomfortable. His very presence forced people to react and, for the most part, ultimately change.

For instance, ballplayers traditionally react strongly when a teammate is spiked, tagged too roughly, or suspiciously hit by a pitch. And Jackie in '47 was getting that kind of treatment, as well as the unmentionable verbal abuse. This troubled some of the white Dodgers, especially since they knew Jackie was pledged not to respond in any way. I remember before one game at Ebbets Field, some of the Dodgers talking about it, out of Jackie's earshot. It was almost as if they were forced to think in new ways about race. Pete Reiser offered the tentative thought "Well, democracy means that everyone is the same, so that means we should treat everybody the same way." He meant well, but in this situation that came down to "it's not proper for us to do anything special about it." This didn't quite satisfy Pee Wee Reese, the team captain, "That's true," he said in his Kentucky drawl, sort of thinking while he talked, "democracy means everyone is equal, but Jackie's the only colored guy in the league and he's catching special grief because of it. Maybe we ought to try to make things more equal for him."

Now this is twenty-five years before affirmative action was ever heard of. Pee Wee wasn't an ideologue. He would have laughed and shrugged if you put a larger social significance to what he said. So how does a white Dodger actually go about trying to make things a little more equal for Robinson? Captain Reese led the way a short while later when the Dodgers went to Cincinnati, kind of a southern city, across the river from Kentucky. There are loud boos the moment Jackie takes the field for pregame practice, and some loudmouth is shouting vile things about Jackie and the white players' sisters. Reese walks over to Robinson, casually drapes his arm around him, and chats with him. Doesn't sound like anything special today, but it was electrifying back then.

They're talking about having that moment as a piece of sculpture in front of the new Coney Island minor-league ballpark in Brooklyn. Here's another example. Earlier I talked about Carl Furillo telling Branch Rickey,

"I ain't gonna play with no nigger!" Well, one day about two months after the season opener, when I got to Ebbets Field a little early, there were numbers 6 (Furillo) and 42 (Robinson) paired off, warming up together. The racist abstraction was fading for Furillo.

Now fast forward to a game two years later. It's midsummer 1949, Dodgers versus Braves, now the defending league champs, at Ebbets Field. It's a night game, full house. An important game in a close race, scoreless tie top of the fifth. Nobody on, one out. Preacher Roe of Ash Flat, Arkansas—coolly correct about Jackie's presence on the Dodgers—gives up a walk. The next batter, Clint Conatser, drives an outside pitch into the open spaces of right center. Jim Russell, the Brave runner on first, after hesitating to make sure the ball can't be caught, takes off. Furillo, the right fielder, catches up to the ball at the base of the wall about 380 feet from home plate, wheels, and cocks the game's strongest arm as the crowd rises to its feet in anticipation.

Freeze the action for a moment. The long-legged Russell is in full cry, tearing through third in a wide turn. Conatser digs toward second. Robinson, now a second baseman, eases out some fifty feet into the outfield, half-facing Furillo. Shortstop Reese moves to cover second. First baseman Gil Hodges moves into position to possibly cut off the throw to the plate. Catcher Roy Campanella, the team's second black player, who came aboard in '48, waits slightly up the third base line. Roe ambles from the mound to back up the plate. It's the full panorama of baseball, a team game, in a moment that no television camera can encompass.

Okay, unfreeze. Furillo cuts loose. The noise begins swelling as the ball bullets into Robinson's glove, head high, slightly to his right, making it unnecessary for him to pivot his feet before throwing. Robinson's throwing arm is the least imposing of his nonpareil skills, possibly due to two years of pounding as a running, blocking, pass-catching back for UCLA's football team, but he made the throws when he had to. Campy snatches the ball waist high and dives for the tag as Russell plummets in feet first. Up through the dust comes the thumb of umpire Larry Goetz. He's out! The next batter pops up for the third out. Furillo lopes in from the outfield with a huge grin. The crowd roar starts up again. Robinson, Roe, and Campanella wait for Carl at the lip of the dugout, then envelop him into an exuberant foursome. I lean out of the press box above to watch them descend into the dugout together, then turn my gaze to the people in the stands, those raucous, salty, kidding, good-natured, integrated Ebbets Field stands, unlike any before or since. I imagined the continuing crowd roar merging with the animation of all Brooklyn listening to Red Barber on the radio. Here, two years later, was the full-blown aura of the magical Jackie Robinson years and a measure of how Robinson had changed baseball, and America. Oh, yes. The Dodgers won that game 4–0 en route to the pennant, one of six in the ten Robinson years. [Without two last-day-of-the-season fluke endings, it would have been eight out of ten.] A payoff for the game's first integrated team.

Now take the little Furillo-Robinson human drama further. It's 1955, eight years after the breakthrough, the night after the Dodgers finally beat the Yankees in the World Series, and there's a festive victory party for the team and the Brooklyn writers in Brooklyn's old Bossert Hotel. And here's Furillo ("I ain't gonna play with no niggers") rushing to greet Jackie and Rachel Robinson as they come in. Carl and Jackie, friends, hugging with cheeks pressed together, saying, "We did it, we did it." Baseball, democratic baseball, can do that. To be sure, there were some Dodgers—Gil Hodges, Ralph Branca, Carl Erskine, Duke Snider, and of course that special Kentuckian, Harold "Pee Wee" Reese—to whom baseball integration was pretty much a shrugging "Why not?" from the start.

Here's another specially dramatic example of the conflicted emotions and the waves rippling around the country at the time. Even in southern cities that didn't have a Big League team. This is the spring of 1949. The Dodgers are heading home after spring training, and they're stopping off in Atlanta for an exhibition game against the Atlanta Crackers. This is long before the Braves moved to Atlanta.

It's gonna be Georgia's first interracial game, and as you can imagine, there's tension in the air. The Grand Dragon of the state Ku Klux Klan issues a statement saying the game cannot be tolerated. The Dodgers get into town, and when they get off the train Pee Wee Reese nudges the ground with his toe, peers down as though he's looking under a rock, and asks, "Where's the Dragon?" Campanella told me this story. Meanwhile, black fans have been streaming into Atlanta all day from outlying towns and the countryside for the night game. There are still separate stands for blacks, of course. But the black stands are small and fill up quickly. So the management, not happy about turning away cash customers, and perhaps also with some dim sense of history in the making, allows the overflow to pour on to the field behind hastily erected rope barriers along the walls. Other blacks climb and cling to the terraced right-field fence.

When Robinson emerges from the visiting dugout, with Roy Campanella and Don Newcombe close behind, a deep roar emerges from the sea of black fans. This touches off heavy booing from the white stands. Then there's a third reaction—other whites begin to clap. All eyes turn that way, where maybe about a third of the white fans are getting to their feet, standing as if to differentiate themselves from the booers and continuing to clap.

Can you imagine the drama of this brand new racial experience in the Georgia of 1949? The bedlam of mixed sounds, the cheering, the booing, the standing up and clapping. Who were these white Southerners who stood and clapped? For sure they couldn't all have been Southern liberals, Lillian Carter, Ralph McGill types, suddenly coming out of the closet. You can only conclude that they were first and foremost sports fans, weaned on sports along with white supremacy, caught this night in a head-on collision between the two as they looked down at those magical men, Big League players. You're not supposed to "mix the races," yet all these guys in Dodger uniform were part of the elite four hundred of almost every American male's dreams . . . sixteen teams, twenty-five per roster, that's all. I think you can throw into the mix the fact that Atlantans felt they were the hosts this night, and "host" is another pretty significant word down south.

Part of the magic of Jackie was that he actually changed some people. There were the blatant racists who yelled obscenities. Then there was a bigger body of fans who weren't happy about integration but wouldn't join the overt racists in shouting ugly stuff. Some with mixed feelings, like the ones in Atlanta, their "normal" aversion to integration colliding with feelings about sportsmanship, which they also grew up with. Some who played baseball themselves had to have a reluctant appreciation of Jackie, and maybe even of what he was doing under the intense pressure. Plus a certain number who we wouldn't call "socially conscious" but basically decent folks who couldn't see why a good enough player with black skin shouldn't play if he could cut the mustard. And, of course, the still smaller number of political progressives who were enthusiastic backers of baseball integration from the get-go.

How would I know all this? I didn't take a poll. But I did follow the Dodgers closely almost every game with my antennas out. And I engaged in a certain amount of mingling with crowds before and after games. Anyone could see and sense a steady change in crowd reactions. I'd say that late in Jackie's second year it was clear that the outspoken racists were a shrinking minority. Maybe some of them actually changed too, but even if they didn't they sensed they were on the losing side and they at least shut up.

The change was most striking in the South. In 1946, the city of Jacksonville, Florida, padlocked the ballpark to thwart a game between the Dodgers and their Montreal farm team because of Robinson's presence. Seven years later, same ballpark. Packed stands cheering. City fathers beaming. A young man at home plate is receiving a trophy as the Most Valuable Player in the Sally League, made up of such cities as Montgomery, Savannah, Macon, and Jacksonville. The young man, with "Jacksonville" sewn across the chest of his uniform, is Hank Aaron, same color as Robinson.

For years the racists and the cynics had said it couldn't happen. That's what Burleigh Grimes told me in 1937. Never in Memphis, they said. Never in New Orleans. Never in Mobile. Never in Shreveport. All those cities saw the moment when the umpire called, "Play ball!" and black and white players trotted onto the field at the same time.

You know that horseshit about the Dallas Cowboys, they put a lot of red, white, and blue on their cheerleaders and they're "America's team." But in the decade 1947–57, the Dodgers were really America's team. They had fans cheering for them in St. Louis, Chicago, Pittsburgh, wherever. Mostly black fans, of course, but not a small number of fair-minded white fans too. Even in cities with no Big League baseball, the exploits and even the box scores of the Dodgers were closely followed by lots of blacks and many whites. How many other teams can you say that about?

Sportswriters were changing too. When I started the sports section for the *Daily Worker* in 1936, there wasn't a single sportswriter who was writing about this stuff except for a very few sporadic mentions by Jimmy Powers of the *Daily News* and Dan Parker of *The Mirror*. They weren't all bad guys. There were even some liberals. It was just the accepted culture of the times. But by 1939, they were becoming more aware. The campaign was picking up speed and supporters after the very lonely agitation by us and the black weeklies.

You could say they were Johnny-come-latelies, but I felt good about it. I never wanted the campaign to be our exclusive story. I was in it because I wanted the damned ban to end, to bring elementary democracy to the game I loved, and to see the banned black players get their chance to show they belonged. Sure, I pointed out that we were the only daily pushing the campaign. But if it stayed our story for years, that was never something we wanted, even in journalistic scoop terms. When the other papers finally ended their shameful silence, I was tickled pink. Or maybe I should say red.

The big-time baseball radio announcers were also impacted—none more so, perhaps, than Red Barber, who was famous for his coverage of Dodger games. Barber was from Mississippi, and in later years he wrote about his inner conflicts when Jackie Robinson and then other black players broke the color line. He certainly wasn't an enthusiastic advocate. He concedes as much. He was proper. Naturally. He had to hold his job and all. But slowly he began to change, and I'd say by mid-season of '49, which is two and a half years after Robinson broke in, Barber was different.

To some extent you could sense it just in the tone of his voice. And then, after a while, he'd be saying things on the air like "this great interracial crowd" and "This is America," stuff like that. Even from the start, he never spoke condescendingly or disdainfully about the black ballplayers on the Dodgers. Condescension came from some of the old-line guys on the *New York Times*—Roscoe McGowan, John Drebinger—the "gentlemen" from the *Times*. I never saw them warm up to the changed scene.

Barber was a very interesting guy. There was great curiosity in the press box about him. Some thought he would quit. They assumed that a white guy from Mississippi couldn't adapt. But he did.

Like a lot of others, he got caught up in the character of Robinson. He had to make certain adjustments. He used to speak to groups in Brooklyn about that. He'd say, in his Mississippi drawl, "You may wonder what I think of Robinson coming into Big League ball, and I must admit that at the beginning I thought different than I do now." It was a real conversion. Not fake. Brooklyn was a special case in those years. An announcer had to be with that. He couldn't just sit back and continue as before. He had to capture that new spirit of Brooklyn in his announcing. And Barber did. I remember some of the sportswriters talking about him: "Hey, what about Red Barber?" This Deep Southerner. They pretty much agreed that he adapted as a human being and broadcaster.

Mel Allen broadcast the Yankee games on radio, and the differences you might expect between a southern Jew and most southern Bible-belters of that time were there. His case was different from Red Barber's, though. He wasn't in the middle of a pulsing change.

He was an apologist for the Yankees being lily-white for so long. In fact, he was just a paid shill for the Yankees, so he wasn't going to rock the boat. Mel didn't have to deal with the Dodger fans. He broadcast Yankee games.

By the early 1960s, new black players coming into organized baseball were no longer news. In the early years after Robinson literally changed the complexion of the game, a black ballplayer had to be a lot better than good. If he couldn't make it big, and quick, if all he had was a "fair-to-middling" batting average, he couldn't expect a seat on the bench at Big League pay. What's more, he was expected to comport himself at all times and under all provocations as a colored Little Lord Fauntleroy toward the opposition and to his majesty, the umpire. But by the early 1960s, blacks of varying abilities—stars, almost-stars, journeymen, and short-lived flops—were to be found throughout the Big Leagues. Colored athletes had achieved what is pretty much taken for granted today: the inalienable right to be ordinary and even relatively mediocre Big Leaguers—just like whites.

The growing presence of black ballplayers brought into clearer view the fact that baseball wasn't integrated at every level.

It was 1966 before major league baseball had its first black umpire—Emmett Ashford. He was hired nineteen years after Jackie Robinson broke the color line. His first assignment was the season opener in Washington, D.C., where the Senators were playing the Yankees. Vice President Hubert Humphrey was scheduled to throw out the first ball, and with all the controversy over the Vietnam War, the Secret Service was out in full force. When Ashford got to the parking lot, he was stopped by a Secret Service man who wanted to know who he was. Told Ashford was there to be an umpire in the day's game, the agent laughed and said, "Who you kidding?" When Ashford insisted, the Secret Service man thumbed through a folder. When he came to the last page, the agent said, "What's that name again?" and stared in utter disbelief when Ashford repeated his name. Ashford was finally let in, but the scene was repeated two more times before he could get to the umpire's room. "But after I got dressed and went out on that field and saw the full stadium," Ashford would say later on, "there was a lump in my throat. Then I knew all those years of perseverance and labor were well worth it" (Ashford 1992, 78).

But the higher echelons of the game remained overwhelmingly white. In 1969, twelve years after he hung up his spikes and three years before his premature death, Jackie Robinson was invited by the Yankees to appear at their Old Timers game. Robinson had become an increasingly deep critic of the stubbornly remaining racial inequities in American society, and he refused the invite, saying, "My pride in my blackness . . . requires that until I see genuine interest in breaking the barriers that deny access to managerial and front office positions, I will say no" (Robinson 1972, 260).

Over the course of the next two decades, three blacks briefly held managerial positions. Larry Doby with the Chicago White Sox and Maury Wills with Seattle were fired after less than a season and weren't recycled into the musical chairs so common for white managerial retreats. Frank Robinson lasted a little longer—three and a half years with San Francisco and Cleveland.

Since then, there has been progress in the field manager position. The day finally came when a black manager, like so many white managers before him, could be fired by one team and hired by another. And there's no to-do when a manager like Dusty Baker is twice named Most Valuable.

By the mid-1980s, the gap between the number and caliber of black ballplayers and the overwhelmingly white makeup of on- and off-the-field managerial and executive personnel had become a touchy subject for the game's top brass. Pressed to explain this inconsistency by TV interviewer Ted Koppel, Los Angeles Dodgers general manager Al Campanis reached back into the past, when baseball executives claimed they couldn't find any "qualified" black players, to say, "They may not have some of the necessities to be a field manager or perhaps a general manager." Ironically, the occasion of the interview, April 5, 1987, was a commemoration of the fortieth anniversary of Jackie Robinson's coming to the Dodgers.

When an incredulous Koppel asked him, "Do you really believe that?" Campanis replied, "Well, I don't say all of them, but they certainly are short. How many [black] quarterbacks do you have, how many pitchers?" (from ABC *Nightline* transcript, April 5, 1987).

The Campanis interview generated an immediate firestorm.

Hank Aaron called Campanis's comments "the tip of the iceberg." Although Campanis had befriended Jackie Robinson when he first came to the Dodgers, Rachel Robinson, Jackie's widow, was "appalled and angered." Baseball Hall-of-Famer Willie Stargell organized a hastily called conference of current and former Big Leaguers to discuss what could be done. Some two hundred showed up, among them Frank Robinson, Dusty Baker, Don Baylor, Chris Chambliss, and Bob Watson.

Kenneth Shropshire, a professor at the University of Pennsylvania and a sports industry consultant, attended the meeting and subsequently wrote an account of it:

Stargell urged individuals to come forward and tell their stories. One by one, the African-American baseball heroes of my youth stepped up to microphones and spoke of how the teams that formerly employed them as players had treated them. Some went on to talk about the baseball futures they had sought but been denied due to their color.

Many sportswriters and fans likewise registered their displeasure at Campanis's remarks. But the Dodgers general manager had his defenders too. Some pointed to Campanis's support for black baseball players in the early days of desegregation. Others defended him for being willing to speak out on a subject usually not mentioned in public—the disproportionately large number of black athletes in three of the country's main professional sports—basketball, football, and baseball. Campanis, said many, was the victim of "political correctness" from those who wanted to deny genetically racial differences between whites and blacks as the reason for black domination in certain sports and certain positions in these sports.

Campanis himself, trying to undo the damage and oblivious to the paternalism by which many whites seek to rid themselves of the taint of racism, noted that he had many black friends and that "they are outstanding athletes, very God-gifted, and they're very wonderful people . . . gifted with great musculature and various other things. They are fleet of foot, and this is why there are a number of black ball players in the major leagues" (from ABC *Nightline* transcript, April 5, 1987).

"What's really being said in a kind of underhanded way," commented Harry Edwards, sociology professor at the University of California at Berkeley, "is that blacks are closer to beasts and animals in terms of their genetic and physical and anatomical make up than they are to the rest of humanity" (*Colorado Springs Independent,* November 16, 2000).

But Campanis was doing no more than giving voice to a mind-set widespread in the sports hierarchy. For no matter how much they praised the athletic skills of black players, they simply could not imagine a black man in a position of authority over whites.

LR: In the years since Al Campanis asserted that blacks "didn't have the necessities" to make it as major-league pitchers—let alone field managers and general managers—much has changed in major-league baseball. Outstanding black pitchers have become commonplace and black field managers are no longer a novelty, although many teams continue to rotate white managers and coaches with mediocre records while ignoring blacks. Although the numbers are still small, blacks have begun to break into front offices, and a few have even gotten executive positions. But the ultimate authority—team ownership—remains all white. I'm not privy to these things anymore, but with black athletes so prominent, sports-minded blacks with money, like Bill Cosby and Michael Jordan, might be at least sounded out about buying into our national pastime.

Nevertheless, the desegregation of baseball has had a profound effect on sports in general. Baseball was the best known die-hard institution of a racialized America. It certainly paved the way for the full integration of pro basketball and football. In both those sports, the pros had been second in popularity to the college game. That changed when blacks came in. Althea Gibson broke the barrier in tennis in 1950. Arthur Ashe established a black player as number one in the men's game, and the Williams sisters [Venus and Serena] have inspired a whole new generation of tennis-minded black youngsters. And now there's Tiger Woods. All these break-throughs owed a lot to Jackie Robinson.

The breakthrough in baseball also had an impact for racial change in the larger society. Segregation laws took a big hit in many Dixie cities when baseball broke the color ban. I talked about this once at Ebbets Field with Roy Campanella, who argued that baseball was *the* most important factor in the Supreme Court's 1954 decision ruling school segregation un-constitutional.

I always had a better, more casual relationship with Campy than with Jackie for that kind of thing, though Jackie was professional and coopera-tive with me. Anyhow, when Campy said that, I gave him one of those quizzical come-on-now smiles, but without blinking he insisted, "All I know is that the ball clubs going down there and playing together, and travel-ing together, and then eating together and all, we were the first every time, we were like the teachers of it." We had a piece on that. The headline was "Baseball Had Something to Do with that 9–0 Score—Roy Campanella."

Of course, Campy was a ballplayer, and he was shortchanging the full spectrum of the Civil Rights movement. Still, in calculating such things, it might be pertinent to recall that when Martin Luther King Jr. first met Don Newcombe, he said, "You'll never know what Jackie and you and Roy did to make it possible for me to do my work."

Although the *Daily Worker* was certainly a catalyst in bringing about the desegregation of baseball, a new historical dynamic was at work after Franklin Roosevelt was elected president in 1932. Not that FDR did anything significant about racism in the South; the white South was too important a political base for the Democratic Party. But the New Deal projected a kind of common-man outlook that helped open doors elsewhere. Some racial stereotypes were starting to break down in the arts and in sports, thanks to people like Marian Anderson, Paul Robeson, Jesse Owens, and Joe Louis. The growing black migration out of the South brought tens of thousands of blacks into northern industry and into the labor movement. The CIO itself, particularly because of the influence of the Communists in it, adopted an anti-racist stance. All this brought blacks and whites in closer and more equal contact with each other than ever before. World War II accelerated the process. In short, the general culture was changing. A few of the old walls began to come down.

LR: The color line in baseball wouldn't have been broken when it was without the petition campaign—a million, a million and a half, two million signatures piling up on Judge Landis's desk. Then there were the things that flowed from that, like when Landis had to meet with Paul Robeson, which put him on the defensive. In 1942 the *Daily News*, the largest circulation daily in the country then, wrote that our petition campaign and our getting people like Dodger manager Leo Durocher on record was threatening to democratize baseball.

Even the wartime stuff by itself wouldn't have done it—you know, just saying that Negroes are dying so why shouldn't they be in the Big Leagues. We did a lot. Putting pressure on the owners, arranging tryouts for black players, and turning up the heat on Landis. And so did Wendell Smith and the *Pittsburgh Courier*. Getting white managers and players on the record in favor of ending the ban was a very big deal. But a lot of decent newspaper people and celebrities were increasingly on board. That made a big difference in the timetable. All that paved the way for Rickey to make his move. Yet you can't really say there was a swelling national tide to force integration.

Without that campaign, even if Rickey somehow out of the goodness of his heart decided he wanted to break the color line, he would have been slapped down by the other owners. And by Landis. As it was, the other owners did try to sabotage him.

One sign of the impact made by Jackie Robinson on society as a whole was his appearance in 1949 before the House Committee on Un-American Activities [HUAC]. The committee and the FBI both had been after Jackie to make an appearance for quite a while. The FBI had actually opened a file on Robinson in 1946, probably because of our role in the campaign. This was right at the beginning of the cold war, 1946, '47. They were concerned that the *Daily Worker* and the Communist Party were getting credit for the racial breakthrough. Not so much by whites, most of whom—except for baseball and newspaper people—had no idea of our campaign. But many blacks were aware of the role we played, and our standing was relatively good in the black community in those days, in part because of the campaign.

During the McCarthy years, when the Communist Party wanted to hold a public meeting in New York, the only place we could get a hall was in Harlem. And because of the standing of people like Ben Davis and Paul Robeson, we knew we weren't gonna be subject to the kind of harassment we'd have gotten in white areas or even if we could have found a place elsewhere that would rent to us.

There was a lot of pressure put on Jackie to testify. Even from Rachel. She wanted to keep Jackie clear of the radical movement. Someone from HUAC talked to Rickey about wanting to get Robinson to testify, and Rickey began urging Jackie to do it. He even offered to write Jackie's speech for him. Then, after Paul Robeson caught so much flack for saying it wasn't in the interest of American Negroes to fight in a war against the Soviet Union, the pressure on Robinson was stepped up, and he finally agreed. It was a big coup for the committee, although if you go back and see what Jackie actually said in Washington, it was more about racial discrimination in America than about Robeson and communism.

At a hearing before HUAC in Washington, D.C., on July 18, 1949, Robinson declared:

The fact that it is a Communist who denounces injustice in the courts, police brutality, and lynching when it happens doesn't change the truth of his charges. . . . Negroes were stirred up long before there was a Communist Party, and they'll stay stirred up long after the Party has disappeared—unless Jim Crow has disappeared by then as well. (Falkner 1995, 200)

After saying that if Robeson actually made the statement attributed to him, "it sounded pretty silly to me," Robinson closed saying the words the committee wanted to hear above all else: "We can win our fight without the Communists and we don't want their help" (Robinson 1972, 86).

Afterward, Robinson had some doubts about the wisdom of going before the committee—not because of what he said but because he knew that his testimony would be used to justify the harassment of Robeson, a man whose courage in fighting racism and whose accomplishments as athlete, actor, and musician he greatly admired. Two months later, after racist whites backed by local cops in Peekskill, New York, attacked a crowd leaving a Paul Robeson concert, Robinson gave a rare response to a political question put to him by *Daily Worker* sportswriter Bill Mardo.

LR: Bill was covering the Dodger game for us the day after Peekskill—the second Peekskill, the riot where they blocked people from getting back to their cars and buses and ran right up to the cars and buses and threw rocks while the police stood by and laughed.

Bill took a copy of the story—both from the *Daily Worker* and the *New York Times*—to show Jackie this isn't something we made up. Anyway, Jackie read the articles all the way through and then turned to Bill—this is in the dugout where other players and sportswriters could hear—and he said, "This is a damned shame and I don't care who knows it. That's not democracy. Paul Robeson is a great man and they should respect him." Stuff like that. Part of it was probably trying to counteract his uneasiness about having testified against Robeson before the committee.

Twenty years later, in his autobiography, *I Never Had It Made,* Robinson wrote:

I would reject such an invitation [to testify against Robeson] if offered now. . . . I have grown wiser and closer to painful truths about America's destructiveness. And I do have increased respect for Paul Robeson who, over a span of that twenty years, sacrificed himself, his career, and the wealth and comfort he once enjoyed because, I believe, he was sincerely trying to help his people. (Robinson 1972, 86)

In the climate of the times, however, it would have been hard to turn HUAC down. Even Wendell Smith, who had once "congratulated" Rodney and the *Daily Worker* for their "great efforts" in the campaign, would later say, as the post–World War II Red-hunting hysteria began to unfold, that "the Communists did more to delay the entrance of Negroes in big league baseball than any other single factor" (*Pittsburgh Courier,* August 23, 1947). The fact that Smith was working for Rickey by that time is hardly irrelevant.

It was only many years later that the actual role of Rodney and the *Daily Worker* began to be acknowledged. One of the first people to do so was Jules Tygiel, in his widely acclaimed book *Baseball's Great Experiment: Jackie Robinson and His Legacy:*

The American Communist Party played a major role in elevating the issue of baseball's racial policies to the level of public consciousness. . . . The *Daily Worker,* led by its sports editor, Lester Rodney, unrelentingly attacked the baseball establishment. Negro League games were headlined as "Chance to See Great Jim Crow Colored Stars." Editorials assaulted "Every rotten Jim Crow excuse and alibi offered by the magnates for this flagrant discrimination."

The Communists did not confine their campaign to newspaper rhetoric but challenged the baseball executives with political action and direct confrontations as well. Delegations to major league teams demanded tryouts for black players. Petition drives collected signatures to protest discrimination. (Tygiel 1993, 36–37)

And in 1997, on the fiftieth anniversary of Jackie Robinson's entry into the major leagues, the *New York Times* wrote:

> A reader seeking the best, liveliest coverage of Robinson's breaking the modern major league color barrier did not get it from the mainstream New York newspapers. Completeness, plus cheerleading, corniness and opinion, came in a torrent from black weeklies such as *The* (Pittsburgh) *Courier,* the (Baltimore) *Afro-American* and the *Amsterdam News,* as well as the *Daily Worker.* Both segments of the media had pushed hard for baseball's intransigent hierarchy to sign worthy Negro Leaguers since the 1930's.
>
> These newspapers were required reading if you wanted to read about efforts to find Robinson and his family a home in Brooklyn; about the type of fan mail he received; about how Robinson's teammates were expected to react to his joining them; speculation about the impact of Robinson's breakthrough, and the broadest use of Robinson's own words. (*New York Times,* April 13, 1997)

HOT CORNER

- *What We'll Talk About*
- *Rookie Pitchers Bother Us*
- *Where Yanks Get Players*

By RED ROLFE
(N. Y. Yankees 3rd Baseman)

FROM a seat in the grandstand, baseball is a spectacle which looks different to every fan. The game is like that accident which a hundred witnesses saw—and no two could agree on exactly what happened.

Out on the field, it's a different story. Sometimes I wish microphones could be hung over the diamond so that the crowd could hear exactly what Lefty Gomez is saying to himself when his curve fails to cut the corner of the plate or what George Selkirk sounds like when he chuckles over those home-run smacks of his.

And I'd like the fans to know more about the inside game, the "skull work" that makes baseball the pastime it is. I think a ball player has an unique opportunity to bring baseball closer to the public. I'm not hinting that the newspapermen up in the press box don't know their stuff when I say that it's a happy privilege for me to be able to write this column and to record in it what's going on behind the scenes in baseball.

You see, the players are not just names in a box score. And the games aren't just pitch, smack, catch or hit. Baseball is the great American national game because it reflects in its daily play both the individual effort to win and the teamwork, the unity which brings victory. I've heard and read that the Yankees are the greatest team in the history of baseball. Neither I nor anyone else know whether this is true or not but I do believe the Yankees of today are a great team because of the way they play together. There is a certain team spirit which makes the individual player shine all the more brilliantly.

It's something of this that I hope to write about in this column. And something else. For it isn't only the team on the field which counts; it's the team off the field, the way the boys think and act when they're not playing baseball.

With this introduction I'm setting down to my job of writing about the season of 1939 as I see it from the hot corner of the Yanks. I'm not going to compete with the press box boys. I'm planning to tell of the things that happen on field and off to a ball player—what he thinks, does and what the good old game means to him.

Chapter 7

The Ballplayers and the Communist

ALTHOUGH RODNEY'S FELLOW SPORTSWRITERS were quite aware of his political affiliations, few athletes knew that a Communist sportswriter was covering their exploits for a Communist newspaper. Most ballplayers had never heard of the *Daily Worker*, especially those who came right off the farm from places like North Carolina or Georgia. And even those who had heard of the *Daily Worker* didn't necessarily associate it with the Communist Party.

Lester Rodney: I never thought of myself as a "Communist sportswriter," no more than I thought of Jimmy Powers as a Republican sportswriter or Leonard Koppett as a Democratic sportswriter. I was a sportswriter. Sure, your political leanings will inform some of the things you write, even in sportswriting. And of course, a sportswriter who was a Communist and worked for a Communist newspaper was hardly an ordinary occurrence in the press box. Still, I was a sportswriter for a Communist newspaper. And that's not the same.

I was a sportswriter who happened to be writing for a Communist newspaper. By the time the *Daily Worker* was something the players might react to negatively, they knew me as a sportswriter and a person. And I think they respected me as both. If I had constantly ground an ideological ax (which isn't my style anyway), the first thing to cross a ballplayer's mind when he saw me would have been "Communist," and I never would have been able to establish the rapport I had with so many different athletes over time.

On the morning of October 7, 1937, a startling sight greeted readers of the *Daily Worker.* There, on the front page of the Communist newspaper that, just a few years earlier, had dismissed professional baseball as a capitalist device to undermine working-class consciousness, was an account of the first game of the World Series between the New York Yankees and their cross-town rivals, the New York Giants. Even more startling was the byline on the article: "Red" Rolfe. Readers who didn't follow sports may have been reassured by the "Red" sobriquet. But the *Daily Worker*'s growing legion of sports fans who knew that Red Rolfe was the Yankees star third baseman couldn't have been more amazed—and thrilled. Aside from the exclusive enjoyment of reading Rolfe's comments throughout the series (won by the Yankees, four games to one), the fact that a major-league ballplayer would be willing to write for the *Daily Worker* signified a degree of legitimacy for the Communist Party—or at least its newspaper—that could hardly have been imagined a few years earlier.

LR: It was unique, a real scoop. There was talk then about it being precedent-setting. There have been articles under a player's byline since then, but they were ghost-written. Rolfe's was the real thing. He wrote them himself. And we said this was because we give players credit for intelligence. It ran for the whole Series.

Readers loved it, of course, but the really fascinating thing was the next day after the story came out. I'd go into the dressing room before the game and—just picture this—there are the Yankees, *the New York Yankees*—sitting around the dressing room reading the *Daily Worker.* If Colonel Ruppert [the Yankees' owner] had walked in then, he would have had a heart attack. Of course, they were reading Red Rolfe. And someone would say, "Hey, Red. Did you really write all this highfalutin' language?" Not a word of Red-baiting.

Rolfe, being a Dartmouth grad, which was kind of unusual in baseball in those days, knew the *Daily Worker* was a Communist newspaper, but he wasn't thrown into hysterics by it. He knew me as a knowledgeable baseball writer from my being around the field and the dugouts before games at the stadium.

I proposed the idea to him at a good time. He had just gotten married —to a young woman who had graduated from Smith or Wellesley, one of those—and he wanted to impress her with the fact that he wasn't just a jock, which he wasn't. So the idea of a ballplayer presenting his own ideas in print, in a newspaper, intrigued him. His nickname had nothing to do with politics. He had red hair. He was just a tough New England democrat with a small "d," from a small town, Penacook, in New Hampshire. I think he may even have been titillated by having it appear in the *Daily Worker.*

He was an individual. And he was a Yankee, one of the pinstriped lords of the universe. He felt he could do what he wanted. No one would give Red Rolfe bullshit. Plus we had McCarthy's agreement. [Joe McCarthy was the Yankees manager from 1931 to 1946, during which time the team won seven American League championships and four consecutive World Series, 1936–39.]

The only problem for me was that Rolfe really wanted to dictate the piece each day, not have it ghost-written. Which was fine. That was the big idea after all, to actually give voice to the player, let him really write it. The problem was that we had a very early deadline. I'd rush down from the press box to the Yankee dressing room after the game and stand scribbling my notes as he talked so I could get the piece for the next day's paper. World Series games were all in the daytime then. Rolfe took it seriously. If I tried to rush him, it only made matters worse. In addition to getting his stuff down on paper, I also had to write my own story of the day's game when I got back downtown to the office on the good old Jerome–Woodlawn subway.

Of course, his whole column would be about the World Series game just played. Mostly he would focus on the key play in the game or explain the strategy behind a particular move. Naturally, he was respectful of the other team, but he also could be pretty blunt. After one game with the Giants in the '37 series, which the Yankees won 8–1, Rolfe wrote, "National League ball as played by the Giants had its test in today's game and from my position at third base, it looked pretty weak compared to the game we play in the American League." And when the Series was over and the Yanks had won in five games, he summed it up: "This series proved again that no defense can withstand power at the bat. That's what gave us the championship."

Irwin Silber: Did he catch any flack for doing it?

LR: Sure. Some people didn't like Rolfe writing for the *Daily Worker*. He told me he'd gotten a bunch of hostile letters and a few anonymous threatening phone calls in the middle of the night. That just got his New England back up. He said, "Can you imagine these people? I'll write whatever I want for whoever I want." Of course, he also got letters of praise.

IS: Did you pay him anything?

LR: Yeah. Not much. Some nominal amount. That actually protected him from any accusation that he was "supporting" a Communist newspaper. And it certainly was worth it to us. The first time we ran Rolfe's column, we sent a circulation truck up to Times Square that night with bundles of the next day's paper. There was a guy standing out in the back of the truck shouting, "Red Rolfe covers today's game!" By eleven o'clock that night we sold thousands of copies right off the back of the truck.

Rolfe wrote for us again in the '38 series with Chicago. But this time we also got a Cub player, Rip Collins, the Cub first baseman and a good hitter. Rip was a smart veteran who'd played on two of the Cards' pennant-winning teams before going to the Cubs. He was also one of the early switch-hitters. Collins was strictly a working-class stiff. He worked as a coal miner in Pennsylvania before making it as a ballplayer. And he was a card-carrying member of John L. Lewis's United Mine Workers.

IS: How did you get him?

LR: The Party was growing fast in the Midwest, especially in Detroit and Chicago. Mostly because of our work in helping build the CIO. So earlier that year, the Party started a daily paper in Chicago called the *Midwest Daily Record*. It was what we called a "progressive" paper. But it was run by Party people. And it had a sports page, sort of patterned after ours. So when the Cubs won the pennant—they overtook the Pirates in the last days of the season—we wired them asking if they could get one of the Cub players to cover the World Series for us the way Rolfe was doing. They'd established pretty good relations with a number of Cub players, and they came up with Collins. I'm sure it helped when they told him about Rolfe doing it too.

IS: Did he know he was writing for a Communist newspaper?

LR: I'm not sure. We never hid who we were, but we didn't go around shoving it in people's faces either. On the other hand, anyone reading even one issue of the *Daily Worker* would know what kind of paper we were. He obviously was familiar with the *Record*, so he had to know he was writing for at least a left-wing newspaper.

His columns were fine and he didn't drive me nuts like Rolfe by insisting that everything had to be exactly his words, but he didn't do too much at bat. None of the Cubs did. The Yankees won the Series in four straight. They were riding high. They did the same thing to Cincinnati the next year, their fourth straight championship.

Rolfe wrote a few more columns for us early in the 1939 season. But then McCarthy told him to stop, that the writing was diverting too much of his time and concentration from the game, and he was probably right.

IS: Did you ever ask Rolfe about the color line and the campaign?

LR: No. I was working with him on articles, so I could have. I had his confidence. But the way I thought about it at the time was that the main value of getting Red Rolfe in the first place was to show that we were a real sports section on a real newspaper. It was also a prestige thing.

If I had immediately said to Rolfe, "What do you think about Negro players? Shouldn't the Yankees have a Negro player?" somebody probably would have said, "See. They only wanted you to get the nigger question in." And McCarthy might well have said, "That's it! As long as it's baseball, okay. But don't put us on the spot." He knew the Yankee ownership almost certainly would have called him in about it. Remember, this is back in the thirties, before the campaign had picked up steam, before the breakthrough of '39 when managers and players spoke up for publication. No player had yet been quoted against the ban.

Some people may fault me for this retroactively, but I didn't want to prematurely push mixing the campaign with our basic coverage, which we were establishing. We wanted Red Rolfe just for baseball. Not for anything else. That was the point of it. To make the point about who we were. You want an American sports section? You got one. The *Journal-American* doesn't have Red Rolfe. Getting Red Rolfe was a big feather in our cap, and I guess the bottom line is, I didn't want to jeopardize that.

IS: How about other Yankees? Joe DiMaggio, to begin with.

LR: Usually you think about Joe in two ways: Joe the man and Joe the ballplayer. In his last years, he was Joe the icon—admired, dignified, largely inaccessible. Self-cultivation of his mythology. But even during his ballplaying days, the writers weren't fond of Joe. They mostly found him aloof, almost monosyllabic, and sometimes curt.

But I also remember Joe for two moments early in his career which contrast sharply with that later image. The first, in 1936, came about when the IWO [International Workers Order, closely associated with the Communist Party] was starting a kids' softball league and someone from the organization asked me if there was any chance I could get Joe DiMaggio to come to their grand opening. Joe was still a rookie, but he was already something of a sensation. So I asked him and he said okay. The event was taking place on a Sunday morning in Brooklyn, just a few hours before a doubleheader, and the two of us went racing down there. Joe said a few words, threw out the first ball, and went racing back to Yankee Stadium. And of course, everyone was thrilled.

IS: Why did he do it?

LR: Well, for one thing, ball clubs always encouraged players to make those kinds of community gestures—especially with kids. Certainly there were no evident social or philosophical views to suggest that Joe had a particular sympathy for the Left. But looking back on it today, I think it's a fair supposition that in his first couple of years in the Big Leagues, while he was very young and before the aura of celebrity superstar had fully socked in, Joe felt closer to his roots as the son of a hard-working immigrant fisherman, and an invitation to do something nice for working-class kids just struck a responsive chord with him.

The other moment was in 1937 when Joe said visually for the record that Satchel Paige was the best pitcher he ever faced. That was an honest and decent thing.

So there's more than one truth about Joe DiMaggio. One is that he was a simple kind of guy. Too simple, it turned out, for Marilyn Monroe, who worked in a high-powered atmosphere of creative ideas and had upward cultural aspirations. After some years in New York, Joe found his social niche at Toots Shor's nightclub, actually a kind of secluded corner of it. This had something to do with Toots himself, who was a genial and reasonably perceptive guy. Naturally, Toots didn't scorn Joe as a simpleton jock. But he also didn't fawn over him. Of course, Joe was something of an ornament for the place, but Toots didn't exploit that. Joe was comfortable there and even expanded in little social ways—though always carefully, with just a few people of his choosing.

Not that he ever evolved into any kind of bon vivant or self-assured conversationalist. Nor was there ever the slightest hint of the playful rowdiness of guys like Mickey Mantle or Whitey Ford. None of that was in him. He wasn't even a happy user of the big money he began making. Joe was a tightwad. Certainly he wasn't much of a father. Yet another plus in my book: He risked booing from fans around the league by holding out stubbornly for what he was worth before the 1938 season. Nor did that hurt him with the other Yankee players. It always helps the rest of them when the top guy holds out for more.

So you can say Joe was a simple person, with simple tastes and no sophistication, who devoted his postbaseball years to making more dough and embellishing and protecting his image. Yet you also have to say that Joe DiMaggio was the possessor of an extraordinary baseball intelligence, which was very much part of his greatness in the field, at bat, and on the base paths.

As a ballplayer, Joe was also an artist. If Joe DiMaggio wasn't ballet, what the hell is ballet? Floating all that distance—you'd look at where he started when a ball was hit and then where he caught it taking it gracefully in full stride. It's not just physical. It's not just balletic grace and speed of foot. There was a mental side. He had to be a center fielder for this. He couldn't be a left fielder or a right fielder. The center fielder—even if he's shaded to the left or right a little—has the clear view of the pitcher throwing to the batter, and where the catcher is set up to receive it. On every pitch in every ball game.

I talked to Joe about this once. His baseball mind was like a computer. He could never have been a manager because of his personality and communication shortcomings, nor did he have anything like the breadth as a person that managing others needs. But he sure was a baseball student. When a batter stepped into the box, Joe would automatically and instantaneously weigh different factors. I suppose he might not even be fully conscious of his thought process. This is what he told me. Depending on who was pitching, and what velocity he had, who was batting and what were his tendencies, and the location the catcher set up at the last instant before the pitch, Joe would be leaning in the direction he calculated the ball would go. He sometimes gave the appearance of taking off in the right direction before the crack of the bat. For example, this batter has such bat speed that even a pitch slightly outside by a pitcher without terrific velocity or who threw a lot of breaking stuff would be pulled rather than hit to the opposite field. And many variations depending on the hitter and the pitcher.

That's the "secret" he described to me, and I suppose he talked about to other sportswriters, though I don't remember seeing it really developed in print. "Do all center fielders do that?" I asked. Joe shook his head no. "It needs a lot of patience."

Mickey Mantle, on the other hand, was just sheer blazing speed. That's why he wasn't a truly great defensive outfielder. That's one of the reasons I put DiMaggio on my all-time, all-star outfield. Ruth, Cobb, and then DiMaggio by a slight margin over Willie Mays. That outrages the generation right after me. Mays, of course, leads my second outfield, with Hank Aaron and Ted Williams. But Joe DiMaggio—he was a beautiful ballplayer. And not only that; he hit .381, .357, .352, .346, for Christ sakes, and with power. If he had been just a super defensive player—as he was—and a .285 leadoff man, he would still have been a great all-time star. I loved his stance, spread, poised, none of all the fidgeting and stepping out and back in. Now combine his nonpareil fielding with his batting, his smart base-running—nobody could remember him being thrown out stretching a hit or going from first to third—his arm. Everything.

But the guys I knew the best were the Dodgers, because I spent more time with them. This wasn't just because I grew up in Brooklyn and was a diehard Dodger fan. Once the Dodgers broke the color line, they became the most newsworthy team in baseball. I got along well with them even after they became aware of the fact that I was a Communist.

For instance, Gil Hodges was a big, funny guy. He liked to chat baseball with me and kid around. There was one time when Erv Palica—he was a pretty good relief pitcher for the Dodgers—had pitched in five consecutive games. Some of the players thought that Burt Shotton, who was the manager that year, was overusing him. You know, players knew better about "rubber arms." They know the arm is bone, flesh, and tissue. But no one's likely to question the manager openly on that. Anyway, I happened to be in the Dodger dugout before the game the day after Palica's fifth straight stint on the mound, and Hodges comes over to me and calls Palica over. Gil picks up my right hand and Palica's right hand, tells us to shake, and booms out with an eye on Shotton, "Daily worker, meet *Daily Worker*."

Another little Hodges story. We moved out to southern California from New York in '58, the same year the Dodgers moved. The first time I get to a Los Angeles Dodger game I'm sitting in the press box at the Coliseum, because I'm still an active member of the Baseball Writers' Association. Anyway, Hodges glances up at the press box and spots me. A big grin busts out on his face and he bellows out so everyone in shouting distance can hear, "Hey! The Commies are following us!"

Another time, I was chatting with Leo Durocher when he was managing the Dodgers. This was just after a pretty important game. Leo was some kind of tough guy. He got into a few fights both off and on the field and was once suspended for a whole year for provoking a brawl in a restaurant. We were talking about game strategy. Suddenly Leo leans over to me, grabs my arm, and says, "You know, Rodney, for a fucking Communist, you sure know your baseball!" So, as I told my children, now if anybody asks me what kind of Communist I was, I can tell them.

Most ballplayers, of course, were vaguely anti-Communist, like the general population. But only a handful would make anything of it. Like Dixie Walker. He was a racist, and explicitly anti-Communist too. Actually, he merged the two in '47, saying the move to integration was a Communist plot, not an unknown view for ignorant southern racists. Whitlow Wyatt, who pitched for the Dodgers for a few years, was somewhat hostile because of who I was. Not because of anything I wrote or because of the race question. I could easily imagine him going to another guy I had chatted with, out of my earshot, saying, "Why do you talk to that goddamn Commie?" It was written all over him. Kirby Higbe, another pitcher. He was from South Carolina, which maybe excuses him. So there were some. But most were nonpolitical and took people as they came.

There were other guys I could talk to on a serious level—not just about baseball. Roy Campanella, of course. Then there was Clyde King—also on the Dodgers. A bespectacled relief pitcher from North Carolina who was kind of an intellectual. He'd come to me with questions about literature and all. We talked up a storm about Thomas Wolfe, also from North Carolina. I guess he sensed I was somebody he could talk to about some of that stuff and not just baseball.

Dodger pitcher Carl Erskine was a highly intelligent, thoughtful, sensitive, and sometimes philosophical guy, also a practicing Christian in the best sense of that word. Meaning not a "God Squad" nuisance but quietly decent on things that matter, including Jackie and race. He's a church elder in Anderson, Indiana, and a leading figure in educating about retarded kids.

Another guy like that was Joe Gordon, who played for the Yankees and Cleveland. A guy who read a lot and played a Reeselike role with Larry Doby. He was the only one to stick his hand right out when Lou Boudreau introduced Larry to the players in '48. Larry told me about a "gentleman's agreement" scene in a Washington hotel when the Indians were checking in and he wondered about registering in a traditionally white hotel. (I think it was the Shoreham.) Doby seemed a little uncertain, so Joe told him, "You're a member of the Cleveland Indians and this is where we all stay in Washington." So the two of them—Larry and Joe—walk up to the desk together, and after a moment's confusion and hesitation by the clerk, Doby was registered. It seems like a small thing now. It wasn't then.

Then there was a Jewish guy who pitched briefly for the Dodgers, Saul Rogovin. His parents were probably Lefties. Once Durocher got on his case on the train going to one of the out-of-town cities, and at one point, Leo says something nasty like "Boy you made a couple of stupid pitches." And

Rogovin snaps back, "Stupid? You can bet your ass I'm the only guy on this team that reads the *New Masses*." And he pulls a copy of the magazine out of his back pocket. He wanted to needle Durocher. That's gotta be one of the great pieces of dialogue in Big League history. "You can bet your ass I'm the only guy on this team that reads the *New Masses*."

IS: How did you get on with the black players?

LR: Very well in most cases, but it varied from one individual to another. Roy Campanella was my buddy. I must have interviewed him more than fifty times. He was a mild-mannered kind of guy, unlike Jackie Robinson, who was intense. This led people to think that Roy was not much of a thinker and not interested in racial and political issues. No way. Roy may have been soft-spoken, but he was fearless and he had a strong social conscience. He was a member of the executive board of the New York NAACP [National Association for the Advancement of Colored People].

This will tell you something about Roy. During the McCarthy period in the early fifties, there was a publication called *Counterattack* that undertook to "expose" not just Communists but anyone they deemed Communist-leaning.

Naturally, they monitored the *Daily Worker*, and they picked up one of my many interviews with Campanella. This was in 1955 before the season began. McCarthyism was still pretty strong then. Anyway, they wrote what was, in effect, an open letter to Roy, saying something like "We're not blaming you. You probably don't realize you're doing a wrong thing for your race by talking to a hardcore Communist." Implicit, though, was a warning: "We'll let you off this time, but if you keep it up we'll get you banned from baseball. You'll be seen as a Commie. We're not calling you a Commie but . . ."

It was just about that crude. I didn't keep a copy of it, but that's close. So I wrote a column saying the *Daily Worker* was the first daily newspaper in the country ever to mention Roy Campanella as someone who should be in the Big Leagues, and where were these fascist-minded *Counterattack* crumbs then? And who were they anyway—a couple of punk dicks with a typewriter who have terrorized Hollywood and made abject cowards of college presidents, and so on. But, I said, they're not going to intimidate me, nor are they gonna intimidate Campanella. And let them continue to check the *Daily Worker* and they'll see by the breadth of the athletes, managers, and owners I interview that they're not gonna make any headway.

Roy simply ignored it and kept right on in our normal professional relationship. It had no effect at all.

Another incident involved Dick Young of the *Daily News*, who wrote a book in an annual series called *The Most Valuable Player*. This was after Roy won the award in '51. So, he's working with Roy on the book and, naturally, asks him at some point how he got to play in the Big Leagues. And Roy says to him, "Well, the *Daily Worker* was—"

"Oh, no!" says Dick. "We can't put that in the book!"

"What do you mean?" says Roy. "You asked me the question and I'm telling how it happened. You've got to put that in."

And in it went. As Casey Stengel would say, you could look it up. This is what Young wrote: "As the [1939] season got underway, agitation for the admission of colored players to organized ball was resumed. Roy found himself accosted by a man who introduced himself as a reporter from the *Daily Worker*, a communistic organ which pounded hard and unceasingly against the color line in organized ball." Of course, I wasn't "accosting" him. Roy knew me well, I knew him from the Negro Leagues, and all the black players knew of the campaign by '39.

IS: You don't often think of Roy Campanella being especially race-conscious.

LR: A lot of people don't realize that Roy was mixed. His father was an Italian grocer in Philadelphia. His mother was black, which is the opposite of Franco Harris—the Pittsburgh Steelers running back, whose father was black and his mother Italian. I asked Roy once when we were chatting, "What threw you in as a kid on the black side? Why weren't you an Italian?" "I didn't get to make that choice," he said. "It was made for me."

There's another side to Roy and Jackie that I've never read about. One day I get a call from one of our readers who worked in Harlem, saying, "Do you know that Campanella and Robinson come up once a week to the Harlem Y and work with kids there?" I asked Ben Davis if he knew anything about that, but it was news to him too. So I decided to check it out for myself. I didn't even tell Robinson or Campanella or the Harlem Y that I was coming.

When I get there, sure enough, Jackie and Roy are shooting pool while a few kids are standing around jockeying for "next" and making typical kid remarks. One kid, he couldn't have been more than eleven, pipes up, "Beat him again, Campy, so's I can get even with you!" Roy runs out a string of five to clean up the table and then they come over to me and say hello, Campanella more cordially than Robinson for reasons I've explained. "Do you mind if I just hang out and watch?" I ask, and of course they say okay.

I was especially interested in the way the kids related to these guys who had to be superheroes to them. They didn't have the kind of stultifying awe you see today with Michael Jordan. They'd kid around with them. These kids knew them close up. It wasn't a one-shot magic appearance. They might have been more starstruck the first time. But now it was more natural. They all wanted to know about baseball strategy. "I'm a catcher, too," says one youngster to Campanella. "Tell us about picking a guy off base. Like, when do you throw to first base?" And everyone asks Jackie about stealing home. The exciting things. And Jackie slyly shakes them up. "You know," he says, "I have a teammate, Pete Reiser, who stole home seven times one year. More than I did."

I also remember them giving the kids little fitness exercises to write down and take home with them. Stretching before you play. "What do you mean, stretching?" the kids would say. And they'd show them, things like bringing your leg up to your chest before you play ball and how to cool down after you run a lot. Slow up. Things like that. Like big brothers. They were teachers.

You could see it was a great thing for the kids. And for Roy and Jackie too. There was another interesting thing about this. You know, there used to be some talk of tension between Roy and Jackie. Some sportswriters like to play up sexy angles. What's sexy? Jackie Robinson is outspoken and very militant. Roy Campanella is passive and so on. So there must be tension between them. This is sheer bullshit. They're different personalities. So what's the tension? They're both black men who know what black people go through. Campanella knew exactly what Robinson did. He just wouldn't be caught dead saying some of the things that Robinson said. He wouldn't even accuse the umpire of a double standard. Robinson would. Roy would just turn to the umpire and say, "But I had the plate blocked." That was Campanella. Robinson might say, "You wouldn't do that with so-and-so." And that's why Robinson was disliked. That's why Robinson, after leaving the Dodgers, was never considered as a manager or [for] the front office.

First the Dodgers tried to trade him to the Giants after 1956, which fell through when Jackie refused and retired. They were embarrassed. So he never had a shot at being a manager. He was a fiercely intelligent guy. He knew baseball from A to Z. He'd probably have been a wonderful manager. Or at least an adjunct to the manager, teaching base-stealing, batting, base-running, fielding. Work with the infielders. But they never dreamed of taking him on. Had Campanella not been crippled in an accident, they might have taken him on when he retired, as their catcher-coach, their bullpen coach, and so on. Because he wasn't as "threatening" as Robinson. So that's one of the things I felt was a good reason for going up there and doing that column. There were Jackie and Roy, working together with black kids. End of silly myth.

Even at the LIU [Long Island University] conference on the fiftieth anniversary of Jackie ending baseball discrimination, there were people who had read that stuff and were curious and asked us, "How about the rift between Robinson and Campanella?" That's what some sloppy sportswriting can do. There was never any rift.

And then there was a poignant little thing. Somebody said to me, "Campanella's granddaughter is here." I went over to her between sessions. She was a young woman of about eighteen, nineteen. And I said, "You're Campanella's granddaughter." She said, "Yes." And I said, "I thought you might like to know I was a sportswriter and I knew your grandfather very well." (Roy had died by then.) "I wrote about him and Jackie Robinson a lot. I know you may have heard that your grandfather was just a ballplayer, as opposed to Jackie Robinson. That he wasn't a strong advocate of correcting injustices. Well, let me tell you, in his own quiet way, he knew exactly as much as Robinson. He just projected himself in a different way. I thought you might like to know that."

You could tell, she was glad to hear that. And she cried a little.

IS: Did you run into any other ballplayers you might call socially conscious?

LR: Well, there was Dizzy Dean, who was an underrated guy in many ways. He was a great pitcher, a thirty-game winner in 1934, led the Cardinals to two World Series championships and was elected to the Baseball Hall of Fame. He was also a sharp and focused guy and very class-conscious. He was constantly battling the magnates for better pay and usually was able to get more than they offered. He knew his own worth as a pitcher—but also as a draw. And he spoke his mind.

Dizzy wasn't the dumb Okie he was often made out to be, butchering the language and so on. When he became a sports announcer broadcasting St. Louis Cardinal games on radio after he retired, his language was certainly colorful and often original. Like he would say that a player had "slud" into third on a close play, or the base runners had returned to their "respectable" bases after a fly ball.

Grammar wasn't Dizzy Dean's strong point, although after a while you could tell he was going out of his way to avoid "correct" English. The fans loved it. At one point, the St. Louis Board of Education demanded that he be taken off the air because he always used the word "ain't." Unfazed, Dean said, "Let the teachers teach English and I'll teach baseball."

One time Dizzy was guest speaker at a banquet sponsored by the local chamber of commerce honoring the Indianapolis Indians of the American Association—the top Triple A League at that time—after they won the pennant. An array of speakers coughed pompously and uttered the usual platitudes about the glory of bringing the pennant to "our fair city" and so forth. Then came Dizzy:

Now you guys on the team a-settin' here have heard a lot of stuff and had a lot of bouquets throwed at you but, brother, you can't eat bouquets. Remember this, you won a pennant. You guys here in Indianapolis drew almost twice as many paid admissions as the St. Louis Browns have so far this season. But when you're filling the park like that, don't forget the boss is settin' back there computin' the dough as it rolls in. He's makin' money and plenty of it. That's about all he thinks about. Why, in St. Louis, I seen the time when we played in a downpour of rain just to get in five innings so the boss wouldn't have to issue rain checks.

Next spring is another story. Another season will be startin' and you guys will have contracts to sign again. You guys have established yourselves. You don't have to play for peanuts any more. When you start talkin' contract, remember that attendance record you set this year. Don't sign for peanuts. Make him kick in some of that dough he made off you this year. You guys won't always be playin'. The time will come when you can't throw and run and hit like you do now. But the owners will still be makin' dough. There ain't no age limit on that. Take a tip from ol' Diz. They can afford it and don't let them kid you. (*Daily Worker,* September 24, 1948. From notes taken by a *Daily Worker* reader in Indianapolis and sent to Rodney)

LR: The very next day, Dizzy gets a telegram from the baseball commissioner himself, Happy Chandler, calling him in to explain himself. That was a mysterious interview. Why did Chandler summon Dizzy? What happened? Nothing was ever written about that. I look at this now and I kick myself for just writing a column. It should have been a screaming headline: "Why Chandler Called Dean: Diz Rips Greedy Magnates." Wow!

And he wasn't the only one. Look at the baseball strike of a few years ago. The owners obviously felt that they could crack the ballplayers' unanimity. But a week before the season opened, not a single player had defected. What is that? Maybe not class-consciousness as we know it. But the solidarity of guys who work for a living, no matter how much money they make. After all, Michael Jordan was for the basketball players union; and Patrick Ewing, he's not hurting for money, why was he heading up the basketball players' union? These guys believed that the big-shot owners shouldn't get away with it. It's obvious to me because I saw that in other ballplayers, like Dean, in my working years.

Babe Ruth was like that too. Coming out of a Baltimore orphanage, the Babe was always highly aware of the size of his paycheck. He was appreciated by the other Yankees for holding out for top dollar. At his peak in 1930, he got $80,000 a year—big money in those days. When someone noted that Ruth, a baseball player, was being paid more than President Hoover, Babe replied in that Depression year, "I had a better year than him."

Player resistance to the owners actually goes way back. It's not well known, except maybe for history buffs. In 1890, embittered players organized their own Brotherhood League and took 80 percent of the National League's players, including the entire New York, Chicago, and Philadelphia rosters. The immediate issue? First, the owners colluded to impose a $2,000 salary maximum. Next, they said no player could get an advance on his salary. Remember, these were guys who had no other livelihood. Some of them had pregnant wives and were in desperate financial straits. No matter. Finally, the owners said that henceforth "habits and earnestness" would be a factor in determining pay. That blew the lid off.

But the Brotherhood League players also had a larger perspective. In an eloquent appeal to the general public explaining their action, the players said, "Reservation—that's what they called the Reserve Clause—became for them [the owners] another name for property right in the player. By a combination among themselves stronger than the strongest trust, they were able to enforce the most arbitrary measure, and the player had either to submit or get out of the profession in which he had spent years attaining a proficiency." I'd call that class-conscious.

IS: What happened to the Brotherhood League?

LR: Pretty much what you'd expect. The press called them bums and unpatriotic. The *Sporting Times*, the National League newspaper, labeled them "ingrates, men without principle, drunken knaves, men who would be idling on street corners but for the opportunity the National League had opened for them." One newspaper claimed that members of the Washington team smoked opium. The owners, of course, set out to sabotage them. They made it very tough for the Brotherhood to rent suitable playing fields, deliberately scheduled their games to conflict with every Brotherhood game, and got the newspapers to refuse to carry the Brotherhood schedules. Even then, the Brotherhood League actually outdrew the National League in attendance.

But the owners held the economic cards. They were able to block several of the franchises from getting suitable facilities. As a result, the new league was backed to the financial wall despite relative success in other cities. They were finally forced into a merger with the National League—which was really a surrender—but they did win a guarantee of no reprisals.

The owners' chief stooge was Cap Anson—today often called the "father" of Big League baseball. He's the same guy who, more than anyone else, fought for and won the imposition of Jim Crow on organized baseball. It figures. The game's number-one fink and number-one racist were one and the same.

There were sporadic outbursts of militancy in the years that followed, but mostly "resistance" to the owners took the form of quiet grumbling or individual holdouts.

IS: What about Casey Stengel?

LR: A wonderful character and a shrewd baseball intelligence. The stuff of legends. Sportswriters loved him, he was a real performer. Always came up with something tart and funny that the writers could use.

Baseball was his life, yet in a strange way he didn't take it too seriously. You know he had a terrible record of managing for the mediocre Dodgers and Braves before moving to the Yankees, where he became an instant genius. He even would kid about that. He knew that no matter how smart you were, you had to have the horses. But Casey showed he knew how to handle them when he got them. He left other managers behind in World Series tactics. Stengel would yank his ace in the fourth inning if he didn't like what he was seeing in a World Series game. He'd say, "It's the World Series! We'll talk about tomorrow tomorrow." He and Durocher were the two innovative Series managers who grasped the need to play the Series differently from regular season games. So there *are* differences in managers.

Unlike most managers, Stengel cultivated a colorful self-image that sometimes obscured his baseball intelligence. His creative usage of language was laced with an irony remarkable for its sophistication. He mastered the art of using self-deprecation and image. But the one thing he apparently never talked about publicly was baseball's color line.

Casey's silence was especially glaring during his first years as the Yankees' manager, from 1949 to 1954. It was during those years that baseball was gradually being integrated. By 1954, twelve of the sixteen major-league teams had at least one African American player. Prominent among the holdouts were the Yankees. "The truth is," general manager George Weiss said to sportswriter Roger Kahn in response to a question about Yankee policy, "our box-seat customers from Westchester County don't want to sit with a lot of colored people from Harlem" (Kahn 1993, 45). Ever garrulous, Stengel remained mute on the subject. He knew who he was working for.

But when, in 1955, the Yankees finally signed their first black player, Elston Howard, Casey came up with a typically ironic Stengelism for the sportswriters: "Well, they finally got me a nigger and he can't run."

LR: I don't think he meant it in a racist way. He wanted Howard and treated him right. It sounds to me like Stengel was subtly knocking the Yankee management and puncturing a stereotype at the same time.

IS: Speaking of managers, what about Connie Mack? Did you have any encounters with him?

LR: Routine stuff when the As came to Yankee Stadium, but no real "encounters." Some writers still call Mack the "Grand Old Man of baseball." What a crock! The real Connie Mack screwed everybody. The players, the fans, the city of Philadelphia.

His Philadelphia Athletics were a great championship team way back before World War I. They won pennants in 1910, 1911, 1913 and '14, and the World Series in three of those years. The team included all-time greats like Eddie Collins, Chief Bender, Jack Coombs, "Home Run" Baker, and Eddie Plank—all at the peak of their careers. After the 1914 season, Mack put all his star players on the auction block and pocketed the cash. As a result, the A's finished dead last for the next seven years.

Was he worried about losing fan support? "They'll come back," he said. And they did. Not too many people were about to take a train to New York or Washington to see a ball game. Mack's ability to find and develop talent was never in question, and by 1929 he had built up another winner. The A's won three straight flags from 1929 to 1931, and two World Series [1929 and 1930] with a lineup featuring Jimmy Foxx, Al Simmons, Lefty Grove, Rube Walberg, George Earnshaw, Jimmy Dykes, and Max Bishop. In '32 they finished second, and then Mack repeated the fire sale. He sold Simmons and Dykes in '33, then Grove, Walberg, Earnshaw, and Bishop in '34. Foxx was the only one left, and Mack cashed him in in '36. [Foxx had seven more good years with the Boston Red Sox.] From '35 on, the Athletics were a pitiful last nine times, seventh [next to last] twice, and sixth once. The old buzzard made out like a bandit, but the royal screwing twice was too much. The A's never regained the fan following they had enjoyed in Philly and eventually were moved to Kansas City.

Did this bother Mack? Hardly. As a result of these monumental rake-ins, Mack was able to entrench himself and his family in the organization until he owned the whole shooting match. He was manager and magnate. What did he think of his ballplayers? Here's what he told a reporter in the spring of 1948: "If there are any holdouts on the A's you can say for me they can hold out forever. I will rewrite none of the contracts I sent out. If any players don't like it, they can stay home." Those were the days of the reserve clause, of course, when a player either signed on management's terms or couldn't play.

Granted, Mack was an unusually crass example of an owner milking the game for all he could while not caring one hoot about the city, the fans, tradition, community. But what an example of utter contempt for the people in what was officially supposed to be a game, not a business! To me, he was the embodiment of hypocritical, voracious capitalism. Mack even looked the part, a taller Henry Ford. He never put on a baseball uniform in the dugout. He used to wear a stiff-winged collar, like Herbert Hoover.

The guys who worked in the *Daily Worker* print room were part of the Big Six, the printing trades union. We could appoint a foreman who was friendly to the paper—that was our prerogative—but the jobs had to be held by whoever the union sent. So we had all kinds of people, including, of course, anti-Communists. I used to chat with them down in the composing room when I made up the sports pages. There was one very skilled worker, a big old Irishman name of Jack Foley, who was an ardent baseball fan, and we'd get into baseball arguments every once in a while. He'd say, "You communists exaggerate everything," a comment sometimes not without reason, I have to admit.

Anyway, one day after I wrote a blistering column about Mack and his treatment of a particular ballplayer, a wounded war vet, Jack came up to me in the composing room and said, "You know that column you wrote about Connie Mack," and I figured he was gonna say something like "Oh, you're too hard on the guy. After all, he's an old man. And that's the way owners are." But what he did say was "That was a great column. I'm so glad you stuck it to that sunnavabitch. I'm ashamed he's Irish."

And wouldn't you know it, Mack was one of the fiercest defenders of maintaining the color line in baseball. In 1946, when the Dodgers were scheduled to play the Athletics an exhibition game during spring training, a sportswriter asked Mack, "Suppose they bring Jackie Robinson along?" Mack snorted, "I wouldn't play him. I used to have respect for Rickey. I don't any more."

Grand Old Man?

As the *Daily Worker* gained a growing but begrudging legitimacy in the sports world, it was able, from time to time, to convince athletes to support causes backed by the Communist Party.

LR: One time we got a group of outstanding college basketball players and a team of trade unionists to play each other in a benefit for the Spanish Loyalists—the ones who were fighting Franco. This was sometime in the winter of 1937. It was held at the old Hippodrome on Sixth Avenue. It's not there any more. I organized it, so everyone knew it was a *Daily Worker* thing. But Spain was something that went well beyond Communist politics, plus we were starting to get kind of mainstream in those years. So it wasn't "The *Daily Worker* Presents . . ." It was called "Games for Spain: Athletes Make Their Feelings Known."

The event was a tripleheader. The Hippodrome was sold out and we raised something like $7,000 for Spanish War Relief—a big sum in those days.

One game was between two women's teams from different locals of the International Ladies' Garment Workers' Union [ILGWU], perhaps the largest union in New York City in those days. Another between an IWO team and a team from the Furriers Union.

(The IWO was brought into being by Communists. As with many other immigrant-based groups, its main function was to provide low-cost insurance and burial benefits for workers. It also developed a wide variety of cultural and sports programs and was one of the most important Left institutions of the period. At its peak, it numbered several hundred thousand members.)

The "feature" attraction was the college players (present and ex-) and the trade unionists. The names probably wouldn't mean much to anyone today. But some of them were really well-known marquee players in the college game. The coach at Brooklyn College, Art Musicant, was a big supporter, so we didn't have any problem getting a couple of players from there. We got Max Kinsbrunner, who was a famous basketball player from New Utrecht High School and St. John's University; all-city. I had gone to summer camp with him. The trade union team included three staff members from the *Daily Worker*. We qualified because we were all members of the Newspaper Guild.

They were Mike Singer, who had been the eighth man on the St. John's "Wonder Team," and Mac Gordon, who fancied himself a basketball player—and myself. Then there was Wee Willie Marron. He had been a substitute on the fabled Original Celtics. Later on he became a Communist Party organizer in New Jersey, using the name Bill Norman. I once told Nat Holman, "Regards from Wee Willie," and Holman said, "Oh, Wee Willie. How is he? He was a good little player. I heard he was a Communist." Willie actually sunk a couple of pregame practice shots from mid-court that night, though he had gray hairs by then. And then he made a courtesy appearance in the game—he was already out of shape playing with the trade union guys against the college guys. He played about ten minutes and scored four points, if I remember right.

It may be hard to imagine now, but Communists had a lot of respect in those days. Our support or even sponsorship of some big event gave it credibility. It was usually for a cause with broad popular support, and everybody knew all the money would really go to help that cause. After the success of Games for Spain the Scottsboro Defense Committee asked if we could do one for them. And we did later that year.

The "Scottsboro Boys" were nine black teenagers who, in 1931, were arrested in Alabama on charges of raping two white women. Even before the hastily invoked trial began, Alabama newspapers proclaimed the young men's guilt in screaming headlines. Typical was one declaring, "All Negroes Positively Identified by Girls and One White Boy Who Was Held Prisoner with Pistol and Knives while Nine Black Fiends Committed Revolting Crime!" (Linder). Two white attorneys were appointed to defend the youths: one was a real estate attorney who came into the courtroom drunk; the other was a seventy-seven-year-old lawyer who hadn't tried a case in decades.

The charge was totally spurious. Although the evidence was shaky and the witnesses unsavory, the nine young men were quickly convicted by an all-white jury and sentenced to death. The NAACP at first shied clear of the case, concerned that some of the boys might turn out to be guilty. But the Communist Party jumped right in. The Party-organized International Labor Defense (ILD) called the case a "murderous frame-up" (Linder). Eventually, the ILD succeeded in becoming the attorneys for the defendants.

The Communist Party was able to make the case a national and then an international cause célèbre. The ILD convinced the famous non-Communist defense attorney Samuel Liebowitz to take on the case. Liebowitz forced a retrial, but another all-white jury still voted to convict, even though it had become overwhelmingly clear that the defendants were being railroaded. In 1935 the U.S. Supreme Court threw out the convictions. A third trial in the summer of 1937 resulted in charges being dropped against four defendants, but the other five were still found guilty and sentenced to long prison terms. The protests continued until the last of the Scottsboro Boys, Andy Wright, was paroled in 1950.

The Scottsboro Defense Committee sports event was a boxing exhibition put on at the Rockland Palace, a popular boxing venue in Harlem.

LR: Al Douglas, the owner, let us have it rent-free because the money was going for the Scottsboro defense. It created a big stir in Harlem. A crowd of thirty-five hundred jammed the place. We had a card, I think, of six bouts, the main eight-rounder featuring heavyweight contender Jersey Joe Walcott.

As a result of its role in the Scottsboro case, the Communist Party gained a significant political foothold among African Americans. Years later, during the McCarthy years, when almost all public auditoriums were denied them, the Communists were still able to hold public rallies at Rockland Palace.

The *Daily Worker* also gave active support—not just with coverage but through actual participation—in trade union struggles. One such was a 1937 strike by the Newspaper Guild at the *Brooklyn Eagle.*

LR: I remember one day when several of us from the *Daily Worker* joined the picket line in front of the *Eagle*'s building in downtown Brooklyn, and I found myself right behind Heywood Broun, who was founder and president of the Newspaper Guild. Broun was best known, of course, as a prominent nationally syndicated columnist. Hard to imagine someone like that today being a union president on the side.

It was a bitter strike. Newhouse [the chief strikebreaker] was a miserable bastard. The *Eagle* sports columnist, Ed Hughes, who I knew pretty well, was beaten up by anti-union thugs after he came out of a church mass.

We helped organize a Citizens Committee in Support of the Brooklyn Eagle Strike and—in part because of what happened to Hughes but also because of their general sympathies with working stiffs—some of the biggest names in baseball and boxing joined it. The ones I remember offhand were Joe DiMaggio, Lou Gehrig, Lefty Gomez, Bill Dickey, Red Ruffing, Red Rolfe; also Burleigh Grimes, who was the manager of the Dodgers. Plus Joe Louis, Jack Dempsey, Jim Braddock, Mickey Walker, and Tommy Farr of the boxers. Harold Parrott, the only *Brooklyn Eagle* sportswriter to scab during the strike, later became director of publicity for the Brooklyn Dodgers. At least one ballplayer spit on Parrot's hand when offered a handshake when the strike ended.

In the end, management agreed to a contract with the Newspaper Guild, but there were no pay raises and some of the scabs were kept on.

Perhaps the most significant labor action by ballplayers before the 1970s was in 1941, when seventeen members of the Chicago Cubs received contracts from Jim Gallagher, the new general manager, calling for wage cuts. Gallagher was a one-time sportswriter for the *Chicago American* who had scabbed during a long newspaper strike. I guess that made him an ideal choice for Cubs owner Phil Wrigley. But much to Gallagher's surprise, seventeen players banded together and refused to sign the new contracts. The mass holdout included star regulars Billy Herman, Stan Hack, Phil Cavaretta, and Augie Galan. It lasted several months and won the players some raises. The *Chicago Sun-Times* called it "baseball's first general salary strike."

The first major attempt to form a players union was in 1946, when a Boston lawyer, Robert Murphy, who had no baseball background, simply started walking into hotel lobbies where ballplayers were staying and began talking union to them. He focused on a decent minimum wage and the right of a player to get part of the purchase price when sold. In just a few weeks he'd won a majority on at least five teams. One guy.

Murphy decided to concentrate on the Pittsburgh Pirates. When Pirate owner Benswanger refused to consider collective bargaining, Murphy passed that news on to the players just before a game with the Dodgers. When the players discussed how to respond to Benswanger, Frankie Frisch, their manager, warned them, "You guys will be out of baseball. We'll get you out of baseball. And you know, if we fire you, you won't be able to play on any other team." Under the old Reserve Clause system, they were indentured for life to that team. It didn't matter if they quit for five years and wanted to come back, they'd have to come back to that team. Nevertheless, the players voted in favor of sending Benswanger an ultimatum:

bargain or we won't play the game with the Giants two nights later. This is amazing stuff that never got the publicity it deserved in the big newspapers at the time.

Just before that Giant game at Forbes Field was about to begin, with a pretty good Friday-night crowd, Benswanger went into the Pirate dressing room to talk with the players. This time he was all soft words and vague promises. Benswanger told them he had no idea there were grievances and that a strike was not only very serious but unnecessary. Then the players locked the door and talked it over. Think about it. Here were ballplayers organized by one man who had no standing in the trade union movement. The unions, in fact, had studiously avoided getting involved with athletes, probably figuring that was too trivial when compared to steelworkers or auto workers or what have you. They had no evidence of support from the players on the other fifteen teams, no evidence of fan support, a virulently hostile manager, a hostile press, paying customers already in the stands—and all this in the face of an entrenched monopoly holding a blacklist over them.

Yet the Pirate players voted twenty to sixteen to drop their gloves and bats and strike. But it wasn't the two-thirds vote they had agreed to earlier, so, tight-lipped, they came out onto the field, brushed past the reporters, and went on to wallop the Giants 10–5. So the strike never materialized, but the alarmed magnates quickly made some concessions, announcing a $5,000 minimum salary—the first minimum in baseball history—and some other minor reforms.

That was the end of Murphy's attempt to form a union. It would be another twenty-five years before the next serious attempt, which ultimately succeeded.

Terry May Return to 1st for Stretch

| Champion Joe Louis | | Challenger Tommy Farr |

Fascist Story A Phony, Says Farr in Answer To Open Letter

Was Misquoted, Threatens to Sock Press Agent

By LESTER RODNEY

Tommy Farr is NOT for fascism. And the English heavyweight who fights Joe Louis for the world's heavyweight championship tomorrow night denies emphatically having made the statements attributed to him in the Toronto "Star Weekly."

He's so mad over these and other misquotations in the press about him that he wanted to take a healthy sock at Jersey Jones, his hired press agent yesterday.

Farr's heated denial of having predicted fascism for England and calling Hitler, Mussolini and Mosley "great men" came in response to open letters to him in the Daily Worker and the Toronto Clarion.

In confirmation of Farr's denial, we learn from England that he has always had a record of standing four square with the working class and trade unionism. Tommy was a Welsh miner in Tonypandy, and as he says, "felt the lash of hard grueling work in the pits at long hours and little pay."

After becoming a boxer he sponsored and helped into realization the National Union of Boxers in England, an organization that won decent wages for preliminary fighters.

As far as his fistic qualifications go, Tommy seems to have little

Championship History from John L. Sullivan to Joe Louis

'Dempsey Never Punched Like Louis,' Braddock Warns Farr

Chapter 8

Boxing: The Brutal "Sport" and the Class Angle

U NLIKE ORGANIZED BASEBALL, which began systematically excluding black ballplayers in 1889 and became all-white ten years
later, boxing never banned African American fighters completely.
But their careers were severely restricted by a pernicious racism that, while
unofficial, was ubiquitous. Especially guarded as a white preserve was the
heavyweight crown—a prize that almost automatically designated its
holder "the greatest fighter in the world." When, in 1903, a powerful young
black heavyweight named Jack Johnson publicly challenged Jim Jeffries,
the world heavyweight champion, Jeffries's unabashed response was
"When there are no white men left to fight, I will quit the business. . . . I
am determined not to take a chance of losing the championship to a
Negro" (Jakoubek 1990, 43).

Five years later, however, Johnson got his chance. The title holder then
was Tommy Burns, a colorless Canadian who got small purses and little
press. Meanwhile, Johnson had acquired a top-flight white manager, Sam
Fitzpatrick, and was terrorizing those fighters willing to take him on. Guar-
anteed a $30,000 purse by Fitzpatrick, Burns finally agreed to a match
with Johnson. The fight, held in Sydney, Australia, was easily won by Johnson, leading the novelist Jack London, who was covering it, to declare:

"There was no fight. No Armenian massacre could compare with the hopeless slaughter that took place in the Sydney stadium today" (Jakoubek 1990, 53).

While Johnson's win rankled the boxing establishment and much of white America, his almost seven-year reign as world heavyweight champion (1908–1915) was a white nightmare. Johnson was the quintessential "uppity nigger"—a term of abhorrence and fear to whites and, by the same token, a statement of approbation and pride to blacks. Johnson was smart, insolent to whites, and publicly defiant of the mores and racial restrictions that permeated early twentieth-century America. Especially galling was the fact that he openly consorted with white women, some of whom he even married. Promoters immediately began searching for a "white hope" to rescue the crown for the white race, but Johnson disposed of all the top white challengers as quickly as they appeared. Increasingly desperate, the boxing establishment convinced Jim Jeffries to come out of retirement in an effort to bring Johnson's reign to an end.

Two days before the Jeffries fight in 1910, the *New York Times* warned, "If the black man wins, thousands of his ignorant brothers will interpret his victory as justifying claims to much more than mere physical equality with their white neighbors" (Roberts 1983, 97). (The "much more" feared by the *Times* was *social* equality.) But Jeffries was no more successful than were the "white hopes" who had preceded him. Completely overwhelming the over-the-hill ex-champion, Johnson humiliated Jeffries by keeping the bout going for fourteen painful rounds before knocking him out in the fifteenth. Whites greeted Johnson's victory with attacks on celebrating blacks. At least eight blacks were killed and many more injured.

Black reaction was captured in a folk ditty:

Amazing grace, how sweet it sounds,
Jack Johnson knocked Jim Jeffries down.
Jim Jeffries jumped up and hit Jack on the chin
And then Jack knocked him down again.
The Yankees hold the play,
The white man pull the trigger;
But it makes no difference what the white man say;

The world champion's still a nigger.
(Lipsyte and Levine 1995, 50)

As the dream of a white hope to take the title back from the black "usurper" collapsed, boxing officials and the Justice Department colluded to strip Johnson of his title, bankrupt him financially, and throw him in jail. Ultimately, they succeeded in all three objectives. The heart of the campaign was an indictment charging Johnson with violating the recently passed Mann Act (referred to at the time as the White Slave Act), which made it a crime to transport women in interstate or foreign commerce "for the purpose of prostitution or debauchery, or for any other immoral purpose" (Roberts 1983, 144). Johnson's flaunting of his affairs with white women—the ultimate insult to white sensibilities—may well have triggered the legislation, which was enacted in 1910. Rarely enforced, the government found in the Mann Act the precise legal tool it needed to crush the black champion. After Johnson was found guilty and sentenced to a one-year jail term by an all-white jury, Assistant U.S. Attorney General Harry Parkin acknowledged the government's real motive for the prosecution: "This verdict . . . will go around the world. It is the forerunner of laws to be passed in these United States, which we may live to see—laws forbidding miscegenation. This Negro, in the eyes of many, has been persecuted. Perhaps as an individual he was. But it was his misfortune to be the foremost example of the evil in permitting the intermarriage of whites and blacks" (Roberts 1983, 178).

Johnson jumped bail and fled the country, but the white boxing establishment eventually maneuvered him out of the championship in 1915, and the heavyweight title was put out of bounds for blacks for the next twenty years.

When Jack Dempsey won the heavyweight crown in 1919, he made no secret of his intention not to permit a black fighter to contend for his crown. True to his word, Dempsey gave the runaround for the full seven years of his reign to Harry Wills, a superb African American heavyweight long ranked the principal contender for the title. Wills never got his chance. If he had, he might have been the one to beat Dempsey before Gene Tunney did in 1927.

It would be another ten years before a black heavyweight would come close to the title, a distinction that went to Joe Louis, who knocked out the reigning champ, James Braddock, on June 22, 1937.

Irwin Silber: Did you have any qualms about covering boxing as a sport?

Lester Rodney: I certainly had mixed feelings about it. The downside, of course, was the sheer brutality and the corruption surrounding it. At the same time, as the *Daily Worker*, we had to consider the very meaningful significance of Joe Louis and Henry Armstrong as champions when most whites considered blacks inferior and when the fear of another Jack Johnson was still very real.

Then there was the Louis–Schmeling fight in '38 with all its racist overtones, with Schmeling as the representative of Hitler against the *Untermensch* two years after the German had knocked out the young Louis. Probably the most dramatic single sports event ever. We had to cover all that, big time.

After all, what's at the heart of racism? We know that economics plays a big role. But to the individual, the deep-down thing is that the targets of racism are inferior people. That's the rationale that allowed men and women who considered themselves righteous and decent to look away, to accept the horror of seeing other human beings treated like animals. Now along comes Joe Louis. Rightly or wrongly, a black guy taking on all the strongest and best-trained white guys in a roped-off ring away from Jim Crow court rulings and intimidation became socially significant in America. I remember Armstrong's wonderful quote: "You can't discriminate against a left hook." You know Louis had to shake up many whites. And certainly for blacks, his accomplishments were a source of great pride.

Apart from race, there was also what you'd have to call the good old class angle. Is the *Daily Worker*, of all papers, going to call for the end of prizefighting and piously tell youngsters from poor families that they can no longer take their toughness, skills, and determination into the prize ring to make money?

You know, you didn't have to be a Marxist to see that the people at the bottom of the economic ladder at any particular time supplied double their quota of great fighters and champions. In the late nineteenth century, when it was normal for employers to say "No Irish need apply," you had John L. Sullivan and Jim Corbett and Bob Fitzsimmons. And then when the ghettos were teeming with Italians and Jews, you had Tony Canzoneri and Lou Ambers and Benny Leonard and Ruby Goldstein. Later the blacks came in—they would have been there earlier if it wasn't for Jim Crow—and then the Latinos, and today you can hardly find a white man in the ring. Boxing is one brutal sport. You have to be able to take hurt without panic and not care about minute hemorrhages in your brain. Maybe that's why I never found a boxer who was the least bit troubled by the *Daily Worker*. These were all guys who came from the working class. The Italians and the Jews who came mostly from the East Side, these guys talked to me like a *paisan*. And it wasn't a Jewish thing because the black fighters did too. Blacks generally didn't red-bait. And not just because they knew of our campaign to end discrimination.

Willie Pep; Lou Ambers; Rocky Graziano, whoever, they'd say, "Are you gonna have something in the *Daily Worker* about this?" They'd want copies of it.

Henry Armstrong was an amazing fighter and a special kind of guy. One of the most feared and respected fighters of all time. He was the only man to hold the world championship simultaneously in three different weight classes—featherweight, lightweight, and welterweight. This was back in the late thirties, 1937 or 1938—and I got to know him well.

I remember when Armstrong was getting ready to fight Barney Ross for the world welterweight title. He already held the featherweight crown, and now he was aiming for both the lightweight and welterweight championships. Logically, his next bout should have been with lightweight champ Lou Ambers. Lightweight was the next division up from featherweight. But Ross, apparently, also wanted a shot at Ambers's crown, so an arrangement was worked out whereby the winner of the Armstrong–Ross fight would meet Ambers roughly two months later. Barney was a tough fighter who came out of a rough-and-tumble Jewish neighborhood in Chicago. He had won seventy-two out of seventy-nine bouts, twenty-two by knockouts. He also had an eight-pound advantage over Armstrong, who was fighting above his class. But Henry was three years younger and had an even better record. Since early 1937 he had fought and won thirty-seven fights, thirty-five of them by knockouts. He won the featherweight title later that year, and even though that was the year Joe Louis knocked out Jim Braddock for the heavyweight title, Henry was voted the Merit Award for the year by *Ring* magazine, the bible of boxing.

The buildup for the fight was huge. I started covering it early and visited both training camps. When I went to Armstrong's camp in Pompton Lakes, New Jersey, something happened I'll never forget. The first thing he says to me is "I'd like to congratulate your paper on its fine fight for the freedom of the Scottsboro Boys." [For background on the Scottsboro case, see Chapter 7.]

After a few minutes of talking about the upcoming fight, he says, "Come on back, Les, I want to show you something." It turns out, he wanted to show me a poem he had written. I guess he picked me out because he knew me and he knew I would take it seriously. He might have been afraid that some of the other writers would make a joke out of a fighter writing a poem.

Well, I didn't know what to expect. It wasn't the clever, boastful doggerel Ali would write years later. It was serious.

A few days later, Lester ran the full text of Armstrong's poem on the *Daily Worker* sports page. He wrote:

> There's a poem by Henry Armstrong on this page that you want to read. Isn't Armstrong the fighter, the world champion who has knocked out 35 of his last 37 opponents and fights Barney Ross for a second crown tomorrow night?
>
> Yes, and he's the same Henry Armstrong who went hungry as a kid in St. Louis, the same Henry Armstrong who battled discrimination with flying fists and a will to win, who left his native St. Louis, shined shoes, set up pins in the bowling alleys of the Midwest and worked his way to California. . . . Somewhere along the way he stopped throwing the dynamic fists that brought him fame long enough to pour out an inkling of the latent talents choked up

within him and his persecuted race—to pour it out on the piano and in verse.

In Contemplation of May 26
By Henry Armstrong

Through Pompton's charm of placid lakes,
Baked by rolling hills and lush green maples,
We glide, forgetful of punching bags and title stakes;
And while the days bathe us in an aura of crystalline peace,
And Harry's oars dip rhythmically in the blue water,
I think of how wonderful it would be if fighting everywhere
    would cease.
But alas, man must fight to live it seems;
Fight and give violent expression to his boundless energy.
Accounts of man's eternal fighting have filled reams and reams.
Even now, the journalists are steaming up a bloody combat
Between one Barney Ross, a Jewish boy, and myself, a Negro—
Two fighters of oppressed races fighting each other, just like that.
It doesn't seem exactly sensible or right,
We're not mad at each other; we're just fighting for things we
    need.
It comes right back, the same old thing—to live, man must fight.
(*Daily Worker,* May 25, 1938)

(It turns out that Armstrong had also given a copy of the poem to the *New York Post,* then a liberal newspaper, which ran it in the original longhand around the same time.)

LR: The fight itself was almost anticlimatic. Armstrong took a fifteen-round decision, but it wasn't even close. It was Ross's last fight. Three and a half years later, in his thirties, Barney volunteered for World War II. Like so many other Jewish Americans who wanted to "fight Hitler," he wound up in the Pacific. No safe morale or sports-related service for this famous ex-champ. He was wounded at Guadalcanal while holding down his machine-gun post all night. He came home with a Silver Star for gallantry and the Distinguished Service Cross, plus a morphine habit not uncommon to those wounded and fighting a painful recovery in combat areas. Maybe you could say *that* was Barney Ross's last fight. He won it.

Two months later Armstrong beat Lou Ambers for the lightweight crown. So for a brief period, Armstrong held all three titles. By coincidence, I ran into Henry a week later at Pompton Lakes again, where Joe Louis was training for his rematch with Schmeling. Jim Braddock, who Louis had beaten for the championship a year earlier, was also there. He and Louis had become friends. Henry was watching Louis work out and I joined him to say hello. But Henry was a guy you never could just say hello to. Soon we were talking about music, peace and war, social trends, his early ambitions to be a surgeon, the ongoing fight against discrimination, and his three-year-old daughter. I remember he also wondered what Langston Hughes, who he had met earlier, thought about his poem that we published in the *Daily Worker*. Henry was one of the most thoughtful, worldly-wise guys I ever encountered in the whole world of sports. He also knew his craft and didn't hesitate when I asked him what he thought of Louis's chances against Schmeling this time around. He smiled and said, "Joe will do all right."

IS: What about Louis?

LR: Where to begin. He was certainly the greatest fighter I ever saw. Maybe the best there ever was.

To understand Joe, you've got to remember that when he began his career, it was next to impossible for a black fighter to get a shot at the heavyweight title. When he knocked out Primo Carnera, the *Readers' Digest* came out with an article titled "Why Joe Louis Must Never Be Champion!" You know, there'd be race riots and all that. Today, Joe Louis is honored as a dignified gentleman who is buried in Arlington Cemetery. Only people my age remember that in the thirties, most of the press portrayed him as a semi-moronic automaton.

Louis's road to the crown was not an easy one. Every black fighter in those days walked in the shadow of Jack Johnson. John Roxborough, Louis's first manager, knew that he would have to create an image for Louis that was as different from white perceptions of Johnson as possible. The first thing he did was to lay out a set of "commandments" for Louis to follow:

Never be photographed with a white woman
Never gloat over a fallen (meaning white) opponent
Never go into a night club alone
Live and fight clean
Keep a "dead pan"
(Lipsyte and Levine 1995, 146)

Another African American who played a crucial role in Louis's early career was Jack Blackburn, an astute trainer and ex-fighter who had once been a sparring partner for Jack Johnson. "It's mighty hard for a colored boy to win decisions," Blackburn told Louis. "You gotta knock 'em out and keep knocking 'em out to get anywheres. Let your right fist be the referee!" (Mead 1985, 6).

Heeding Blackburn's advice, Louis launched his professional career with a first-round knockout of Jack Kracken in Chicago on July 4, 1934. Less than a year later he had compiled a professional record of twenty-two wins—eighteen by knockouts—and no losses. The wheelers and dealers of the boxing establishment were sitting up and taking notice. But a black boxer, managed and trained by blacks, didn't stand much chance of getting the choice matches he would need in order to compete for the heavyweight title.

At this point enter Mike Jacobs, a flamboyant promoter with a great flair for publicity, who had three advantages: He knew everyone in the business end of the fight game, he was based in New York, and he was white. In coming to an arrangement with Louis and his triumvirate of manager-trainers, Jacobs endorsed Roxborough's "commandments," adding only that Louis "can win every fight he has, knock 'em out in the first round if possible. I promise if Joe ever gets to the top, he'll get the shot at the title" (Mead 1985, 43).

True to his word, Jacobs quickly got Louis a bout with former heavyweight champion Primo Carnera, who at 6'5" and 260 pounds was the largest heavyweight title holder ever. Louis knocked him out in six rounds.

Two months later, Louis took on Max Baer, another former heavyweight champion, who had won the crown from Carnera. Baer was disposed of in four rounds.

Describing the spontaneous celebration in Chicago's black communities after Louis's victory over Baer, black novelist Richard Wright wrote:

> Two hours after the fight the area between South Parkway and Prairie Avenue on 47th Street was jammed with no less than twenty-five thousand Negroes, joy-mad and moving to they didn't know where. . . . They seeped out of doorways, oozed from alleys, trickled out of tenements and flowed down the streets; a fluid mass of joy. . . . Something had happened, all right. . . . Something had popped loose all right. And it had come from deep down. . . . Four centuries of oppression, of frustrated hopes, of black bitterness, felt even in the bones of the bewildered young, were rising to the surface. . . . From the symbol of Joe's strength, they took strength, and in that moment all fear, all obstacles were wiped out, drowned. (Cited in Lipsyte and Levine 1995, 149)

The victories over Carnera and Baer immediately made Louis a top contender for the heavyweight crown. Now the challenge facing Jacobs was to burnish the image that Roxborough had earlier fashioned in order to neutralize the anticipated fear of whites at the prospect of a black world champion. The main thing was to make Louis nonthreatening to whites—even while he beat the brains out of white contenders in the ring. Louis would be the most modest and unassuming boxer in the history of fisticuffs. He didn't drink or smoke. Let the press think he was somewhat on the dim-witted side, as long as they added "but with a heart of gold." (Never mind that Louis, while relatively uneducated, was knowledgeable and alert to the world around him.)

One of Jacobs's press agents got Louis's mother to send him a Bible. Immediately, press releases and photos poured forth from Louis's camp. Louis, they said, read the Good Book every night before going to sleep.

Pictures of Louis holding the Bible appeared in newspapers throughout the country. And true to Roxborough's injunction, the only time Louis's numerous romantic attachments received public notice—he had "discreet" affairs with such white Hollywood stars as Sonya Henie and Lana Turner—was when, just before the Carnera fight, he got married. Jacobs, Roxborough, and company were ecstatic. From a public relations point of view, they couldn't have devised a better match if they tried. And perhaps they did. Certainly they encouraged Louis not only to get married but in his choice of bride, Marva Trotter, a secretary in the offices of a prominent black newspaper, the *Chicago Defender.* Not only was Marva smart, beautiful, well spoken, and from a middle-class family, but—most important to the Joe Louis managerial team—she was black.

The image making engineered by Louis's entourage didn't take long to bear fruit in the form of press comments highlighting the difference between Louis and Jack Johnson:

Joe Louis is as different a character from Jack Johnson as Lou Gehrig is from Al Capone. . . . The Brown Bomber is just what the doctor ordered to restore life in the business of boxing. He is a God-fearing, Bible-reading, clean-living young man to be admired, regardless of creed, race, or color. . . . Modest, quiet, unassuming in his manner, he goes about his business, doing the best job he can every time he climbs into the ring. (Richard Vidmers, *New York Herald-Tribune*)

A favorite phrase was to cite Louis as "a credit to his race," after describing him as "nonpretentious," "self-effacing," and other adjectives designed to reassure whites that, while he might be a champion, Louis "knew his place."

Still, Louis's dominance of the ring posed another challenge to the racist stereotypes that kept most of white America comfortable with the de facto second-class citizenship of African Americans. If blacks were—as popularly assumed—inherently inferior to whites, how to explain a black fighter able to defeat all his white opponents? "Something sly and sinister and perhaps not quite human came out of the African jungle last night," began Hearst's *International News Service* account of the Louis–Carnera fight (Mead 1985, 62). Many of the country's most distinguished sportswriters quickly echoed the "not-quite-human" theme.

Bill McCormick of the *Washington Post,* reporting on the Louis-Baer bout, had "the dusky detonator . . . stalking like a panther on the hunt" and then, after knocking Baer to the canvas, eyeing the fallen fighter "with an impassive face, eyes filled with blood lust" (Mead 1985, 72). (Sportswriters of the day outdid themselves in using suggestive alliteration for Louis, who was called at various times the Brown Bomber, the Dark Destroyer, the Tan Tiger, the Chocolate Chopper, the Shufflin' Shadow, the Saffron Sandman, and the Sepia Slugger, among others.)

Grantland Rice, the dean of American sportswriters, also loved the jungle imagery, calling Louis a "bushmaster" with "the speed of the jungle, the instinctive speed of the wild" (Mead 1985, 63).

Joe Williams of the *World Telegram,* in a column titled "Don't Feed the Animals," saw "a glint of animal savagery, a gleam of horrible meanness" in Louis's eyes and wrote, "There is no telling where an exploration of Louis' sprawling family tree would lead. But away back somewhere there must have been more than a touch of the predatory killer. . . . To look at Louis you will never associate barbaric cruelty with him, never suspect he took brutal delight in mangling human frames. . . . Go on over to the zoo and study the jungle acts. We think you'll find several characteristics in common" (*Daily Worker,* May 1, 1939).

Only one sportswriter took Williams to task for his unabashed racist blast—Lester Rodney.

But the ultimate surcease for an anxious and troubled white America was offered by Paul Gallico, sports editor of the *Daily News,* whose widely syndicated column reached far beyond his New York readers. For Gallico, Louis's triumphs in the ring merely reflected the superior physical prowess of the primitive over the civilized, the animal over the human. After watching Louis train, he wrote, "Here was a mean man, a truly savage person, a man on whom civilization rested no more securely than a shawl thrown over one's shoulders. . . . I had the feeling that I was in the room with a wild animal." A short time later, Gallico returned to the theme:

Louis the magnificent animal. He lives like an animal, untouched by externals. He eats. He sleeps. He fights. He is as tawny as an animal and he has an animal's concentration on his prey. . . . What else dwells within that marvelous, tawny, destructive body? The cowardice of an animal? I see in this colored man something so cold, so hard, so cruel that I wonder as to his bravery. Courage in the animal is desperation. Courage in the human is something incalculable and divine. (Mead 1985, 67–68)

But then Louis, well on his way to a title bout, uncharacteristically stumbled, losing to another former heavyweight champion, Max Schmeling, who won by a knockout in twelve rounds. The defeat was a body blow to the spirit of jubilation that had thrilled Wright. Adam Clayton Powell Jr., head of a powerful Harlem church (and later an important congressman), reflected the changed mood in the *Amsterdam News:* "Along came the Brown Bomber, Death in the Evening, and our racial morale took a sky-high leap. . . . Then the Yankee Stadium fiasco. . . . Gone today is the jauntiness, the careless abandon, the spring in our stride—we're just shufflin' along" (Mead 1985, 199).

Immediately after this devastating setback, Louis set out on the comeback trail. Over the next ten months he would defeat all eleven opponents he faced, ten by knockouts, finally getting his shot at James Braddock's title in June 1937.

But the loss to Schmeling encouraged many to revert to those classical stereotypes that were the mirror image of white jungle fever. Leading up to the championship fight with Braddock, some suddenly found that Louis was lazy, gorged himself on fried chicken, was prone to fall asleep as soon as his attention wavered, and—perhaps the most ludicrous of all—couldn't take a punch. The racist overtones to these commentaries were barely, if at all, disguised.

Typical was a piece by Jack Miley of the *New York Daily News,* who wrote:

Any young fellow accustomed to earning his bread by the sweat of his brow, who now sleeps ten or twelve hours a day and stuffs himself with food like a gourmand isn't the kind of guy I wish to bet my dough on. . . . Joe was a natural fighter. He will never be any better than he was the day he first pulled on a glove. He performs by instinct and nobody will ever be able to pound anything through his kinky skull. (Mead 1985, 120)

Jack Dempsey, who had labored to find a white hope who could block Louis's seemingly inevitable road to the title, was gleeful after the Schmeling fight. "Schmeling exposed the fact that Louis has a glass jaw and consequently cannot take a punch," declared the one-time heavyweight king, who had steadfastly refused to fight any of the black contenders of his era. "All you have to do to beat him is to walk into him and bang him with a solid punch. I don't think he'll ever whip another good fighter" (Mead 1985, 99).

Bill Corum of the *New York Journal* called Louis "a big, superbly built Negro youth who was born to listen to jazz music, eat a lot of fried chicken, play ball with the gang on the corner, and never do a lick of heavy work he could escape. The chances are he came by all those inclinations quite naturally" (Mead 1985, 120), while *Life* magazine had Louis hating workouts and getting out of bed.

John Kieran of the *New York Times,* the sportswriting fraternity's intellectual-in-residence, dubbed Louis "Shufflin' Joe" and wrote numerous columns on his presumed sleeping habits.

But Jim Braddock, who had to face Louis in the ring, knew better. Despite a game battle, Braddock succumbed to Louis's punches in eight rounds. The world and the country had a new and—for the first time in more than two decades—black heavyweight champion. Ten years before Jackie Robinson broke the color line in major-league baseball, a twenty-three-year-old black man born in a sharecropper's shack in Alabama, the seventh of eight children, had reached the pinnacle of his profession and changed its face forever.

LR: Joe Louis was nothing like that stereotyped cartoon image of a sleepy, animal-like man of subpar intelligence promoted by so many sportswriters. Sure, Joe was uneducated and his speech reflected that, though he steadily got more articulate. He certainly didn't feel at ease early on when he was thrown into the bedlam of shouting reporters, photographers, and microphones. He answered questions tersely and maintained a sort of passive exterior. But those of us who got to know him saw a different Joe Louis. At the training camps or in the boxing offices at Madison Square Garden, he would talk freely and easily with those he knew and trusted, about boxing techniques or the baseball races. He would talk about jazz, which he seemed to know a lot about.

Joe wasn't a "politico" as such, but he was quite race-conscious and pro-union. Someone at the Newspaper Guild once asked me if I could get Joe Louis down to one of our big affairs. The Guild had a pretty strong Left leadership in those days.

This was in the late thirties, maybe 1940. Anyway, I asked him and he wanted to know what the Newspaper Guild was, and I told him it's the national union of newspaper people and this was the New York chapter. That got him interested. You know, before he turned pro, Joe worked at the Briggs auto-body plant in Detroit. That was before the UAW [United Auto Workers] won recognition, but he knew what the union meant for workers in the auto industry. So he says, "What will I have to do? Make a speech?" "No," I said, "just say hello and how glad you are to see them—whatever you want to say. Nothing fancy." And he says, "Okay, I'll come." I met him at his hotel and we took a cab to the Guild hall. They had a good turnout. He was great.

He said something like "I'm a fighter, and we don't have a trade union for fighters"—I remember him saying that—"but I'm a union man at heart." I was a hero in the Guild that night.

Joe hung around for a bit afterwards and chatted informally with the Guild members. Who else was there? A famous actress. She had one name, like Margo. Somebody else had gotten her to come. She was very interested in Joe. She was buzzing up a conversation with him. And he knew her name. She had on a low-cut gown. The edge of the nipple was . . .

IS: I see you paid attention to the details.

LR: But not her name. Another time—this was in 1948—one of our reporters was covering a Henry Wallace campaign meeting at the Golden Gate arena in Harlem when he spotted Joe standing in the back of the hall. Some other reporters did too, and naturally, they went over to him. "What are you doing here, Joe?" one of them asked. And Joe says, "I'm listening. And I like what these people are saying." When the usual collection pitch was made, Joe quietly kicked in a hundred.

One of my best memories is not about Joe but about his mother. I was in Detroit to cover Louis's second fight with Bob Pastor. This was September 1939. Joe had beaten Pastor two years earlier before winning the title, but it was one of the few by a decision rather than a knockout. Pastor had gone the distance mostly because, as the writers said at the time, he had gotten on his bicycle and managed to keep out of the range of Joe's heaviest punches. I should say Bob wasn't a bad fighter and could take a punch. Not one of the "Bum of the Month" types. So he got a rematch, this time for the title. Joe knocked him out in the eleventh, at Briggs Field, the Tigers' ballpark. There were lots of auto workers in the stands.

The day before the fight, Joe gave me his mother's address and I went out to get an interview. Her name was Lily Brooks Barrow. Mrs. Barrow was usually portrayed as a kindly, loving mother whose main goal in life was to cook up platters of fried chicken and pork chops for her famous son. But she was a lot more than that. She was a community leader who could often be found on picket lines and was active in fighting for better housing for blacks in Detroit. A lot more "political" than her fighting son!

I brought along a cartoon that had appeared that very morning in one of the Detroit papers. It showed Joe reclining under a tree, dozing, with a chicken in one hand, "training" for the fight. I showed it to Mrs. Barrow and asked her what she thought about it. She looked at it, smiled gently, and said, "Now how could anybody be lazy and get to be the best in the world at what he sets out to do?"

Then she told me how the young Joe would go straight from a long day on the assembly line to a smoky little gym where he was learning to be a fighter. He'd come home, bone-weary, bruised, often discouraged. "But he stuck with it," she said. "Then he began to bring home watches, which was the prize for amateurs. We pawned them. We needed the money. . . . All that foolishness about being a natural and born fighter.

Nothing comes natural without hard work. I saw Joe work hard. I could tell there were times he didn't want to go on. But he did." It was a page-one feature story for us.

IS: What was his greatest fight?

LR: There were so many. But the one that will be most remembered, for sure, was the second Schmeling fight. There was so much riding on that fight. This was June 1938. The world was beginning to wake up to the true nature of the Nazi regime. Schmeling had been proclaimed a national hero in Germany after knocking Louis out two years earlier. German newspapers called it "a victory for Hitlerism." And for Joe, it was the first defeat in his professional career. Meanwhile, Schmeling was playing psychological games, claiming that he had figured out Joe's secret weakness. Joe was a 2–1 favorite but even his staunchest fans had to be more than a little uneasy. And to top it all off, this time it was a fight for the heavyweight championship of the world. Talk about high drama.

The beyond-the-ring significance of the second Louis-Schmeling fight (the night of June 22, 1938, at Yankee Stadium in New York) is hard to overstate. Hitler, still smarting from the gold medals won by African American athletes at the 1936 Olympics in Berlin, looked to Schmeling not only to win a championship but to reassert the "proof" of Aryan supremacy, which had been embarrassingly damaged by the exploits of Jesse Owens, Ralph Metcalfe, Mack Robinson (Jackie Robinson's older brother), and other black athletes from the United States. Just before the fight, Hitler personally sent a telegram to Schmeling expressing confidence that he would defeat the *Untermensch* again.

LR: In the months leading up to the fight it became clear that this would be no ordinary ring battle, not even an ordinary heavyweight championship contest. Schmeling saw himself as the Great White Hope who would end the black dynasty in boxing. The newspapers were filled with news, speculation, and trivia about the two boxers and their entourages. Sportswriters swarmed to both training camps. To give you an idea of the intensity of feeling, Jewish organizations originally proposed a boycott of the fight, saying why buy tickets for an event in which a German would wind up taking money to Hitler Germany. As the fight neared, with the Nazis practically hanging their swastika on Schmeling's chin, the overwhelming desire to see Louis blast the German (no TV then, remember) took over and the boycott happily collapsed in a mad rush for tickets.

IS: Did you go to Louis's training camp before the fight?

LR: Before a big fight I'd usually visit the training camp. Only this time I went with Richard Wright, the famous black novelist, who was a member of the Party at that time. Somebody high up in the Party—it might have been Ben Davis—told me that Wright was interested in meeting Joe and asked me if I could arrange it. I was already booked to go up to the training camp at Pompton Lakes, so I called Harry Markson, who was head of publicity for Madison Square Garden—they ran all the big New York fights in those days—and I asked him if I could bring along a well-known Negro writer (as we said in those days) and Markson said it was fine. So Wright rode along in the limo that Markson provided and I introduced him to Joe.

I'll never forget that fight. Me and eighty-five thousand other people, except I was in the second press row, about six feet from the ring. I've been told that I'm the only sportswriter still perpendicular who was at that fight.

Given all the prefight hype, the thing that impressed me most was Joe's absolute confidence. He came out so purposefully with the opening gong, there never seemed to be the slightest doubt about what was going to happen. He waded right into Schmeling and he never let up. He had the fighting skills to back up the confidence. He wasn't just defeating another boxer. You could tell Louis was making a statement to the world. Then there was the fan reaction. When Schmeling went down for the last time, there was a moment of stunned silence. Everyone had waited for this fight for so long and suddenly it was over. I guess it took a moment for the full impact of it all to register. But then the most remarkable thing happened. It started with a few shouts that were quickly picked up by thousands of others: "Back to Hitler, bum!" A classic New York send-off.

In the dressing room afterwards, Louis lay back on the fighter's table smiling slightly, and he said to the reporters, "I feel like a real champ now."

When one of the writers asked him whether he had gone into the fight with any personal feeling against Schmeling, Joe said, low-key, "I was sore at some of the things Schmeling said." It was probably the understatement of the year. Someone else suggested that maybe Schmeling hadn't said those things, that perhaps they had been "planted" in his mouth. "Well," said Joe, "he didn't deny them, and that's just as bad to me." Frank Murphy, the governor of Michigan, came in to congratulate Joe. And then the mayor of New York, Fiorello LaGuardia, his trademark huge hat in his hand, grinning ecstatically from ear to ear as he walked across the dressing room, finger wagging to hug the still sweaty fighter.

Richard Wright wrote a great piece on the fight for us. He called it "And Oh—Where Were Hitler's Pagan Gods?"

Time: When fascist Hitler and his world allies of repression are trying to conquer all mankind by force of arms and intimidation.

Scene: An oval sea of faces of all races, criss-crossed by powerful floodlights and centered about a snow-white squared circle.

Place: New York City, where a foul nest of Nazi spies has just been routed.

Characters: Joe Louis, Negro Boxing Champion, once defeated by Schmeling, and who is circumscribed because of his color as to where he must eat and live despite his success in the ring; and Max Schmeling, friend of Hitler, who believes that his mere "white" presence is enough to throw fear into the heart of a Negro.

Quick as a panther, Joe was out from his corner with the sound of the bell. There was a brief lull during which each fighter looked the other over; it was here that it seemed the entire fight hung in the balance. But if there was any doubt which way the battle was going, it was dispelled when Joe shot two straight left jabs to Schmeling's chin and followed them with a blunt, vicious left hook that must have jarred Hitler's Charlie Chaplin moustache, if only slightly, in faraway Fascist Germany.

Schmeling . . . backed away with amazement showing all over his face. But Joe was razor-edged and mad; he followed his challenger. Maybe he was thinking of those countless jibes and taunts let loose upon him for having let a man like this beat him. He let fly a shower of fistic destruction, included in which was a nerve-shattering right to Schmeling's chin. . . . [A]ll the pagan Gods of Dr. Goebbels could not have saved him from the next left hook, which staggered Schmeling and rocked his very senses.

Hitler's wilted pet looked like a soft piece of molasses candy left out in the sun; he drooped over the ropes, his eyes glassy, his chin nestling in a strand of rope, his face blank and senseless and his widely heralded powerful arm hanging ironically useless.

The fight really ended right there. It was the shortest and most lop-sided heavyweight bout on record, two minutes and four seconds of the first round, and it left no doubt in anybody's mind as to the caliber of the fighter who won. There was a lot of cheering when Joe's hand was hoisted in victory, but there was a lot of stunned silence too; silence stemming not from a lack of respect for Joe, but from inability to grasp the fistic and political significance of what had happened so quickly.

But if the spectators did not respond quickly, Harlem did. The quarter of a million Negroes who live within these narrow confines knew what this fight meant and they gave vent to it in a demonstration wholly political in character such as Harlem had never seen. (*Daily Worker*, June 24, 1938)

LR: There was joy about it everywhere in the country, not only in Harlem, where after eerie silence as everyone in town was glued to the radio, the streets instantaneously swarmed with jubilant crowds. Spontaneous parades formed down the center of the avenues with arms raised in a mocking Nazi salute. There were street demonstrations in every large city. You could feel it on the subway and in the streets the next day as strangers stopped to talk to each other about the fight, what they were doing at the moment of the knockout. That was the fight that was much more than a fight.

IS: In Louis's heyday, the sportswriters loved to debate who was better— Louis or Dempsey. Who would you pick?

LR: Louis would have killed Dempsey.

First of all, if you look at his career, after Dempsey won the title he defended it against carefully selected opponents a total of six times in the next seven years, losing finally to Gene Tunney. He beat [Georges] Carpentier, a glamour-created middleweight who didn't belong in a heavyweight ring. Then there was [Luis] Firpo, a huge, wide-open mauler, perhaps about as dangerous as Buddy Baer, who Louis knocked out twice. Dempsey was a very good fighter, but there was a lot of phoniness to his record.

While Dempsey and his manager, Jack Kearns, blatantly ducked Harry Wills, the black contender who would have given him his toughest fight, one of Louis's first acts as champ was to reschedule Max Schmeling, the only fighter to beat him. I don't think Dempsey ever fought as tough and well-rounded a heavyweight as the Max Schmeling Louis destroyed in a little over two minutes. Louis fought everybody who wanted to fight him, and he fought them a second time around if they wanted. He fought a guy like Bob Pastor, who went the distance because he ran away, and then he fought him again and knocked him out. He fought Max Baer—and then he fought his kid brother, Buddy. Dempsey never fought a guy who could hit like Louis. Nobody, not even Muhammad Ali, hit with such blinding speed and power with two hands. He must have hit Schmeling twelve times just while he was on the way down in that first round. And not just jabs. Fastest hands by far that I ever saw.

I never heard a boxing writer in my time who had seen both who didn't feel that Louis would have decimated Dempsey. They'd visualize the fight and write a column about an imaginary fight, and Louis would always knock out Dempsey. Now, Muhammad Ali might have been a different story. I never covered Ali. He was after my time. I saw him a few times on television. If you asked me who would win, I'd say Louis. Ali was a marvelous fighter, and he'd cut you up and wear you out, but Louis could kill you with one punch. Billy Conn, a masterful boxer, was ahead on points late in his fight with Louis 'til Joe connected and it was over. He had a fight with Arturo Godoy, who was a shell-like fighter. Louis was looking for an opening for three rounds, and Godoy would occasionally get in a punch. Everybody came to life in the Garden: "Hey, this Godoy is giving him a fight." Then Joe saw one opening. Godoy moved his left hand and Joe's right shot in and Godoy went down, bloody and out. It took them two minutes to revive him. One punch.

When Louis was the champ he fought so many fights they used to have what they called the "Bum of the Month" club.

Louis over Dempsey, without question. And for my money, over Ali, although that would have been an interesting fight, 'cause Ali was so quick on his feet. He'd have stung Louis and moved around. But Louis would have nailed him.

Later, in the sixties, some African Americans thought of Louis as an Uncle Tom, and some cruel things were said. Even Muhammad Ali, although afterwards he took it back, saying, "That's demeaning."

IS: Considering the kind of icon Ali has become, it's ironic that when he came along as Cassius Clay and changed his name to Muhammad Ali and joined the Black Muslims and then refused to be drafted to fight in Vietnam, he was criticized by many white sportswriters for not being more like Joe Louis, who was "a credit to his race."

LR: Louis was a man of the thirties in a new era when blacks were beginning to emphasize race pride and independent political action. But he himself, while not articulating it, was a major catalyst in the emergence of militant black pride. Like it or not, you can't take a man like Louis out of historical context when what he was doing as a fighter represented a formidable challenge not only to the racist stereotypes but to the racialized segregation of his time.

Sure, Joe was not a racial militant. Partly that was a conscious strategy asked of him, designed to portray him as nonthreatening to whites. But partly it was also Joe's personality. Joe had grown up at a time when young black boys, especially in the South where Joe was raised, were taught by their parents to be obsequious to whites simply to survive. He outgrew that, of course, but he was still formally uneducated and taciturn by nature.

Joe had a world impact, especially in what was then the colonial world. During the war, I was stationed for a while on the island of Tonga, where we set up a field hospital. I got pretty good at the language, and a

Tongan who was being trained by us as a medic startled me by asking if it was true that Louis knocked out the best white fighters. When I assured him it was, he gave me a smile a yard wide. This was an isolated little Polynesian island.

But maybe Joe's most important contribution was in his impact on blacks themselves. In his time, Louis was the quintessential symbol of black aspirations in America, a larger-than-life champion whose success stirred racial pride and whose breaching of racial barriers seemed certain to open doors for African Americans. Considering it was a decade earlier than Jackie Robinson's debut, I guess you could make the argument that Louis was even more important to African Americans than Robinson.

IS: I've seen columns of yours that were highly critical of boxing. Not just of those exploiting the fighters but of the basic concept of the sport, men punching each other to inflict as much physical damage as possible. There were columns about deaths in the ring and the cynicism of almost everyone involved in the fight game—promoters, managers, ringside doctors. To say nothing of the corruption and the encouragement of brutality. But I never saw anything you wrote calling for the abolition of boxing. How come?

LR: Well, when I first came on the scene Joe Louis was just starting out, and it was obvious that the desegregation of boxing was completely bound up with Joe's career in the ring. That's not something I concocted. Joe's feats in the ring were destroying the myths that justified Jim Crow—not just in boxing but in all sports. On top of which, he had generated a whole new level of excitement for African Americans and no small amount of anxiety for the racist boxing establishment—including much of the press. As a sportswriter—especially one who was a Communist—you'd have to be a weird, out-of-it aesthete to even think about calling for the abolition of boxing then.

But after the war [World War II], there was a big upsurge in ring deaths. I remember writing a piece called "Indict the Boxing Commission." Did you know there were eighteen known boxing deaths in the country in 1949? And many more near deaths. I raised some hell about a kid named Carmine Vingo, a young Bronx heavyweight. Vingo was fighting the awesome Rocky Marciano and had little to defend himself with but raw courage. Marciano was pounding him with powerful shots to the head at will, and Vingo was reeling, staggering, swallowing blood. People at ringside, usually a hard-hearted lot, were yelling, "Stop it!" Dr. Vincent Nardiello, the official physician at every fight in Madison Square Garden and St. Nicholas Arena, was sitting in the second row but did nothing to stop the mayhem. So Vingo was allowed to come out for the third round and was finally knocked out so cold, they had to rush him straight from the ring to nearby St. Clare's Hospital.

Carmine lived, but came out partially paralyzed. I wrote a blistering piece about the incident that provoked an editorial in one upstate New York paper. attacking the *Daily Worker* "party line" on boxing and saying that the fans, the workers, liked boxing or they wouldn't keep paying to see it. As if the fans approved of a defenseless guy being nearly killed because of callous indifference.

In 1950, I watched a raw youngster named Laverne Roach thrown in against the hard-hitting topnotcher Marcel Cerdan at the Garden, an obvious mismatch. Roach was knocked down seven times, four times in one round, and the good old commission doctor let it continue. Shortly afterward, the obviously befuddled Roach was cleared for a couple more fights, which he lost badly, and he retired. Then, surprise, one year later the International Boxing Club gave a big buildup to a "successful comeback" by Roach, leading to a fight at the old St. Nicholas Arena with a hard hitter named Georgie Small. In the ninth round Roach was reeling around, arms down, blood pouring from his mouth, people were screaming, "Stop it!" But the fight went on. He was knocked cold in the tenth and died a few days later. Obviously he never should have been cleared for a "comeback." That's what prizefighting had degenerated to.

IS: Yet you wrote about boxing often as a fan.

LR: Sure. It's basically a terrible "sport," yet there it was, with interesting men developing the art of fighting, with courage, setbacks, man-versus-man drama. I look back and if I want to be honest, I have to confess that I often got caught up in and enjoyed some of the fights . . . completely apart from social and racial angles. Like those wild Tony Zale–Rocky

Graziano fights. Yet I have to hope that the way we dealt with the worst abuses may have helped a little.

Maybe someday when the almighty buck isn't corrupting and degrading things, where there is real supervision of youngsters who enjoy sparring and boxing for the sport of it, it might be better. I don't know.

Garden Row Stirs Coaches

Holman, Lapchick to Act Against Anti-Semitic Wyoming U. Coach

By Lester Rodney

New York City's basketball coaches reacted swiftly yesterday to the disgraceful anti-Semitic, anti-Negro exhibition put on in the Garden by the Wyoming University coach Saturday night, and a boycott of the foul-mouthed Everett Shelton began to take shape.

Nat Holman, whose unbeaten CCNY team whipped Wyoming 57-48 in a near riotous game, said flatly that City would never play against a Shelton coached team again.

Joe Lapchick, coach of St. John's of Brooklyn, added that he would move for action against Shelton by the National Coaches Association.

The big blowoff came near the end of the CCNY-Wyoming game, which was the first of a doubleheader before a capacity Garden crowd. It had been a close, furiously played game, with City ahead at the half 32-30 and the score tied 43-43 with seven minutes to go. At this point the City players, who had maintained a relentless, sizzling pace throughout, began to break away from the tiring Westerners for the winning points.

Holman suddenly got up from his seat on the City bench, walked quickly over to the Wyoming bench and shook his folded program vigorously under Shelton's nose. Nobody except those in the immediate vicinity of the players' benches knew what was going on but Holman and CCNY players later revealed that Shelton had shouted "Those damn Jews get away with anything in New York" and had also slurred Joe Galiber, Negro player on the City team.

When Holman shook the program under Shelton's nose he said "I'll punch you right in the nose if you say anything like that about my players again." He returned to his seat on the bench as the CCNY squad applauded him vigorously. Shelton made no more remarks from the bench, but the trim 50-year-old Holman, once renowned as the world's greatest basketball player while a member of the immortal Original Celtics, was still boiling with rage. He got up again, went back to Shelton, and emphasized his previous point with a doubled up fist close to the Wyoming coaches' face. Though he bravely popped off again in his dressing room after the game when Holman wasn't around, Shelton sat stock still under Holman's threat.

City Pours It On

TAKES NO GUFF

NAT HOLMAN

The 'Daily' Roundup

Illini Hard Hit; Baltimore in AA

THE ILLINOIS football team's Rose Bowl stock was down ? Coach Ray Eliot found it hard to whip his sports. But next year the Maryland city will pop up with an All American Ass'n franchise, taken from

Picking Locals Over USC, UCLA

COAST TEAMS HERE TONIGHT

A hot holiday week schedule of intersectional double-headers starts at the Garden tonight as the University of California at Los Angeles and its crosstown rival, Southern California, meet New York University respectively. (from here on it's initials)!

The West Coast teams come in fresh from a dual triumph in Philly Saturday night, where UCLA nipped St. Josephs 50-48 and USC trounced Temple 68-54.

The once beaten UCLAns, rated

> **WE PICK:**
> NYU over UCLA
> LIU over USC
> RECORD: 21 out of 24)

favorites for the Southern Pacific Conference crown, are sparked by players in Don Barksdale, 6-6 center, and Davage Minor, a transfer from Toledo who may be remembered by Garden fans. Barksdale is the key operative as his 15 points against St. Joes suggests. Another star is Dick West, All Coaster in '43 and '44. Their game with NYU will feature the program. The locals bounced back from their upset by Oregon to whip Colorado last week.

Tall and also once beaten LIU catches a good squad in USC in the opener. The Trojans won four of five on the Coast before embarking

Chapter 9

Hoop Dreams— and Scandals

I N 1936, WHEN THE *DAILY WORKER* launched its sports section, major-league baseball was number one in popularity with New York City fans. But in baseball's off-season—mid-October to late March—the city was a hotbed of basketball. Certainly it was the sport of choice for *Daily Worker* readers, especially the young working-class readers who had attended schools where basketball was the main athletic activity.

But where baseball was predominantly a sport in which salaried professionals only occasionally played for their own hometown teams, the popularity of basketball at that time was largely in the college game; and in New York especially, the players were mostly graduates from local high schools. It was not until the late 1950s that the pro game began to attract more and more fans, eventually matching the popularity of the collegians.

The game itself was relatively recent. Invented in the early 1890s by James Naismith, a physical education instructor at a YMCA training school in Springfield, Massachusetts, basketball quickly became popular on both college campuses and the YMCA circuit. Nominally a no-contact sport—at least in those days—it was also taken up by women's colleges, with Vassar and Smith adding it to their athletic programs early on.

Within a year, thanks largely to its promotion by the YMCA, basketball was being played in Kentucky and the prairie states. By 1896 it was a favorite sport in New York City, where the Original Celtics—known as the New York Celtics—were spawned.

Lester Rodney: The Celtics were really a national team. They weren't based anywhere. They traveled the whole country. They'd go to a gymnasium in Terre Haute, Indiana, and play a local team; they'd go to Oklahoma or they'd go to the West Coast. They never lost. They were like a white Harlem Globetrotters—except they always played serious basketball. They were the Johnny Appleseeds of basketball, planting the seed of the game in places that had never seen it played the way it could be. They also made money. [Later on, when the pro league came into being, Boston—which is supposed to be the home of the Irish—immediately took the name Celtics to capitalize on their reflected glory.]

Basketball was extremely popular among blacks long before they came to dominate the game in the latter part of the twentieth century. The game had become the major schoolyard sport of youngsters who did not have the resources, equipment, or playing fields that might have attracted them to baseball, football, or hockey. The first black all-star men's team was the New York Renaissance (better known as the Rens), founded in 1923. They took their name from the famed Renaissance Casino in Harlem. They were joined a few years later by the Chicago-based Harlem Globe-Trotters. Although banned from the newly formed American Basketball League, both teams frequently played against all-white pro fives. Games with the Original Celtics were always feature attractions in which the Rens and Globe-Trotters, demonstrating a talent that never got full recognition until the color line was broken in the 1950s, clearly held their own. In 1932, the Rens beat the famed Celtics, laying claim to the sport's world championship. In the years immediately afterward, the Globe-Trotters became the better team and won a sizable following not only among blacks but among many white fans as well.

For the most part, blacks were barred from college teams and banned completely from the all-white pro teams. Among the exceptions were Paul

Robeson, famed for his prowess on the gridiron, who was varsity center on the Rutgers basketball team in 1917, and Ralph Bunche, the Nobel Peace Prize laureate, who played for UCLA in the mid-1920s, the same school at which Jackie Robinson starred in basketball in 1939–1940. One of the greatest of the black basketball players of the pre–World War II era was William "Dolly" King of LIU (Long Island University), who may have been the very first African American to play for an NBA (National Basketball Association) team, with a brief sojourn with the Rochester Royals in 1946.

But it wasn't all cheers and roses for these pioneering black athletes, who suffered all the indignities, insults, and threats that were the lot of those breaking the color barrier in every sport. They were often benched when their teams played against southern schools, who threatened to cancel their games otherwise. On the road, decent hotel accommodations were rare, as were restaurants. Racist epithets from hostile fans were commonplace, nor were the players always supported by teammates and coaches.

LR: I remember Clair Bee, who hailed from West Virginia, making a very dramatic statement at a gathering of sportswriters after he came back from a tour with his LIU team. This was before the fixes. He had a couple of black players. "We played in Oklahoma and different places," he said, "and I was stunned at the racism these kids encountered. The things people called out. What's going on in America? Do we realize the extent of this?" I ran that in a column the next day and I named every paper that was at that meeting. I think there was one line in one of the papers— maybe it was the *Herald-Tribune*—which mentioned in passing that Bee was critical of a few incidents that happened on the road. Nobody took up this statement by a veteran coach challenging racism in America.

By the 1930s, New York had emerged as the mecca of college basketball. Madison Square Garden had become the venue that was able to attract the best college teams in the country to play against New York's best. That is where LIU, CCNY, St. John's, NYU, and Manhattan took on teams like Kentucky, Bradley, Notre Dame, UCLA, Stanford, and DePaul. The Garden also hosted the National Invitation Tournament (NIT), then the only culminating event of the season. The winner was considered the national champion of college basketball.

Over the years, spontaneous adjustments and innovations by players and coaches transformed basketball into the game we know today.

LR: One significant change came in 1937, when Stanford came to New York, with Hank Luisetti shooting the first one-handed shots. They ended LIU's thirty-seven-game winning streak. The classical New York coaches were appalled, Holman especially. His CCNY teams had many ways of scoring—on fast breaks, layups after a whirlwind of quick passes—but all outside shots were with two hands. Even from pretty much designated areas on the floor. Now here comes this Stanford team flinging the ball up with one hand from anywhere.

Then a few years later, as the game grew in popularity throughout the country, the giants came in. Bob Kurland at Oklahoma A&M, a seven-footer, and George Mikan of De Paul, also seven feet tall.

But every good coach adapts, and Holman did too. Nat kept his basic controlled rapid-fire passing game to free up a shooter from close up or a layup. But he also incorporated the freer shooting style and greater spontaneity he had seen by Stanford—what you might call the first West Coast offense. You could still tell a Holman-coached team. That was pretty much the style of the great New York Knicks that Bill Bradley played on, along with [Dave] De Buscherre, [Willis] Reed, [Walt] Frazier and [Earl] Monroe; they were coached by one of Nat's guys, Red Holzman.

Perhaps the most exciting moment in college basketball—at least for New York fans and *Daily Worker* readers—came in 1950 when CCNY's (City College of New York) "Cinderella Team" won both the NIT and National Collegiate Athletic Association (NCAA) tournaments—the only time the same team had won both.

LR: Actually, CCNY had a bunch of Cinderella teams starting back in the 1920s. CCNY dominated New York basketball then. They won the national championship in 1928. A Communist Party guy, Lou Spindell, was on that team. He went on to play pro ball for ten years. Later Lou became head of the Trade Union Athletic Association, which was run by the organized Left. He was an important guy in New York trade union politics. Lou went on to become basketball coach at Textile High School in New York and was fired in 1952 after being called up before HUAC [House Un-American Activities Committee]. There were Party guys on many New York teams in those days.

IS: Who were they?

LR: I don't want to mention names.

IS: Seventy years later? What's the big secret?

LR: There's a principle involved. People went to prison to uphold the principle that their politics was nobody's damn business. But I can tell you there was one exuberant CCNY player who was a member of the YCL [Young Communist League]. After making a basket he would clench his fist to his YCL *paisans* in the stands. The clenched-fist salute. This was soon after the war.

Then there was Wee Willie Marron, who was a substitute on the Original Celtics. Later on he became a Communist organizer in New Jersey under the name Bill Norman. And Mike Singer, one of the real bright guys on the *Daily Worker*. In college, he was the eighth man on the St. John's "Wonder Team." Later he was our state correspondent in Albany.

There were quite a few. Not just on CCNY either. But they or their descendants might not like being named. It's really nobody's business.

IS: Well, you didn't send them in there to infiltrate. They were just good basketball players and they liked the game.

LR: I know. But they didn't play as Communists any more than other players played as Republicans. Same as I wasn't in the army as a Communist but as a soldier. It was understood, if you look at the proportion of progressive and Left kids at CCNY, why not on the basketball team? These weren't imported players recruited from other states. They were students who rode the subway to class.

But back to Nat Holman and the "Cinderella" team.

In those days the NIT was the big prize. The best teams in the country were invited to play. In 1950, number one was Bradley; Ohio State was number two and Kentucky number three. CCNY had a good record and some great players, but they made it into the NIT only by the skin of their teeth. It was a twelve-team tourney, and they were picked number twelve. Their first game was against the University of San Francisco, the previous year's champs. City demolished them 65–46.

Next was Kentucky, one of the all-time powerhouses in basketball. At that time they were seen by many sportswriters as the New York Yankees of the college game. The experts figured this was the end of the road for the City College Beavers.

LR: Adolph Rupp, maybe the most arrogant coach in basketball, was so sure his Wildcats would win in a walk that he didn't even bother to scout City College. He was also a dyed-in-the-wool racist. He had publicly announced he'd never have a black player on his team. CCNY had three: Ed Warner; who was their top scorer; Floyd Lane, the sixth man; and Joe Galiber, a reserve.

Nat Holman was sure his team could tame the Wildcats and decided to use Kentucky's racial bias against them. He told his players to offer to shake hands with the Kentucky players before the game. He thought one of the Kentucky players was likely to do something stupid. And sure enough, it happened. When Floyd Lane offered his hand to one of the Kentucky players, the Wildcat player turned his back. Furious, Lane shouted out, "You're gonna be picking cotton in the morning." Maybe Lane, anticipating something like that, was ready to respond the way he did. In any event, the effect was electrifying. A chorus of boos from the fans. A disconcerted Kentucky team. And a galvanized bunch of CCNY players who beat the famed Wildcats 89–50. It was the biggest loss in the history of Kentucky basketball.

CCNY went on to beat Bradley, the number-one team, in the finals. But that wasn't the end. The NCAA was next. CCNY wasn't seeded, but after winning the NIT, they got to play in the NCAA. And all they did was beat two powerhouses, Ohio State in a squeaker and North Carolina State. And then, once again, they were matched against Bradley in the finals.

That was a game for the ages. CCNY led by eleven points with nine minutes to play, but Bradley rallied and with forty seconds left, City was ahead by just one. City had the ball, trying to run out the clock, when Gene Melchiorre stole it and headed for what looked like a sure-fire basket. But [Irwin] Dambrot caught up with him, the two collided, no foul was called, and Dambrot came up with the ball. A quick pass down to the other end to Mager, a substitute, gave City its clinching basket for a final score of 71–68. Pandemonium. It was the first time any team had won *both* the NIT and the NCAA. They don't enter both tournaments anymore. Much to the chagrin of those who don't like New York City, Nat Holman and the Beavers were the kings of the hill, the toast of the town. There was a spontaneous parade down Broadway after the game.

And then the shit hit the fan!

Almost a year after CCNY won its historic double crown, college basketball was rocked by revelations that players on some of the best teams in the country—including City College—had accepted bribes from gamblers for shaving points in key games. The scandal broke when Junius Kellogg, mainstay of Manhattan College's basketball team and its first black player, told coach Kenny Norton that he had been offered $1,000 to keep the team under the point spread in an upcoming game. Norton put Kellogg in touch with the district attorney's office and a trap was sprung against the man who had offered the bribe, Hank Poppe, Manhattan's former co-captain. The next day the story broke in the New York papers, sending shock waves through the basketball world.

But Manhattan was just the tip of the iceberg. In the months that followed, CCNY, NYU, and LIU were implicated. A wave of self-righteous indignation emanated from some of the premier schools in the Midwest, who attributed it all to the cesspool of New York. Bradley University announced it would no longer play in New York. But then Bradley, Toledo, and Kentucky were also shown to have fallen prey to the fixers. Among those found to have been on the take were Ed Warner, Al Roth, Ed Roman, and Floyd Lane from CCNY; Sherman White and two other players from LIU; Ralph Beard and Alex Groza from Kentucky; and Gene Melchiorre and some other Bradley players. All told, thirty-three players and one referee were implicated in fixing games over a period of more than three years.

LR: I was horrified. This may sound pompous, but I think that because of my political background, I looked more at the underlying causes of the mess rather than just coming down like a ton of bricks on the players who foolishly succumbed to the gambling atmosphere all around them. Nevertheless, I didn't think the players should get off scot-free or anything like that. They were guilty as hell for violating the law, the trust of their fellow students, their schools, and ordinary fans. Not to mention all the high school players looking ahead to college. The whole thing was shattering—and sickening.

But we focused on the real culprits, those who permitted the gambling element to fester around the games. Plus the big-money bookies and the vermin who seduced the players. This was a lonely fight for us. The sports editors who cynically ran the point spread every day, in effect as a service for the bookies and a convenience for the gamblers, were shocked—shocked!—with pious horror. That's why I was so outraged by those sportswriters who demanded no mercy for the players without saying a word about their own newspapers' culpability by printing the point spread. It's so blatant, too. This team to beat that team by eight and a half points. What's a damn half point in basketball? There's no such animal. It's strictly a gambler's device.

Milton Gross was the worst. He wanted harsh jail sentences for every compromised player. There must have been a lot of *Post* readers who couldn't stomach that stuff, because after a while he backed off. Then there was Joe Williams of the *World Telegram and Sun*. Colonel Joe was a stone racist who used the fixes to make it seem as though the black players were the main culprits. Although ten players were involved in the first splash, Williams mentioned just two players by name: "One of the LIU traitors, Leroy Smith," and "[Sherman] White, another Negro key man on LIU." What would *you* call that?

(Note: Lester says all this, especially talking about Gross, with a great passion in his voice and a sense of indignation that still reverberates half a century later.)

LR: One of the ploys used by the fixers was to tell the players they weren't being asked to dump games. If they were favored by ten points, for instance, all the fixers cared about was that they didn't win by more than nine points. That's what "point-shaving" means. And then they'd say, "Everybody's doing it. Why shouldn't you get a piece of it?"

IS: Wasn't it obvious to the sportswriters and the fans that something hokey was going on?

LR: Not really. These are skilled athletes, and keeping the score down a bit doesn't need to look like something out of the ordinary. I can't say I ever noticed anything suspicious. But just about everyone attending one of those games, especially in Madison Square Garden, knew there was a lot of betting going on. You'd see hundreds, maybe thousands near the end of a game, cheering or groaning at inconsequential points when the winner was already determined. Big bets were being put down; and where there's that kind of money being tossed around, it's almost inevitable that someone was going to try to manipulate the outcome.

The lead story in the March 16, 1950, edition of the *New York Post* makes no bones about it: "Unseeded City College, 5½ points over third-seeded Duquesne. Top-seeded Bradley, 4½ points over fourth-seeded St. John's. That is the verdict of the pricemakers who will play tonight's NIT semifinals at the Garden without firing a shot." The gamblers' odds on all the NIT and NCAA games were featured prominently almost every day. The other New York dailies, with the exception of the *New York Times,* which never carried the odds, did the same.

LR: The biggest tragedy was what happened to the players. They had been exposed as cheaters, their careers were down the toilet. Their futures were wrecked. Talk about being punished. And the black players were hit the hardest. The Jim Crow walls were just coming down and Sherman White, maybe the best basketball player of that year, was a sure shot for the NBA. The scandal was the end of his career. He never played a game of basketball again except for pickup and semi-pro games. Beautiful athlete.

Of the thirty or so players nailed in the scandals, only four were sentenced to jail. Two were black—Sherman White and Ed Warner. The other two were white—Al Roth of City and Connie Schaff of NYU. All those from Manhattan, Bradley, and Kentucky were freed with suspended sentences.

Eventually, Roth and Schaff were also able to avoid jail. Only White and Warner did time. In sentencing White to a year in prison, Judge Saul Streit said, "With his limited judgment and insight, he became greedy and glamour-struck and developed an insatiable lust for nightclubs and girls." The same judge sentenced Ed Warner to six months, calling him "retarded and aggressive."

For us, this was a long-running story. I went up to the schools and talked to students on the campuses. A few weeks after the scandals broke, a reconstituted CCNY team played Lafayette at the Garden. Over three thousand CCNY students attended, and they came with big banners. The biggest one read "Jail the Gamblers—Reinstate Roman, Roth, and Warner." That tells you something. They may have been heartbroken by what happened, but by and large they didn't see the players, their fellow students, as the bad guys. And I talked to the coaches too. Clair Bee, of LIU. Kenny Norton of Manhattan. And, of course, Nat Holman.

Bee was much more honest about it all than Holman. Nat tried to protect his ass. Only in later years did he take a deeper tone, more charitable to the players who succumbed to the gamblers. Bee was much better from the start—on the players and the whole scene. I absolutely believe he had no notion of what was going on. I'd bet my right arm on it. Holman I wouldn't. He was always looking out for himself.

Not that he was part of any gambling. But he was the type not to rock the boat. I didn't have the same respect for him that I had for Bee in all this. Bee's point, and he said this publicly, was "Why are they picking on the kids? It's really the big gamblers, the coaches who allowed it, the athletic directors who knew that gambling was going on, and the newspapers playing up the odds." Bee actually defended the players. He said, "They're my boys; they're not the ones who should go to prison." Stuff like that. Holman never talked like that. He just said, "Oh, I'm heartbroken, I'm heartbroken." Me, me, me.

I'll give Holman this. Before the scandals, he and Bee would often challenge the sportswriters at the weekly basketball writers' luncheons. "Why does your paper run the gambling odds? You know that's helping big-time gambling." They were uneasy.

So they were critical. But it didn't go anywhere. The sports editors would say, "People bet. You're not gonna change that. We're not on a crusade to end gambling in the United States. It's human nature. The readers want to know who's favored and by how much." A couple of months after the scandal, the papers stopped publishing the point spread. That didn't last long.

Kenny Norton called me and said, "Look, don't put this in your paper." Manhattan is a Catholic college. They wouldn't be happy to have him quoted complimenting the *Daily Worker*. But still, he's calling me and he says, "You're the only one who's got the real stuff about this." He was in accord with Bee, that they're jumping on the wrong people.

I also talked to the players. Sherman White sounded ashamed. But he also talked about the gamblers and the other outside forces. So I ask him, "Why did you do it?" And he just looks at me. Finally he says, "Because I was stupid. The first time this guy came with his sweet talk I shoulda kicked him out on his ass. But I didn't. He told me it was easy and no one had to know. He says, 'Everybody's doing it. Don't be a damn fool. You're not gonna lose games. Just shave points.'"

Of all the players caught up in the scandal, Sherman White paid the highest price. The first breakthroughs of black players in the NBA had already occurred, and White, who needed just seventy-seven more points to break the NCAA scoring record, was everyone's pick for the one most likely to make it in the pros. "If it weren't for the scandals" said *New York Times* columnist Dave Anderson, "the Knicks would have made White their territorial draft pick and the Knicks, not the [then] Minneapolis Lakers, would have won all those NBA championships in the '50s. White might have become the NBA's best player" (*City Dump*). Instead he wound up with a one-year jail term, the stiffest punishment among the only four to be sentenced to prison.

LR: Bee also put me in touch with Leroy Smith's high school coach, Frank Ceres. Smith, who was also black, was a wizardous drive-in and set shot artist for LIU. I went over to Newark to the school where Smith had started out. I met Ceres in the school gym, and the first thing I saw was a huge picture of Smith hanging on the wall. Underneath were the words "He's still the greatest."

I asked Ceres what he thought had happened. "The schools make money from basketball games," he said. "The coaches make money. The peanut sellers make money. The ushers make money. And, of course, the gamblers make money. These kids truck all over the globe and play their hearts out for the supreme privilege of making a lot of other people rich. Can you really blame them if they make mistakes? I'm not saying what they did is right. But let's put the blame where it belongs. These kids are just that—kids—at the mercy of those older and shrewder. When they see all that money kicked around and passing from hand to hand, what do you expect?"

The other guy from LIU I remember was Adolph Bigos, a white guy. He was a war veteran with six battle stars and a Purple Heart, older than the other players, prematurely balding. Good floor man and a terrific rebounder. When he was arrested, he called his mother and told her to show the detectives up to the attic, where they found $5,000 in the lining of an old coat. He never spent a dime of it. He didn't feel right about it. What a tragedy. All he could say over and over was "Why did I do this?"

But I couldn't talk to the City College players. CCNY instituted a policy of no interviews with the players. The athletic director and Nat Holman. There wasn't a quote from any of the players in any of the papers. Their excuse was that there's an ongoing investigation and the players can't say anything.

The high-class papers, the *Times* and the *Herald-Tribune,* were not as blatant as say, the *Post.* But they were just as bad. When Asa Bushnell—he was the president of the NCAA—targeted the summer resorts in New York's Catskill Mountains as the cesspool that spawned the scandals, both the *Times* and the *Tribune* came close to subtle racism and anti-Semitism.

Many basketball players for the New York teams used to get jobs at these resorts, which were known as havens for mostly working-class Jews when they had their summer vacations. The players would get jobs as waiters or busboys; the pay was low, but they made good money in tips. And they would play basketball in their time off. In time, this became an attraction for the guests, and the practice spread. Charles Rosen, in his definitive book *Scandals of '51,* says that "in any given summer, there were perhaps 500 varsity basketball players employed in the Catskills" (Rosen 1978, 43).

LR: Arthur Daley of the *Times* wrote that the colleges should "prohibit their undergraduates from competing during summer months in the mountain resort league, the famed 'Borscht Circuit.' It was in the Catskills that the spiders began to weave the web that entrapped the flies. That's where the dirty work started." As though none of this would have happened if it weren't for these resorts hiring players for summer jobs.

And the *Trib* ran a photo that showed three people at a swimming pool at one of these hotels, a Syracuse player, a girl who was a guest there, and Ed Warner of CCNY. That was a startling scene in those days. Just about every Catskill hotel—like almost all the resort hotels of the period—had a strict color line for guests. It wouldn't seem like that to us today, but at the time it was a picture designed to shock with its depiction of [implied sexual] interracial mixing. Every newspaper editor would know that.

Afterwards some of these guys tried to find a niche in basketball, but none of them could ever play again either at college or in the NBA. At first all they could get were odd jobs. I remember Dambrot became a dentist. A left-handed dentist. Most of the others pretty much faded into obscurity.

Sherman White played basketball during his year in jail and eventually wound up with a touring team called the New Jersey Titans in the Eastern League. He made a living selling liquor displays. Ed Warner also played in the Eastern League on weekends while working in an automobile plant in Tarrytown, New York. Ed Roman became a psychologist, working with troubled kids in Harlem.

Ralph Beard was drafted into the army, where he started playing basketball again. Eventually he got a job as a salesman for a pharmaceutical company and wound up as sales manager. In the 1970s, Beard's old friend from Kentucky days, Alex Groza, enlisted him as a part-time scout for the Kentucky Colonels of the American Basketball Association (ABA). After the ABA folded, the Indiana Pacers took him on as a part-time scout.

The one who fully worked himself back into the game was Floyd Lane. Early on, he got an offer from the Harlem Globe-Trotters, but it never worked out because Abe Saperstein, the Globe-Trotters' owner-manager, wanted Lane to start out with the Kansas City Stars, a farm team, to see what public reaction would be. Lane did get a job, however, as the recreation director at a community settlement house, where he developed a great rapport with inner-city youths while teaching them the finer points of basketball. Gradually, Lane developed a reputation as one of the most skilled and knowledgeable coaches of the game and got positions at such schools as the College of the Virgin Islands, Harlem's Rucker League, and Queensborough Community College in New York City. In 1975, Lane finally closed the circle that had haunted him for a quarter of a century, accepting Nat Holman's old job as coach of the CCNY basketball team.

LR: Nat Holman was a pathetic story. CCNY fired him and then took him back. In the end he was completely exonerated. They named a hall after him. Holman Hall. He retired in 1960, but he used to hang around the campus. An emeritus icon. Not that he was involved in anything. But how stupid could he be? Where were his antennae? Nat lived to a ripe old age. He died in 1995 at ninety-eight.

Nat never did the honorable thing that Clair Bee did. Stand right up for the players. Saying they're not the real culprits. Bee was under terrible stress. LIU shut down its basketball program. He did get a job as a coach in the NBA later. He died prematurely.

IS: What took basketball so long to integrate?

LR: Actually, blacks were playing on basketball and football teams long before baseball got integrated. Just keep in mind that up until the middle fifties, the college game dominated both basketball and football. Yale–Harvard, Notre Dame–Southern Cal, the Big Ten, the Rose Bowl—these were the big events of football. Same thing with basketball. When CCNY and St. John's were packing Madison Square Garden, the New York Knicks were playing in the 23rd Street Armory to much smaller crowds. Baseball was unique in that the pro game was always far and away the dominant draw. College baseball was never a big spectator event. That had to do with the nature of the sport, the much bigger skill gap between college and pro in baseball than in the other sports. And up until 1947, baseball was totally lily-white. Meanwhile, blacks were showing up on a number of top college teams, at least in those schools that admitted black students.

IS: But what about the pros? Here are the Harlem Globetrotters taking on all comers everywhere. Some of them are clearly pro caliber. But they can't get into the NBA.

LR: With black players dominating professional basketball over the last thirty years, it is sometimes hard to remember that, like organized baseball and the National Football League, the National Basketball Association operated a strict Jim Crow policy until the early fifties. Sure, the Globetrotters had some great players who could easily have made it in the NBA. Meadowlark Lemon would have been a star on any NBA team. And there were others, like Marques Haynes. But the owners simply dismissed them as a bunch of "clowns" and not serious players because of their showboating antics, which were designed by Abe Saperstein to attract bigger crowds.

But in 1948, the Globetrotters played and beat the powerful Minnesota Lakers, an NBA team that featured George Mikan. Even if you want to guess that the Lakers weren't playing at their best, it's clear that the 'Trotters were good.

Saperstein himself, for obvious reasons, was not keen to see blacks admitted to the NBA. He knew that once the color line was broken, the Globetrotters would lose their best players and eventually become history. He was mostly right. They still do fairly well, but nothing like the old days.

Once Jackie Robinson broke the color line in baseball and it became clear that the floodgates had been thrown open, it was only a matter of time before the NBA followed suit. The big breakthrough came in 1950, when the Boston Celtics signed Chuck Cooper, the Washington Capitols signed Earl Lloyd, and Joe Lapchick of the New York Knicks brought on Nat "Sweetwater" Clifton. Years later, Richard Lapchick, Joe Lapchick's son, who is the director of the Center for the Study of Sport and Society, wrote to Lester Rodney saying, "I remember my father expressing his gratitude to you and the *Daily Worker* for your support when he brought Nat Clifton up to the Knicks. He got a lot of hate calls for that action."

Today, of course, it is impossible to imagine an all-white pro basketball team, although some colleges (Gonzaga, for instance, which invariably does well in the annual NCAA tournament) still field an all-white team. Bob Cousy, George Mikan, Bob Kurland, Jerry West, and Larry Bird were great white stars. But who can imagine basketball without Bill Russell, Wilt Chamberlain, Elgin Baylor, Magic Johnson, Walt Frazier, Oscar Robertson, Kareem Abdul Jabbar, Reggie Miller, Charles Barkley, Julius Erving, Michael Jordan, Shaquille O'Neal, or Kobe Bryant?

Postscript

O N A COLD JANUARY MORNING IN 1958, four members of the
Daily Worker staff—Editor John Gates, Managing Editor Alan
Max, Negro Affairs Editor Abner Berry, and Sports Editor Lester
Rodney—held a press conference in New York City to announce their joint
resignation from the U.S. Communist Party.

A few days earlier, in a move to shut down an unprecedented insurrection in Party ranks sparked in large measure by the *Daily Worker,* the Communist Party's top leadership had peremptorily ordered publication of its
own newspaper halted for an indefinite period. The trigger for the insurrection was a leaked "secret" report by Soviet Communist Party head Nikita Khrushchev that laid bare a shocking account of Joseph Stalin's mal-
feasances for a quarter of a century.

As revelations of the history of killings, crimes, and corruption under
Stalin's rule spread, an unprecedented movement for a radical reform and
restructuring of the U.S. Communist Party erupted among Party members,
engendering a deep rift in an organization that had made monolithic unity
a point of fundamental principle. At the center of the maelstrom was the
Daily Worker's editor, Johnny Gates who, along with most other staff members, threw the pages of the Party paper wide open to debate. But while the

heated exchange of views went on, Khrushchev's revelations had resulted in a mass exodus from the Party's ranks.

In just a few years, membership was reduced by two-thirds, leaving the *Daily Worker* and the reformers vulnerable to a leadership that, in the main, was more concerned with keeping the Party's ideology "pure" than with any serious consideration of the shattering revelations from Moscow. As the membership dwindled, the Party leaders struck—their first move being the suppression of the *Daily Worker.* The shutdown made it clear to most in the reform camp that the movement for significant reform in the Party's outlook and structure had been strangled. "Our heady insurrection never had a chance," says Rodney forty-four years later, reflecting on this turning point in his life. "More and more disheartened members dropped away and the old guard took over the remnants."

And so, twenty-two years after launching the *Daily Worker*'s sports section and serving as its editor, Lester Rodney, then forty-seven, found himself without a job and wondering how to support a family with two small children. Employment prospects for a middle-aged ex-Communist whose only professional experience was as a sportswriter for the *Daily Worker* were clearly not promising.

After some deep soul-searching, the Rodney family decided to join the booming westward migration to California in search of a new life, winding up, along with countless other New Yorkers, in Los Angeles. "The midlife change of scenery for this New Yorker made psychological sense," Rodney says. "The major portion of my life had ended. The feisty newspaper at the center of my beliefs had been mortally wounded by the Khrushchev Report of 1956, which blew the whistle on the real nature of Stalin and Stalinism."

Lester Rodney: It wasn't that we on the newspaper ever felt we were some kind of adjunct of the faraway Soviet Union. We were Americans who believed that socialism was a far more equitable, human way to go than anything-for-a-buck corporate capitalism. Starry-eyed over the world's first nation to proclaim itself socialist and place people over profits, we rooted for the Russians to show the world that it worked. In that wishful process, we became victims of do-it-yourself brainwashing, refusing to recognize the sad reality until it was hurled in our face.

Because Lester and his wife, Clare, despite their ages, had marketable skills, the transition from New York to California was somewhat smoother than they had anticipated. The main breadwinner at first was Clare, an experienced schoolteacher, who, due to a shortage of trained teachers in California, quickly found a public school teaching job.

Lester's new career took a little longer to get launched. It included a brief sojourn with the *Santa Monica Outlook,* a staunch conservative newspaper as far from his own ideological outlook as could be imagined; a four-year stint with an advertising agency; a period of freelance writing; and finally winding up at the *Long Beach Independent Press-Telegram,* a major newspaper in what subsequently became part of the Knight-Ridder chain.

It was there that his newspaper career took its most astonishing turn. After a year as an all-purpose writer-editor at the *Press-Telegram,* Rodney was asked to be the paper's religion editor. Reluctant at first to take on the assignment, Rodney had second thoughts when the paper's managing editor said he was looking to shake up the religion beat, moving it away from the traditional dull reports on church bake sales and Sunday sermons to coverage of the sweeping controversial issues confronting both clergy and laity.

So, much to the amazement of family and friends, the Jewish-born, atheistic, one-time Communist sportswriter became the religion editor for the second largest newspaper in the Los Angeles area. No less amazed were the readers of the *Press-Telegram,* who suddenly found their paper's religion section dealing with all the main debates of the major religious denominations in the United States—the role of social action by the churches, racism, capital punishment, the war in Vietnam and amnesty for those who refused service, abortion, Nixon's pardon, nuns wanting to change their habits and be more involved in social work.

Nothing was off limits. Rodney's natural skills and respect for individuals that had earned him the cooperation of professional athletes likewise won him the trust of ministers of every religious and social persuasion.

Soon the *Press-Telegram*'s religion beat became one of the paper's most widely read and popular features. During circulation drives, Long Beach buses carried advertisements proclaiming, "Les Rodney Covers His Beat Religiously."

In time, the past caught up with the Rodneys. When the local school board—egged on by a member of the visiting House Un-American Activities Committee—uncovered Clare's earlier Communist connections, she lost her teaching job, in spite of support from all her fellow teachers. In time, she obtained a position as professor of early childhood education at Long Beach State University, after a stint at a prestigious private school. Around the same time, Lester was eased out as a volunteer leader for a Cub Scout troop on similar grounds.

And then, after Rodney had been running the religion section for several years, a representative of the infamous Los Angeles Red Squad asked the *Press-Telegram*'s editor if he knew that he was employing a "notorious Communist," strongly suggesting that Rodney be fired. When the editor called Rodney in to ask about the charge, Lester acknowledged that he had once been a Communist Party member but that he had left the Party years before coming to work at the *Press-Telegram*. A relieved editor said, "I thought it must have been something like that," and told the agent of the Red Squad to, in effect, peddle his papers somewhere else.

When Rodney retired in 1975, he was given a gala send-off by the paper's entire staff and asked to contribute columns and op-ed pieces from time to time. Some years later, he and Clare moved to a retirement community in the San Francisco Bay Area.

But Lester Rodney never lost his interest in sports. An avid tennis player most of his life, he was active in senior tournaments in California, becoming number one in California and second in the country in the eighty-five-and-over bracket. He also continued to write occasional pieces for *In These Times* and other publications on current sports issues and is regularly invited to speak at conferences and on radio and TV programs on historical and current sports subjects.

Rodney, who still regards himself as a radical in politics, considers himself a baseball traditionalist. He bemoans the designated hitter, having wild-card teams in the playoffs, and the glut of home runs unbalancing the game at the expense of the sacrifice bunt, the hit-and-run, the stolen base.

So how does Rodney, an early campaigner against the Reserve Clause and in favor of free agency, feel about the staggering multimillion-dollar salaries some players are making?

LR: I'm not outraged. Why should it bother me more than similar amounts paid to movie stars and other entertainers? Big League ballplayers are highly skilled performers who have worked at honing their skills from boyhood. They are in a field where most of them will be "old" before forty, long before the CEOs who double their own obscene salaries after sending work to overseas sweatshops and dumping American workers.

Like most sportswriters and many fans, Lester has an all-time, all-star team. His selections, he notes, are pretty traditional.

LR: Lou Gehrig is the unmistakable first baseman. Rogers Hornsby, the best right-handed batter I ever saw, is the second baseman. Honus Wagner by acclamation at short. Mike Schmidt, robust-hitting, great-fielding third baseman, of a more modern era, rounds out the infield.

Babe Ruth and Ty Cobb are givens in the outfield (though Cobb was sure one S.O.B. as a person.) Plus Joe DiMaggio over Willie Mays, a choice that gets me in big trouble with younger generations. Why DiMag over Mays for the third spot? Willie was wonderful, but Joe was not only the consummate defensive outfielder but hit for higher average, and also with power. He had seasons of .381, .357, .352 ,and .346, plus the record deemed least likely to be surpassed, fifty-six straight games with base hits.

You could throw a blanket over three catchers. I settle for Johnny Bench over Roy Campanella and Bill Dickey. Of these eight position players, Wagner is the only one I never saw play. (I'm not that old!) My pitching staff is Christy Mathewson, Walter Johnson, Lefty Grove, Nolan Ryan, Sandy Koufax, Bob Gibson, Randy Johnson, and, another guy I hate to include, Roger Clemens.

A second team would have Jimmy Foxx barely over Bill Terry and Hank Greenberg at first; Jackie Robinson barely over the quietly great

Charley Gehringer at second, with Jackie's unique aggressive base-running value to his team making the difference; the current A-Rod, Alex Rodriguez, over Ernie Banks and Derek Jeter at short; and classic third baseman Pie Traynor rounding out the infield.

Mays, of course, a runaway first choice for the second outfield, followed by Hank Aaron and Ted Williams. Ted by a whisker over Barry Bonds, in spite of Barry's monster 2001 and 2002 years. Williams, the definitive left-handed hitter, in the .350 range over his long, twice war-interrupted career, and the last man to bat over .400 in a season, was an ordinary defensive outfielder, but Barry has some weaknesses too, mainly in the hustle department.

Now these are Big League all-star teams. If you include the many great black players who never had a chance to play in the Bigs, and who cannot be measured by statistics, there would have to be some changes. Josh Gibson, the greatest catcher this land has produced, nothing less than a right-handed hitting Babe Ruth at bat, and the equal of Bench defensively, would be an immediate number one. Satchel Paige, who America saw in the Bigs only from age forty-two on, would join him. And you would have to contend with the likes of legendary stars such as Smokey Joe Williams, who preceded Paige as an all-dominant pitcher; Cool Papa Bell; Oscar Charleston; Mule Suttles; Ray Dandridge; and others.

Among sportswriters, as in many professions, the respect of one's peers is highly valued and is not lightly given. One of Lester's most prized awards, therefore, was being elected a lifetime member of the Baseball Writers' Association of America after his retirement from the *Daily Worker.* Now in his nineties, Lester still occasionally uses his membership card to watch the Giants and A's from the press box—a fitting place for this Press Box Red.

Bibliography

ABC *Nightline* transcript, April 5, 1987.

Ashe, Arthur R., Jr. 1993. *A Hard Road to Glory: A History of the African-American Athlete.* Vol. 2: *1919–1945.* Vol. 3: *Since 1946.* Armonk, N.Y.: Amistad Press.

Ashford, Emmett. 1992. *Get That Nigger Off the Field.* Brooklyn, N.Y.: Book Mail Services.

Brown, Michael E., Randy Martin, and Frank Rosengarten, eds. 1993. *New Studies in the Politics and Culture of U. S. Communism.* New York: Monthly Review Press.

Buhle, Paul, and Michael Fermanowsky. 1984. "Lester Rodney: Baseball and Social Conscience." Interview conducted under the auspices of the Oral History Program, University of California, Los Angeles.

Buhle, Paul, Mari Jo Buhle, and Dan Georgakas. 1992. *Encyclopedia of the American Left.* Urbana and Chicago: University of Illinois Press.

Burghardt, Carl R. 1980. "Two Faces of American Communism." *Quarterly Journal of Speech* 66.

City Dump. Home Box Office original documentary.

Colin, Joseph R. 1974. *The American Radical Press 1880–1960.* Vol. 1. New York: Greenwood Press.

Colorado Springs Independent, November 16, 2000.

Dorinson, Joseph, and Joram Warmund, eds. 1998. *Jackie Robinson: Race, Sports and the American Dream*. New York: M. E. Sharpe.

Duberman, Martin. 1989. *Paul Robeson: A Biography*. New York: Ballantine.

Falkner, David. 1995. *Great Time Coming: The Life of Jackie Robinson from Baseball to Birmingham*. New York: Simon & Schuster.

Fariello, Griffin. 1995. *Red Scare: Memories of the American Inquisition*. New York: Norton.

Foner, Philip. 1978. *Paul Robeson Speaks*. New York: Brunner/Mazel.

Golenbock, Peter. 1984. *Bums: An Oral History of the Brooklyn Dodgers*. New York: Putnam.

Kahn, Roger. 1993. *The Era: 1947–1957*. New York: Ticknor and Fields.

Kelly, William G. 1976. "Jackie Robinson and the Press." *Journalism Quarterly* 530.

Klein, Robert. 2001. "Lester Rodney." In *Dictionary of Literary Biography,* vol. 241: *American Sportswriters and Writers on Sports*. Detroit: Gale Group.

———. 1996. "Sports Reporting in New York City 1945–1960: Arthur Daley and Lester Rodney." An address delivered at a conference for *Nine: A Journal of Baseball History and Social Policy Perspectives*, March 10.

Levine, Peter. 1992. *Ellis Island to Ebbets Field: Sport and the American Jewish Experience*. New York: Oxford University Press.

Linder, Douglas O. "The Trials of the Scottsboro Boys." In the Famous American Trials series, available at <http://www.law.umkc.edu/faculty/projects/FTrials/scottsboro/scottsb.htm>

Lipsyte, Robert, and Peter Levine. 1995. *Idols of the Game: A Sporting History of the American Century*. Atlanta: Turner Publishing.

Mead, Chris. 1985. *Champion Joe Louis: Black Hero in White America*. New York: Scribner's.

Naison, Mark. 1979. "Lefties and Righties: The Communist Party and Sports during the Great Depression." *Radical America* 13. July/August.

———. 1977. "Sports for the Daily Worker." *In These Times,* October 12.

Peterson, Robert. 1970. *Only the Ball Was White*. New York: Gramercy.

Rampersad, Arnold. 1997. *Jackie Robinson: A Biography*. New York: Knopf.

Reichler, Joseph L., ed. 1982. *The Baseball Encyclopedia*. 5th ed. New York: Macmillan.

Roberts, Randy. 1983. *Papa Jack: Jack Johnson and the Era of White Hopes*. New York: The Free Press.

Robinson, Jackie. 1972. *I Never Had It Made*. New York: Putnam.

Rodney, Lester. 1978. "Fair Is Fair and Foul Is Foul." *In These Times,* March 15.

———. 1979 "Managers Play Musical Chairs." *In These Times*, April 4.

———. 1981. "Settling an Old Score." *In These Times,* July 20.

Rosen, Charles. 1978. *Scandals of '51: How the Gamblers Almost Killed College Basketball.* New York: Holt, Rinehart & Winston.

Rusinack, Kelly Elaine. 1995. "Baseball on the Radical Agenda: The *Daily* and *Sunday Worker* on the Desegregation of Major League Baseball, 1933 to 1947." M.A. thesis presented to the Graduate School of Clemson University.

Shoemaker, Martha. 1999. "Propaganda or Persuasion: The Communist Party and Its Campaign to Integrate Baseball." M.A. thesis, University of Nevada, Las Vegas.

Simons, William. 1985. "Jackie Robinson and the American Mind." *Journal of Sport History* 12(1), 1.

Smith, Ronald A. 1979. "The Paul Robeson–Jackie Robinson Saga and a Political Collision." *Journal of Sport History* 6(2).

Sports Jones, August 24, 2001.

Tygiel, Jules. 1993. *Baseball's Great Experiment: Jackie Robinson and His Legacy.* New York: Oxford University Press.

Weaver, Bill. 1979. "The Black Press and the Assault on Professional Baseball's Color Line." *Phylon* 40(4).

Wiggins, David K. 1983. "Wendell Smith, *The Pittsburgh Courier* and the Campaign to Include Blacks in Organized Baseball, 1933–1945." *Journal of Sport History* 10(2).

Index